JAVA
STUDIO

Blue Book

Jennifer Atkinson
Lee Taylor

Publisher
Keith Weiskamp

Acquisitions Editor
Stephanie Wall

Marketing Specialist
Diane Enger

Project Editor
Melissa D. Olson

Technical Reviewer
Craig Swanson

Production Coordinator
Wendy Littley

Cover Design
Jody Winkler

Layout Design
April Nielsen

CD-ROM Developer
Robert Clarfield

Java Studio Blue Book
© 1999 The Coriolis Group. All Rights Reserved.

Limits of Liability and Disclaimer of Warranty
The author and publisher of this book have used their best efforts in preparing the book and the programs contained in it. These efforts include the development, research, and testing of the theories and programs to determine their effectiveness. The author and publisher make no warranty of any kind, expressed or implied, with regard to these programs or the documentation contained in this book.

The author and publisher shall not be liable in the event of incidental or consequential damages in connection with, or arising out of, the furnishing, performance, or use of the programs, associated instructions, and/or claims of productivity gains.

Trademarks
Trademarked names appear throughout this book. Rather than list the names and entities that own the trademarks or insert a trademark symbol with each mention of the trademarked name, the publisher states that it is using the names for editorial purposes only and to the benefit of the trademark owner, with no intention of infringing upon that trademark.

The Coriolis Group, Inc.
14455 North Hayden Road, Suite 220
Scottsdale, Arizona 85260

602/483-0192
FAX 602/483-0193
http://www.coriolis.com

Library of Congress Cataloging-in-Publication Data
Atkinson, Jennifer, 1964-
    Java studio blue book / by Jennifer Atkinson and Lee Talyor.
        p.   cm.
    Includes index.
    ISBN 1-57610-322-6
    1. Java (Computer program language)   2. Java studio.   I. Tayor, Lee (Lee A.)
QA76.73.J38A85   1999
005.7'2 — dc21   98-46083
                                                                                CIP

Printed in the United States of America
10 9 8 7 6 5 4 3 2 1

an International Thomson Publishing company

Albany, NY • Belmont, CA • Bonn • Boston • Cincinnati • Detroit • Johannesburg • London • Madrid
Melbourne • Mexico City • New York • Paris • Singapore • Tokyo • Toronto • Washington

CORIOLIS

14455 North Hayden, Suite 220 • Scottsdale, Arizona 85260

Dear Reader:

Coriolis Technology Press was founded to create a very elite group of books: the ones you keep closest to your machine. Sure, everyone would like to have the Library of Congress at arm's reach, but in the real world, you have to choose the books you rely on every day *very* carefully.

To win a place for our books on that coveted shelf beside your PC, we guarantee several important qualities in every book we publish. These qualities are:

- *Technical accuracy:* It's no good if it doesn't work. Every Coriolis Technology Press book is reviewed by technical experts in the topic field, and is sent through several editing and proofreading passes in order to create the piece of work you now hold in your hands.

- *Innovative editorial design:* We've put years of research and refinement into the ways we present information in our books. Our books' editorial approach is uniquely designed to reflect the way people learn new technologies and search for solutions to technology problems.

- *Practical focus:* We put only pertinent information into our books and avoid any fluff. Every fact included between these two covers must serve the mission of the book as a whole.

- *Accessibility:* The information in a book is worthless unless you can find it quickly when you need it. We put a lot of effort into our indexes, and heavily cross-reference our chapters, to make it easy for you to move right to the information you need.

Here at The Coriolis Group we have been publishing and packaging books, technical journals, and training materials since 1989. We're programmers and authors ourselves, and we take an ongoing active role in defining what we publish and how we publish it. We have put a lot of thought into our books; please write to us at **ctp@coriolis.com** and let us know what you think. We hope that you're happy with the book in your hands, and that in the future, when you reach for software development and networking information, you'll turn to one of our books first.

Keith Weiskamp
President and Publisher

Jeff Duntemann
VP and Editorial Director

Look for these books from The Coriolis Group:

Visual Basic 6 Programming Blue Book

Visual Basic 6 Black Book

Visual Basic 6 Core Language Little Black Book

Visual Basic 6 Object-Oriented Programming Gold Book

Visual Basic 6 Client/Server Programming Gold Book

Visual C++ 6 Programming Blue Book

XML Black Book

For Brian, Taylor, Claire, and baby number 3.

—Jennifer Atkinson

For all the programmers, writers, and content developers who toil behind the scenes and beneath the covers with no control over the ultimate results.

—Lee Taylor

About The Authors

Jennifer Atkinson is a technical writer, manager, trainer, and information development consultant with eight years of experience. Previously, she was a programmer for a solid-fuel rocket-propulsion systems designer and manufacturer. As a writer, she specializes in writing about software languages, applications, and Web-based content. She has created and delivered classes on Web-based multimedia and designing information for the Web. Her clients have included Novell and Deloitte and Touche.

As a manager, Jennifer was responsible for the West Coast operations of PDR Information Services, a technical communication services company. Her clients included IBM, ROLM, Siemens, Borland, Macromedia, 3Com, Digital Equipment Corporation, and AT&T.

Jennifer has presented papers on a variety of technical communication topics and is a senior member of the Society for Technical Communication. Formerly the president of the society's largest chapter, the Silicon Valley Chapter, she currently serves as an associate editor for the Quality Special Interest Group.

She has degrees from Purdue University in technical communication and computer science.

Lee Taylor is the chief operating officer of TixToGo, Inc., a Web start-up company providing online reservation and registration booking services.

In his previous life, Lee was an author, trainer, manager, technical writer, and information development consultant with 16 years of experience. He is a coauthor of three previous books on Web design and development: *The Web Page Design Cookbook*, the award-winning *NetObjects Fusion 2.0: Effective Web Design in 3 Days*, and *FutureTense Texture: Effective Web Design in 3 Days*. He has created and delivered classes in Web design and development, and he has consulted with clients including Novell, John Deere, and IBM.

Lee has also presented papers on a variety of online information design topics and is a senior member of the Society for Technical Communication. He has a bachelor's degree from the University of the South (Sewanee) and a master's degree in creative writing from San Francisco State University.

Acknowledgments

To Brian for supporting me whenever I want to take on a big project that means he has to assume the lion's share of work around the home, and for instinctively knowing when I needed the space, so he took the girls away for some weekend adventures.

To Taylor, for starting kindergarten with such aplomb that I didn't worry hardly at all; to Claire, for being such a trooper when she broke her nose and when she contracted a nasty case of chicken pox; and to our newest baby who's biggest contribution has been to make me nauseous and think longingly about naps.

To Luci for opening her house and her heart to my family, consequently bringing chaos to her life night and day.

To Mom for helping me with the sinking fund factor, and for her trusty HP calculator in verifying the data; to Dad for rearranging the boxes in the garage (or was it the deck chairs on the Titanic?), and hauling stuff to storage. To both of you, thanks for helping in so many ways before, during, and after the move.

To Helen and Bruce, for hosting some of the weekend adventures, and for taking care of Claire during the chicken pox crisis.

To my coauthor, Lee, for agreeing to work with me on this book, even though he was already up to his eyeballs in alligators with TixToGo.

To Melissa for her gentle nagging; to Mary for her terrific eye and wonderful feel for transitions; and to Craig for his tenacity in verifying the technical side of this book and his heart-warming comments that made my day. To the rest of the crew at Coriolis for making this a book a reality: Robert, Wendy, Anthony, April, and Jody.

To Janis Joplin, Barenaked Ladies, Sonia Dada, KFOG, and WTTS, thanks for providing the soundtrack to this book.

—Jennifer Atkinson

Thanks to Billi for the patient support of yet another book project, for putting up with the odd hours and occasional tantrums pertaining thereto, and for knowing that I really didn't mean all those things I said to my computer.

Thanks to my coauthor, Jennifer, for valiantly driving this book to completion, even while handling a major relocation, her husband's job search, a new bun-in-the-oven, and the aforementioned battle with chicken pox. I can't wait to see what she does for an encore.

Thanks to Carole and Stephanie for wading through the transition issues and bulldogging this book project back to life.

Finally, thanks to Bonnie Raitt, the Indigo Girls, and Paco de Lucia for providing the soundtrack to the Colorado-born parts of this book.

—Lee Taylor

Contents At A Glance

Table Of Contents

Introduction

If you bought this book (or are considering buying it, as you stand there in the bookstore, just shy of a cappuccino), then you must want to build JavaBeans. This book teaches you how to use Sun Microsystem's Java Studio 1 to build JavaBeans and assorted other Java-based brews, but it's not just a user manual. If you want a user manual, you could use Sun's slim user manual, which adequately documents the product.

This book goes far beyond simple examples that illustrate features without offering anything useful for your day-to-day struggles. It teaches you how to solve problems using Java Studio, and it equips you with Beans and components ready to run off the book's companion CD-ROM. Not coincidentally, you will use these Beans and components in this book's projects. Now, an explanation of the nature of this book.

Build, Then Understand

This book is part of Coriolis's Blue Book series. The Blue Book series is designed for people with some technical background, who are focused on spending their time as productively as possible. Knowing that adults (and children, for that matter) learn best by example, a Blue Book first walks you through building something. Then, the following chapter explains the concepts underpinning what you just built. You'll notice that the chapter titles in this book alternate between *Building* and *Understanding*.

An Emphasis On The Pragmatic

We're not really talking about understanding with a capital *U*. Yes, you'll get it, but not a deep, meaning-of-life and how it relates to the Zen of JavaBeans understanding. We provide the information (an understanding) that equips you to be up and running as quickly as possible. Just from the heft of this book, you know we're not skimming the surface of the technology. We focused on making this book's contents as practical and immediately useful as possible.

For example, you might consider reading the last two chapters, Chapters 22 and 23, out of order. These chapters address troubleshooting your Java Studio designs, and we offer real-world solutions for problems you may encounter. It may not be the same answers you receive from the technical support people, but we know these solutions work.

As authors, we're working professionals, so we understand your problem with time. That is, not having enough of it. This leads us to a description of you.

About You

You want to build Beans, and we will help you. Of course, you can build applets, Java applications, and Java Studio components with Java Studio, and we will explore those issues in depth, too. We figure that if you're going to add a tool to your toolbelt, it had better be worth the space on your toolbelt. We'll show you how to get the most out of Java Studio. On the companion CD-ROM, we give you the results of each project we build in this book, ready to plug into your Web site. With this book, you can leverage our Beans and build Beans on your own.

We also know a few more things about you.

You're Pressed For Time, Have Intermediate Experience, And Are Undoubtedly Possessed Of Good Taste

A recent study, conducted by the nonprofit Families and Work Institute, found that the average full-time employee in 1997 worked 47.1 hours a week. Compare this to the figure for 1977, when the average was 43.6 hours a week. What happened to

"Work Smarter, Not Harder"? Anyway, if you're in a fast-paced industry, or working for a company that's focused on continuously improving performance and productivity at continuously reduced costs, or both, you probably find that 47 hours of work happens during daylight hours. The rest of the work happens after the kids and animals go to bed.

The bottom line is that we know you're not sitting around looking for something to do. We also know that you have some knowledge about JavaBeans and associated technologies. If you were a technophobe, you wouldn't be reading this far in the book. We assume you have a basic understanding of programming concepts.

But I'm Not A Programmer

That's okay. As long as you're game, we give you what you need to be successful. You do need to be comfortable with concepts such as variables and to have heard of Sun's Java Development Kit (JDK), the software you need to install before developing Java applications or JavaBeans. If you're not comfortable with the concepts and the JDK, maybe a beginner's book on JavaBeans would be a better place to start. But if you know what we're talking about, you're ready to start learning how to build some Beans.

But I Am A Programmer

That's okay, too. We're offering you shortcuts to productivity with our build-then-explain format. Browse the build chapters. If something doesn't quite click, read the explain chapter. If you got it all during the build chapter, just skip to the next build chapter.

You're Using Windows 95, Windows NT, or UNIX

Java Studio runs on Windows 95; Windows NT 4; Solaris (SPARC) 2.5, 2.5.1, and 2.6; and Solaris (Intel) 2.5, 2.5.1, and 2.6.

Sun recommends having a minimum of a 100MHz Pentium processor (for Windows and Solaris Intel) or a SPARCstation 10, but we know from experience that you can get by with a little bit less horsepower in your Intel chips.

You should have one of the following browsers:

- Netscape Navigator 3.0.1 or later, 32-bit version

- Microsoft Internet Explorer 3 or later. If you are using Internet Explorer 3.0.2, you should get the most recent version of the Java Virtual Machine (JVM) from Microsoft's Internet Explorer site at **www.microsoft.com/ie**.

But I Don't Have The JDK Installed

It's okay. Java Studio installs the JDK for you. If you already have the JDK installed, Java Studio installs one anyway, because it needs the JDK in order to run. It's sort of particular about the version of the JDK it uses, so Java Studio takes no chances and installs one whether or not you need one.

Why is Java Studio so particular about the JDK? Because Java Studio uses JDK 1.0.2 *and* JDK 1.1. Because Sun developed the JDK, it can do that. It's the advantage to developing a tool based on a technology that you created.

Yes, We Have A CD-ROM

You probably noticed the CD-ROM tucked into the back of this book. It contains a variety of helpful things, including a demo version of Java Studio and all the examples we use in the book. For more information on the CD-ROM, see the readme.txt file on the CD-ROM.

Conventions And Usages

We use some conventions in this book, as follows:

- *Web versus Web site*—We use Web to refer to the World Wide Web; we use Web site to refer to individual sites on the Web.

- *Internet versus intranet*—Because there is one Internet, it is capitalized. There can be many intranets, so they are lowercase.

- *Double click versus double-click*—Double click is a noun ("A double click starts the application"), and double-click is a verb ("To start the application, double-click on the icon").

- *Select versus choose versus highlight*—When you go to a menu and choose something from the menu, we use the verb choose. For example, from the File menu, choose Save. When you click something to select it or highlight it, we use the verb select. For example, select the connector, and drag it to the other component. We don't use the word highlight.

Also, when we tell you something is on the CD-ROM, we won't specify a CD directory location for the item. The CD is mastered after the book is written, so instead of giving you potentially misleading information, we ask you to look on the CD for a readme.txt file. It orients you to the information on the CD.

Gosh, This Is A Great Book! How Do I Reach You?

We love to hear from our readers. If you'd like to send us a note, you can contact us at the following email addresses:

- Jennifer Atkinson, **jennifer@atkinson-consulting.com**

- Lee Taylor, **leetay@tellword.com**

And now, let's dive into Java Studio!

Chapter 1

Dive Into Java Studio

Sun Microsystems's Java Studio is a tool for creating Java applets, JavaBeans, Java applications, and Java Studio building blocks, which are called Packaged Designs. It's a worthwhile tool, one worth learning and adding to your résumé, because it's a tool that gives you a lot of leverage.

Without too much effort, you can use Java Studio to create some pretty amazing results with some very interesting technologies. So, go fill your cup with your beverage of choice, and let's settle in with Java Studio.

In this chapter, you will start using Java Studio right away. We won't build anything useful quite yet, but we'll get acquainted with the basics of Java Studio so that the rest of the chapters make sense. Consider this chapter a prerequisite before reading the rest of the book. The rest of the chapters in this book come in pairs, with the first one helping you build something and the second chapter explaining what you built. The book is fairly modular, and it makes sense that you might pick and choose where you go from here. But please, start here.

This chapter also puts Java Studio in context for you, so you will know how it relates to some other technologies, and we'll briefly review some issues that might impact your use of Java.

Before We Start

Now, we know you're anxious to jump in, but before you execute the perfect cannonball, let's take a moment to get oriented. Let's review what you have in hand.

1

Sun charges $89 if you purchase Java Studio from the Web site. If you call them and order it, they'll ship you a CD-ROM and charge you $99. Being pragmatists about the dangers that lurk in having software without a CD-ROM around for re-installation, we chose to pay $99.

▶Tip

Introducing Duke

As you get acquainted with Java Studio, or any other Java-based technologies, you will meet Duke. Duke is the mascot for Java, like a warped coffee bean. Don't get us wrong—we like him as well as the next dude. But the reality is that he is omnipresent in Java Studio, especially when you initially start Java Studio. Figure 1.1 displays Duke.

Figure 1.1
Duke is a ubiquitous figure in Java-based technologies.

Are You Using The Demo Version Or A Full Version?

By purchasing this book, you have easy access to the demo version of Java Studio, because it's on the CD-ROM. You can, of course, download the same software from Sun's Web site (look for the Studio Try & Buy link at **www.sun.com/studio**), but that would only make sense if the CD is damaged or if Sun posts a newer version of the application on their Web site.

It's also possible that, prior to buying this book, you've plunked down $89 to buy Java Studio and already have the official, released version of the software on your hard disk.

The main difference between the demo version and the purchased version is that the demo version expires 30 days after you install it, so don't delay too long after installing the demo version before you finish this book. Of course, you can putz around with your system clock and force the demo version to continue functioning, but it's just not worth it. All your files are stamped with the wrong dates and your email messages appear to have been written a month ago. After all, Java Studio is only $89, so if you're even halfway intrigued with this tool and warm up to it within the first couple of chapters, go ahead and buy it. (By the way, we're not employees of Sun Microsystems, and we don't have any other explicit financial connections to Sun. Just wanted to make that clear!)

Diving In

If you haven't already done so, start Java Studio. When it finishes loading, you get three versions of Duke in three windows, as shown in Figure 1.2.

Sun is trying to widen the audience for Java Studio as much as possible, so the window on top is called *Where Do I Start?* It ensures that users are shown helper material right up front, and nobody has a chance to panic. But don't let it put you off, either. The Where Do I Start? window contains four icons representing four types of introductory information: a tutorial, examples, a road

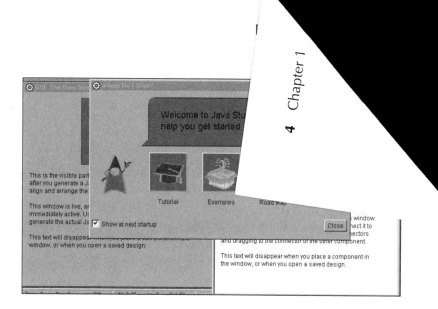

Figure 1.2
Duke introduces the main elements of the Java Studio interface.

map (an interactive quick reference for the Java Studio interface), and frequently asked questions (FAQ). It's not a bad idea to take the time to browse through these items. But if you decide you don't want to, that's okay. You can always get back to the Where Do I Start? window by clicking on the big Duke button, labeled not-so-coincidentally Where Do I Start?, in the upper right-hand corner of your screen, as shown in Figure 1.3.

Before you close this window, click the Show At Next Startup checkbox in the bottom right-hand corner to deselect it. When you close the Where Do I Start? window, you still have three windows open—the Design window, the GUI window, and the Java Studio palette (displayed in your taskbar as "Java Studio—Design1"). The GUI in the GUI window stands for Graphical User Interface.

Your Virtual Whiteboard—The Design Window And The GUI Window

The Design and GUI windows are the visual heart of Java Studio. Consider them your virtual whiteboard, because this is where you build your *designs*.

Figure 1.3
Duke stands by vigilently in case you want to go back to the Where Do I Start? window.

Designs are what you build in Java Studio. After a design is complete, you can tell Java Studio to generate the code so that you can save your design as a JavaBean, Java applet, and so on. Of course, as you are building your design, you are designing with a goal in mind, because it makes a difference as you create the design. But, we'll address this as we build our designs throughout the book.

The GUI window and the Design window are two views of a design—like seeing a set on a stage from the audience's point of view, and then seeing the set from behind, where you understand how it is put together. The GUI window represents how it looks to your users, and the Design window represents the logic of the design. Whenever you take a GUI component, such as a text label, and drop it into the GUI window, the label sits in the GUI window and the corresponding component also shows up in the Design window. If you drop a component, such as the Choice component (what Sun calls a *drop-down field*), in the Design window, the drop-down field appears in the GUI window.

By the way, *components* are the building blocks of Java Studio. They are the items you drop into the GUI and Design windows and use to build your designs. For a complete list of Java Studio components, see Appendix A.

Notice that the GUI and Design windows have their own program buttons on the taskbar, and Java Studio has a separate button on the taskbar for the application itself. If you close the GUI or Design window, you can reopen the window using the View menu. Besides the GUI and Design windows, you have one more tool to learn in the Java Studio interface—the palette.

The Paintbrush In The Logo

You might have noticed the paintbrush in Java Studio's logo. You already know that Java Studio is a visual tool, but Sun also uses the artisan metaphor by calling the area that contains the components a *palette*. This is the third window you see; it is initially identified in your taskbar as Java Studio—Design1. Figure 1.4 shows the Java Studio palette.

Figure 1.4
The palette contains the Java Studio components you use to create your designs.

The palette has tabs, labeled GUI, Data Flow, Computation, Multimedia, Internet, Database, and Debug. The components are organized by their function within the tabs, so, for example, all components used for designing the user interface of your design appear on the GUI tab. To see the available components, click the tabs on the palette. As you'll see in the next section, you build your Java Studio designs by working with components.

Working With Components

Components are the building blocks of Java Studio designs. Each component has a specific purpose, and you can tell the name of the component by holding your cursor over it on the palette for a moment. A pop-up window displays the name of the component.

Adding Components To A Design

Adding components to a design is just like plugging in stereo components—it's not too tricky. So, let's get started, and drop a few components into a design.

1. To bring the GUI components up front, click the GUI tab.

2. Click the Text Field component, the fifth component from the left. Figure 1.5 displays the Text Field component as it appears on the palette. After you click a component on the palette, the component appears depressed, like a button that has been pushed, until you click in the GUI window or the Design window.

3. Click in the GUI window or the Design window. The Text Field component appears as an empty field in the GUI window, and the component appears in the Design window. Figure 1.6 displays the Text Field component as it appears in the GUI and Design windows.

Figure 1.5
Use the Text Field component to collect text and simple numbers.

Figure 1.6
The Text Field component, as it appears in the GUI and Design windows.

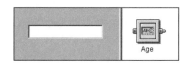

4. The Text Field Customizer window appears (we'll talk about customizers in a moment). In the Name field, type "Age".

5. Click OK.

6. Click the Computation tab on the palette.

7. Click the Arithmetic component, the first component on the Computation tab as shown in Figure 1.7. The Arithmetic Customizer window appears.

8. In the Name field, type "Multiply By 7", as shown in Figure 1.8.

9. In the Function area, open the drop-down field between the labels Left and Right. Choose the symbol for multiplication (*).

10. Select the Set The Right Value To A Constant checkbox. In the field, type "7".

11. Click OK.

Now, you have two components in your design—it's time to hook up your components.

Hooking Up Components

Notice that the components in the Design window have knobs on them. These knobs are called *connectors*, and they generally represent the input and output for the components. Do the connectors remind you of the plugs on stereo components? Your task is to hook up the components—it is much simpler than

Figure 1.7
Use the Arithmetic component to perform simple arithmetic.

Figure 1.8
Use the Arithmetic Customizer window to set up simple equations.

plugging in a new component to your stereo, but the concept is very similar.

1. Click the right-hand plug of the Text Field component labeled Age.

2. Click and drag over to the left-hand plug of the Arithmetic component labeled Multiply By 7. When you get close enough to the input connector on the Arithmetic component, the line turns green. When it turns green, let go.

That's it. You hooked up two components with a connector. The output from the Text Field component goes into the Arithmetic component, where the value is multiplied by seven.

Adding Another Componenet

Let's add one more component, and then we'll talk about customizers. This component allows you to display the result of the arithmetic.

1. Click the GUI tab.

2. Click the Text Field component.

3. Click in the Design window to place the Text Field component to the right of the Arithmetic component.

4. In the Name field, enter "Dog Years".

5. Click OK.

6. Connect the output of the Arithmetic component, called Multiply by 7, to the input of the Text Field labeled Dog Years.

Now, before we turn on this little design, let's quickly discuss customizers, so you will have something to build on.

Customizers: The Devil Is In The Details

Customizers are the mechanism for configuring the behavior of a component. Each component has a customizer, which you can access in one of two ways:

• Right-click a component and choose Customize.

• Select a component. From the Customize menu, choose Selected Component.

In a Customizer window, you can specify items such as:

- Component name
- Label that appears below the component in the Design window
- Size and other visual characteristics of the component if it appears in the GUI window
- Type and number of connectors of the component

Most customizers have a number of tabs. Figure 1.9 displays the Text Field Customizer's Connectors tab.

We'll spend a fair amount of time tweaking customizers throughout this book.

At this point, your design has three components that you have dropped in and wired together. Now what? Let's look at the GUI window.

It's Alive! It's Alive!

See the first text field in the GUI window? Click in the first text field, and enter your age. Then, press Enter. The result is displayed in the second window. Pretty cool, huh? No compiling, no need to even save your design first. The components are alive and functioning as soon as you drop them into the GUI or Design windows.

Figure 1.9
The Text Field Customizer has three tabs, typical of many customizers.

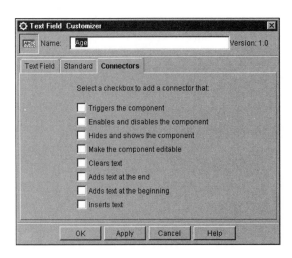

Tip

If You Have Problems Selecting The Label

It might take a little practice before you can easily select an item in the GUI window if you are using Windows 95 (as opposed to a flavor of Unix). Don't click on the text of the label—click a little outside the imaginary rectangle that surrounds the label. If you still aren't selecting it, continue to click in a straight line away from the label, moving only a tiny increment between clicks. After you can start to visualize where the selection rectangle is drawn, it becomes easier.

So, just to maintain good style (and to quell that itchy, not-quite-finished feeling that we suspect you're experiencing), let's add labels to our design.

Adding Labels

Adding labels will help your design make sense to your users. To add labels:

1. Click the GUI tab, and then click the Label component (the first component on the GUI tab).

2. Click in the GUI window below the first text field. The Label Customizer appears, as shown in Figure 1.10.

3. In the Name field, enter "Label for Age field".

4. In the Label Text field, enter "Enter your age, then press Enter".

5. Click OK.

6. If necessary, move the label so it sits directly beneath the first text field. To move the label, select it, then click somewhere along the border but not at the handles. If you click on the handles, you will end up resizing the label instead of moving it. Look for your cursor to turn into four arrows, which indicates moving (two arrows indicates resizing).

7. Repeat the previous steps for the second label. Name it "Label for Dog years", and specify the Label Text as "Your age in dog years".

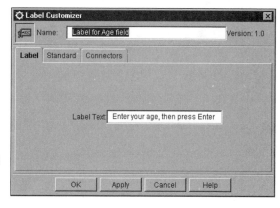

Figure 1.10
Use the Label Customizer to add labels to the interface of your design.

8. From the File menu, choose Save, to save your design. If you want to save your designs in the Java Studio directory, look in your root directory for a directory called *Java-Studio1.0*, then for a subdirectory called *my designs*. When you name your file, don't add a file extension. Java Studio adds the extension .VJ, which stands for Visual Java.

Now, you are ready to generate an applet.

Creating An Applet—Just Say Generate

We have created a Java Studio design. At this point, we can express our design as an applet, an application, a JavaBean, or a Packaged Design. Or we could just save it and close Java Studio so we can ponder our choices. Our little design isn't exactly ready for prime time, but let's go ahead and generate an applet.

1. From the Generate menu, choose Applet.

2. The Generate window appears, as shown in Figure 1.11. You can choose the name of the HTML file generated and the directory where it is stored. To specify the directory, click Browse, and navigate among the directories until you are in the right place. You can also specify the name of the HTML

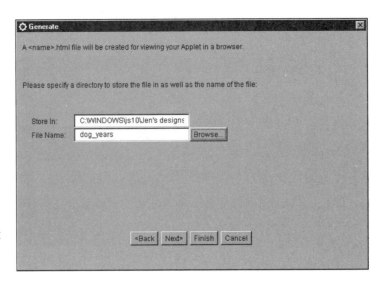

Figure 1.11
The Generate window allows you to specify where to store and what to call the generated HTML file.

file that is generated. (If you're puzzled about why we are generating an HTML file, hold on. We'll get to that in a bit.)

3. Click Next.

4. The Generate window asks if you want to immediately view the applet and, if so, what you want to use to view the applet, as shown in Figure 1.12. Choose Java Applet Viewer.

5. Click Next.

6. The Generate window asks if the applet should display in the browser window (that calls the applet), or in a separate browser window (that is spawned when the applet is called), as shown in Figure 1.13. For our example, choose in the browser window and click Next.

7. Click Finish. Java Studio displays a window with a copyright statement. Accept the copyright statement and click Next.

8. Java Studio compiles the information, generates the code (notice the dialog box showing you the status of the compilation), and creates the necessary applet files. Then, the applet displays in the Applet Viewer, as shown in Figure 1.14.

After you play with the applet a few times, close the Applet Viewer. If you are so inclined, you can open the generated HTML file in the browser of your choice and see the applet load.

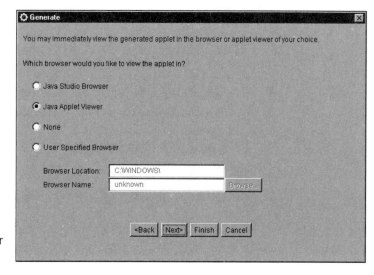

Figure 1.12
Choose the viewer you want to use to view the applet immediately after generating it.

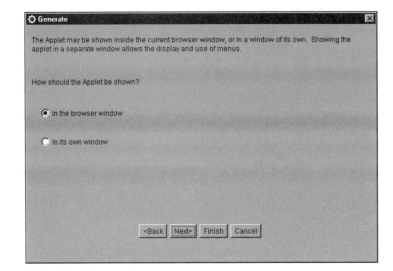

Figure 1.13
Choose whether you want the applet to display in a separate browser window or in the window that calls the applet.

Figure 1.14
Use Java Studio's Applet Viewer to view your newly generated applet.

But Wait! Where's The Code?

Code? You want code? Sun takes the position that Java Studio is a visual development tool and it is therefore unnecessary for the users of the tool to see the code. Java Studio compiles the design and generates a file from the design. It doesn't create any interim files of code for you to browse.

We know some of you may still want to see code, but get over it. Go get an interactive development environment, such as Sun's Java Workshop or IBM's Visual Age for Java, to fill your need. For more information on how to choose your tools, see the section "About Java Studio And Other Tools" later in this chapter.

▶Tip

Why An HTML File?

By definition, a Java applet runs within a Web browser window (or an applet viewer). If your design is meant to run by itself, independent of a Web browser, then it is a Java application. So, an applet automatically needs to be called by an HTML file, which Java Studio kindly creates for you.

Beneath The Surface

When you generate an applet from your design, Java Studio keeps you informed with the Generate Applet window. Java Studio creates several files when generating an item.

When generating an applet, Java Studio creates an HTML file using the name and directory that you specified in the Generate window. The HTML file contains HTML code that looks similar to the code shown in Listing 1.1.

Listing 1.1   The applet tag in the HTML file generated by Java Studio.

```
<applet
    name="chap01_test"
    code="VJad13316356e"
    codebase="classes"
    archive="chap01_test.zip"
    width="392"
    height="373"
>
</applet>
```

When Java Studio generates an applet from your design, it uses the Java compiler to generate a class file, which contains Java *bytecodes*. The class file is a platform-independent file, and (in theory) it can be run on any computer that supports Java. The bytecodes are interpreted by the Java runtime system. The class file containing the bytecodes uses a file name generated by Java Studio, and it is specified by the **CODE** parameter in the **<APPLET>** tag. In Listing 1.1, the class file is **Vjad13316356e.class** (the **.class** part is implied).

Applets do not have a name until you name them with the **<APPLET>** tag. Java Studio uses the **NAME** parameter and names an applet using the name you specified in the Generate window. The **CODEBASE** parameter is used to specify where the class file resides. In our example, the class file is in a subdirectory of the HTML file called *classes*. We will discuss the **ARCHIVE** parameter when we discuss improving the performance of your applets in Chapter 20.

For more information on exactly which files you need to upload to your Web site and how to incorporate an applet into your exisiting HTML code, see Chapters 6 and 7. The next section discusses the technical context of applets and how it impacts your development of applets.

JDK 1.0.2 And JDK 1.1, And The Implications

As you know, the Java Development Kit (JDK) is how Sun distributes the Java language. The JDK contains the Java compiler, Java class libraries, the Java Virtual Machine, the Java Applet Viewer, and the Java Debugger. Sun makes the JDK freely available for anyone who wants to download it. As Sun refines the Java language, it updates the JDK to take advantage of newer features and to fix bugs for previous releases.

This is relevant to you, because Java Studio uses the JDK. Some of the components use parts of JDK 1.0.2 and some components use parts of JDK 1.1. The tricky part is that some browsers support JDK 1.0.2 and some newer browsers also support JDK 1.1. Because the objective is for your users to be able to see your nifty applets, it is a good idea to keep track of the browsers your users are using and which items you build using JDK 1.1. Table 1.1 can help you figure out some of the browser discrepancies.

Java Studio warns you when you use a component that needs JDK 1.1. None of the components that shipped with Java Studio use JDK 1.1. Some of the contributed components do, but we won't add any contributed components until Chapter 14.

Table 1.1 Browsers and the JDK version supported.

Browser	JDK Version Support
Netscape Navigator 3.x	JDK 1.0.2
Netscape Navigator 4.x (starting with Preview Release 3)	JDK 1.1
Microsoft Internet Explorer 3.x	JDK 1.02
Microsoft Internet Explorer 4.x (starting with the beta 2 version)	JDK 1.1

Now that you have an applet, and now that you know which browsers can view your applet, can you proudly display the "100% Pure Java" logo with your applet? Let's talk about exactly what that means.

"100% Pure Java"

So, what does it mean when a vendor brags that its product is "100% Pure Java," and what does it mean to Java Studio? "100% Pure Java" means that Sun has certified that a product uses only Java code as specified in the standard, and therefore, it really will run on every computing platform that has the Java Virtual Machine. This is relevant because some developers are writing code that is not pure Java so they can improve the performance and take advantage of specific parts of an operating system. But, it means that they have software, written mostly in Java, that does not follow Sun's Java vision of "write once, run anywhere." This practice dilutes the power of Java as a truly platform-independent language.

For us, it means that the applets and applications we build using Java Studio are technically pure Java because you know that Java Studio follows the Java standard. Of course, it is unlikely that you will go through the process to get your applets and applications certified by Sun and blessed as "100% Pure Java," so you'll just have to be content knowing that it's true, even if you don't get a certificate proving it. We've already mentioned that Java Studio should be one tool among many in your toolkit. The next section discusses the other tools that you might consider adding to your Java toolkit.

About Java Studio And Other Tools

Java Studio should be just one tool in your collection of tools. This section places Java Studio in context with some other products.

Use Java Studio To Create Applets, (Small) Applications, And JavaBeans

Java Studio is a terrific tool for creating Java applets, small Java applications, and JavaBeans. Its intuitive, visually oriented design allows you to be productive fairly quickly. When your design starts getting bulky, you can slice off a chunk and put it into a Packaged Design. This helps you to keep your design modular and to leverage your designs for more than one purpose. Of course, some of Java Studio's appeal is its ease in creating JavaBeans and its ability to import other Beans. However, don't ditch the rest of your tools in favor of Java Studio.

Use Another Tool To Create (Big) Applications

Java Studio is very good at what it does. But if you want to build a Java application that starts to grow bigger than your Design window, and you've already been using the Packaged Design feature to pack more into the design, then you need to consider another tool. We list a variety of Java development tools in Chapter 9, and we describe some other JavaBean development tools in Appendix B. As you know, Sun also offers some other Java tools, including Java Workshop and the BeanBox.

The Relationship Between Java Studio, Java Workshop, And The BeanBox

Sun has been offering a promotion where you can buy Java Studio and Java Workshop together at a reduced price. This is a great idea, because the two products combine very nicely.

Java Workshop is a visual development tool for professional Java programmers. It offers a compiler, a profiler that pinpoints performance problems in your code, wizards to help you create JavaBeans, and tools to help you design GUIs for your applications.

Think of Java Studio as a screwdriver, and think of Java Workshop as a handheld power tool with a screwdriver bit and maybe a few more bits available for use. For small jobs, it would be silly to plug in anything when you've got a screwdriver in your pocket. For big jobs, you'll be much more efficient if you can apply a little power to the work.

The BeanBox is a tool for testing JavaBeans, and it is part of Sun's Bean Development Kit (BDK) (**java.sun.com/beans/software/ bdk_download.html**). According to Sun, the BDK is offered for free distribution to "support the early development of JavaBeans and to act as a standard reference base." It is not a real development tool. It's more like a tool that Sun developed internally and decided to clean up enough for the rest of the world to play with.

What's Ahead?

The chapters in the rest of the book come two by two. We start by exploring the Design and GUI windows in depth, and then we stroll through building applets, applications, JavaBeans, and Packaged Designs. After that, the chapters focus on topics such as connecting databases with Java Studio, improving the performance of your design, worrying about the security of your design, and testing and debugging your design.

Thank you for sticking with us through Chapter 1. We know you're limited on time, so feel free to jump to the chapters that appeal to you the most. Don't forget to fire up this book's companion CD-ROM to use the designs and resources we've provided to bring you more bang for the buck.

Now, let's start building some serious designs.

Chapter 2

Building Java Studio Designs Using The Design Window

Chapter 1 encouraged you to jump in, feet first and get acquainted with Java Studio. Now, it's time to start swimming. In this chapter, you'll spend considerable time using and familiarizing yourself with the Design window.

In this chapter, you will work through a time-honored ritual—building a "Hello World" design—and then you'll build an ordering form where the work is greatly simplified by Java Studio's Design window. The concepts behind the tasks presented in this chapter are discussed in more detail in Chapter 3.

Let's get started on our "Hello World" design. If you don't have Java Studio running, start it.

Building A "Hello World" Design

Every programmer starts learning a new language by writing a Hello World program. A Hello World program is a very simple program; its purpose is to display the message "Hello, World." Even though you aren't learning a new language, creating a Hello World program is a good way to start learning about the Design window.

As you know, every time you start Java Studio, the Design and GUI windows pop up with our friend Duke lounging about. As soon as you choose a component and place it in one of the windows, Duke disappears. To build a Hello World program, follow these steps:

1. On the GUI tab on the component palette, click the Label component (see Figure 2.1).

Figure 2.1
Use the Label component to display text that is typically going to be unchangeable by the user. Later in this chapter, we will use the Button, Choice, and List components.

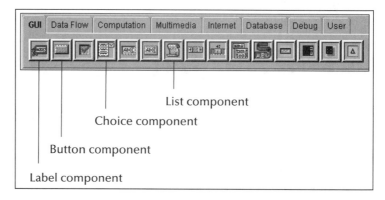

List component

Choice component

Button component

Label component

2. Click in the Design window. The Label Customizer dialog box appears as shown in Figure 2.2.

3. Click in the Name field, and change the text from Label1 to "Hello World Label".

   The text in the Name field identifies the name of this item, so you can tell the difference between it and the other labels in the Design window. The name of the item doesn't display in the GUI window.

4. Click in the Label Text field and change the text to "Hello, World!"

   The contents of the Label Text field are displayed by this component in the GUI window.

5. Click OK.

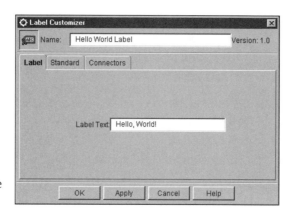

Figure 2.2
Modify the fields in the Label Customizer for the Hello World design.

NOTE

If you have a hard time selecting the text in the GUI window, click on an imaginary rectangle around the text. If you can't find the rectangle, click in a straight line away from the label, moving a tiny increment between clicks.

Figure 2.3
Select the Hello, World! text label, and resize its width to display the text.

Notice how the text appears in the GUI window. The default values for width don't allow enough space for your label text.

6. Select the label text in the GUI window. After the selection rectangle appears, click on the side handle, and drag it until the text fits in the rectangle, as shown in Figure 2.3.

7. From the File menu, choose Save. Choose the directory where you want to save the design, and specify a descriptive name, such as Hello_World. Remember, you don't need to specify a file extension—Java Studio adds a .VJ for you.

That's it. But don't you want more than a basic label?

Jazzing Up Your Label

Now, we think you'll agree that a plain ol' text label just isn't enough for this design. Let's jazz it up a little. After all, you're dealing with a tool that makes jazzing it up easy. Let's add two buttons to display and hide the text label. To do this, you'll use the Merger component so that the input from both buttons can control the text label.

1. In the Design window, right-click on the Label component, and choose Customize.

2. Click the Connectors tab, and select the checkbox Hides And Shows The Component. (See Figure 2.4.)

3. Click OK.

Figure 2.4
Select the Hides And Shows The Component item to add a connector that controls whether the text label displays or hides.

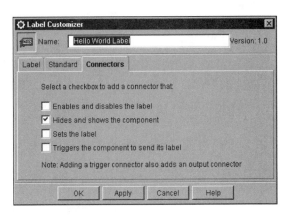

4. Let's add the two buttons. On the component palette, with the GUI tab on top, click the Button component. The Button component is shown in Figure 2.1.

5. After you have selected the Button component, click in the Design window and place the Button component to the left of the Label component, as shown in Figure 2.5.

6. In the customizer for the Button component, name the component Play Button. In the Button Caption field, enter "True". Then click OK. You need to specify the caption this way because the Label component needs a value of True to display (Chapter 3 discusses this concept further). Figure 2.6 shows the settings for the Button component.

7. Add another button below the Play Button. Name the new button Hide Button and name the Button Caption "Hide". Click OK.

Your design should appear similar to the design shown in Figure 2.7.

Figure 2.5
Place a Button component in the Design window.

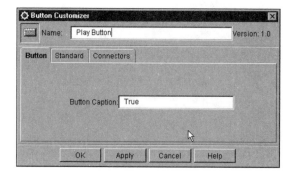

Figure 2.6
Specify the name of the Button component and specify the Button Caption as True.

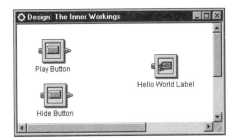

Figure 2.7
The design now has two
buttons, in addition to
the original label.

Next, you need to add the Merger component to function as
the gateway between the buttons and the text label.

8. On the component palette, click the Data Flow tab, and then
   click the Merger component, as shown in Figure 2.8.

9. Place the Merger component in the Design window between
   the buttons and the text label. In the Merger Customizer,
   name the component Button Merger. (See Figure 2.9.)

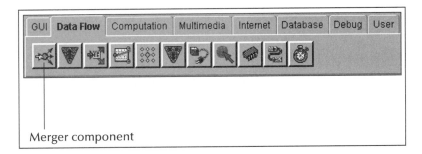

Figure 2.8
On the Data Flow tab,
click the Merger
component.

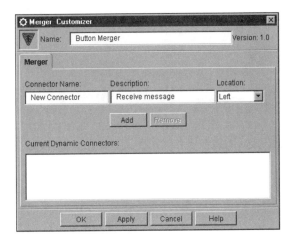

Figure 2.9
Name the Merger
component.

10. You can leave all the other properties in the Merger Customizer as they are. Click OK.

    Now, you are ready to wire the components together.

11. Click the output connector of the Play Button, and drag to the top input connector of the Merger component. The top input connector is called Input 1 (catchy, isn't it?). After the connection line turns green, release your mouse button.

12. Click the output connector of the Hide Button, and drag to the bottom input connector (Input 2) of the Merger component.

13. Click the output connector of the Merger component, and drag to the input connector of the text label (now called Hello World Label) as shown in Figure 2.10.

14. In the GUI window, rearrange the buttons and the label as necessary. Then, click the True button or the Hide button, and admire your work. Your results should appear as shown in Figure 2.11.

15. Save your design.

Figure 2.10
Wire together all the components—this is the fun part!

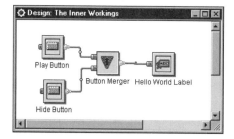

Figure 2.11
The final results are much more interesting with the buttons.

Now, let's adapt the design and create an ordering form in the Design window.

Creating An Order Form In The Design Window

Your job is to create an ordering form for Hello Indiana, Inc., an online company that offers maps and travel guides for cities in the state of Indiana. To simplify the example, let's assume that our customers are domestic and that billing addresses are the same as the shipping addresses.

The first step involves figuring out what information the ordering form needs to collect. For each order, the form should include the following:

- Customer name
- Billing address
- Credit card number
- Credit card expiration date
- City name of each map ordered
- Quantity of each map ordered

In addition to gathering the appropriate information, the form needs to contain a Submit button.

Now, with the preliminary plan in place, let's get started. First, you must begin with a new design. To start a new design, go to the File menu, and choose New. After opening a new design, you are ready to place components. If necessary, save the changes to your Hello World design.

Placing Components

Before you begin placing components, you should identify the components you need. In this example, you'll need to place a component for each item appearing on the ordering form. Table 2.1 shows the components you will use to create the order form in this example.

Table 2.1   Order form components.

Item Number	Item Description	Example	Component
1	Customer name	Sarah Vaughn	Text Field (GUI tab)
2	Billing address	101 Blooz Court Bloomington, IN 12345	Text Area (GUI tab)
3	Credit card number	1234-5678-9012-3456	Text Field (GUI tab)
4	Credit card expiration date	June 1999	Choice (GUI tab); use one Choice component for the month and one for the year
5	City of map	Bloomington, Indiana	Choice (GUI tab)
6	Quantity of map	17	Text Field (GUI tab)
7	Submit button	Submit button	Button (GUI tab)
8	Labels for fields	Your Name	Label (GUI tab)
9	Merge all the items entered on the form, and send them for processing when the user presses the Submit button	(not applicable)	Merger (Data Flow tab)
10	Distribute a signal to all the components to send out the data when the user presses the Submit button; at the same time, distribute a signal to all the components to clear their fields	(not applicable)	Distributor (Data Flow tab)

For this example, you'll use a List component to display the results. If you were setting up this order form to be processed, you would send the results to a file instead of displaying the data on screen.

The upcoming sections show you how to create the components for the order form. The first components that you will add are the customer's name and billing address. Next, you'll add components for the credit card number and expiration date information.

Then, you will add map information and the functionality, until the order form contains all the necessary components.

Add Customer Name And Address

In this section, you'll use a Text Field component to collect the user's name and a Text Area component to collect the user's address.

If you have not already done so, go to the File menu and choose New so we can start a new design.

1. On the GUI tab on the component palette, choose the Text Field component, and place it in the Design window, as shown in Figure 2.12.

2. In the Text Field Customizer, specify the name of the component as Customer Name. Then, click the Connectors tab, and select the Triggers The Component and Clears Text checkboxes. (See Figure 2.13.)

3. Click OK.

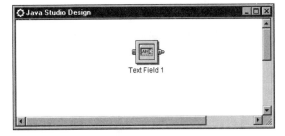

Figure 2.12
Place a Text Field component in the Design window.

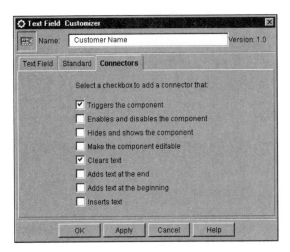

Figure 2.13
Name the component Customer Name, and select two connectors.

4. On the GUI tab on the component palette, choose the Text Area component, and place it in the Design window below the Customer Name component, as shown in Figure 2.14.

5. In the customizer for the Text Area, specify the name of the component as Customer Address. Then, click the Connectors tab, and select the Clears Text and Sends Out Text Via Output Connector checkboxes. (See Figure 2.15.)

6. Click OK. Your Design window should now display both components, as shown in Figure 2.16.

Add The Credit Card Number And Expiration Date

Now, you're going to add the components to collect the information about the customer's credit card.

1. On the GUI tab on the component palette, select the Text Field component, and place it in the Design window, below the Customer Address component.

Figure 2.14
Place a Text Area component in the Design window.

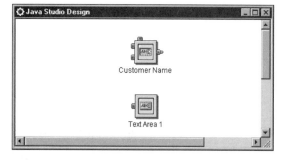

Figure 2.15
Name the component Customer Address, and select the connectors.

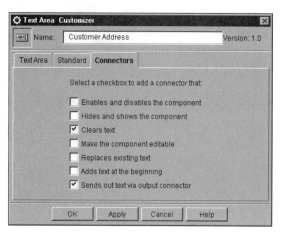

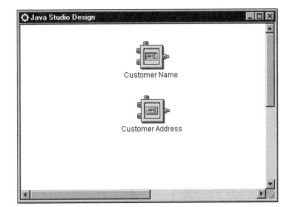

Figure 2.16
The Design window now has the Customer Name and Customer Address components defined.

2. In the customizer, name the component Credit Card Number. Then, click the Connectors tab, and select the Triggers The Component and Clears Text checkboxes.

   Now, you can add a Choice component that enables users to display the month in which their credit card expires.

3. On the GUI tab, select the Choice component. If needed, refer to Figure 2.1.

4. Place the Choice component in the Design window below the Credit Card Number component. In the Choice Customizer, name this component Credit Card Month. (See Figure 2.17.)

   Now, you are going to add the choices to the Choice component. Java Studio supplies one choice by default. Coincidentally, the default choice is called Choice.

5. In the Item field, type "January". As you type in the Item field, the same letters appear in the Value Sent Upon Selection field. To add the item to the list of choices, click Add.

6. Add the rest of the months of the year. Add the months in order, because the order of the choices in the customizer reflects the order in which the choices appear in the component's drop-down field.

7. After you have added the months to the Choice component, select the default choice called Choice, and then click Remove to delete the choice from your selection list.

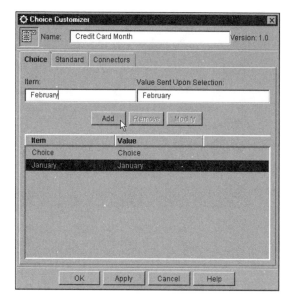

Figure 2.17
Name the first Choice component Credit Card Month. Also, add the months (in order) to the Credit Card Month customizer.

8. Click the Connectors tab, and select the Triggers The Component checkbox, as shown in Figure 2.18. Click OK.

9. Repeat Steps 3 through 8 to add another Choice component for the year that the credit card expires. Name the component Credit Card Year, and place it in the Design window to

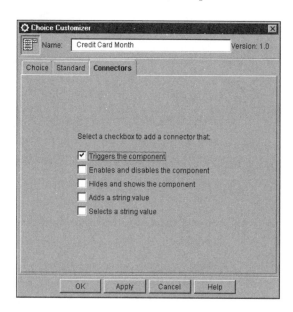

Figure 2.18
Select Triggers The Component in the Connectors tab of the Credit Card Month component.

the right of Credit Card Month. Add the years 1998 through 2003. Don't forget to add a trigger connector.

After you complete the second Choice component, your Design window should look similar to Figure 2.19.

Add Map Information

You are now ready to add Choice components for the city of the map ordered and a Text Field component for the number of each kind of map.

1. On the GUI tab, select the Choice component, and place it in the Design window below the credit card information. Name the component Cities.

2. Add some cities to the Choice component. Just in case you aren't an expert with Indiana geography, here are five cities to add:

   - Anderson

   - Bloomington

   - Carmel

   - Danville

   - Evansville

3. Add a trigger connector, and click OK.

4. Add a Text Field component for the user to specify the number of maps of the selected city. Name the component

Figure 2.19
Your design should now have components for the customer's name, address, credit card number, and credit card expiration date.

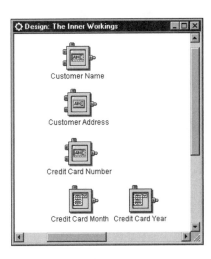

Number Of Maps, and place it in the Design window to the right of the Cities component.

5. Select connectors for Triggers The Component and Clears Text, and then click OK.

Add A Submit Button

In this section, you'll add a Submit button. By necessity, add it to the far left of your Design window. The placement is important because the Submit button needs to send a signal to all of the components in the Design window so it functions as the starting part. By placing it on the far left side of the Design window, it makes it easier to connect it to all of the components.

1. On the GUI tab, select the Button component.

2. Add the button to the far left of the Design window.

3. Name the button Submit Button, and specify the Button Caption as Submit, as shown in Figure 2.20.

When you place the Submit button on the left side of the Design window, Java Studio also places the button on the left side in the GUI window. In Chapter 4, you will rearrange the items in the GUI window.

What About The Labels?

Normally, you would add the label components for your form at this point. But, for now, we're going to delay that process until Chapter 4. In Chapter 4, you will work through the gory details regarding using the GUI window.

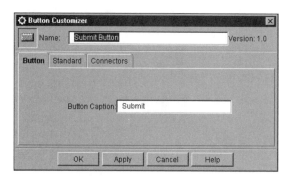

Figure 2.20
Add a Submit button to the design.

Add A Distributor And A Merger

Now, you can add some items to manage the data flow generated by the form's components. As mentioned earlier, you need a Distributor component to distribute the signal from the Submit button to the components, and you need a Merger component to merge the data from the fields for processing. Follow these steps:

1. Click the Data Flow tab on the component palette. Select the Distributor component, and place it in the Design window between the Submit button and the rest of your components.

2. In the customizer, accept the default name of the Distributor. It's the only Distributor component you will use in this design.

   At this point, you will need to add some output connectors to the Distributor component, because the component only comes with two. You need nine more output connectors.

3. Click Add nine times to add the output connectors using the default values, as shown in Figure 2.21.

4. Click OK.

5. On the Data Flow tab, select the Merger component, and place it on right side of the Design window between the rest of your components and the edge of your screen. (See Figure 2.22.)

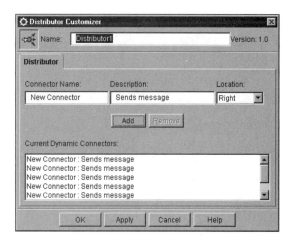

Figure 2.21
Add nine more output connectors to the Distributor component.

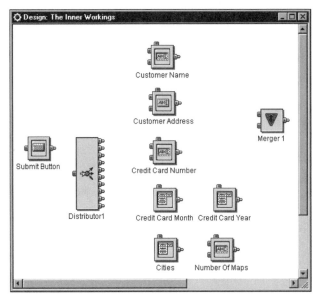

Figure 2.22
Add the Merger component between the rest of the components and the edge of your screen. Notice the placement of the Distributor component and the Submit button from Step 1.

6. In the customizer for the Merger component, accept the default name, because it's the only Merger you will use in this design.

The Merger component only comes with two input connectors, so you will need to add five more.

7. Click Add five times. Click OK. (See Figure 2.23.)

For the purposes of this example, you will send the form's output to a List component. Normally, you would send the data to a file so the order could be processed.

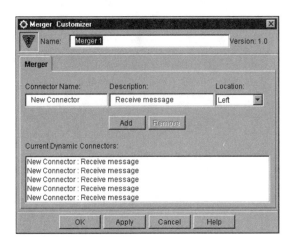

Figure 2.23
Add five more input connectors on the Merger component.

8. On the component palette, select the GUI tab. Select the List component, and place the component in the Design window on the far right side, to the right of the Merger component.

Congratulations! All of the components are in place. Now, you can wire them together.

Connecting The Components

By connecting the components, you allow the components to communicate with each other. The connections are the glue for the design's functionality.

Let's wire the components by starting on the left and working our way to the right.

1. Connect the output of the Submit button to the input of the Distributor1 component. If you're having any problems doing this, review the section in Chapter 1 about wiring components together.

   The Distributor1 component performs two functions: it sends a message to all the form components so their contents are sent through their respective output connectors, and it tells four components to clear their contents. Keep in mind that the information in the components is sent out in the same order that they are connected to the output connectors of Distributor1, because that order determines the order of receiving the trigger signal.

2. First, connect one output connector of the Distributor1 component to the trigger input connector on top of the Customer Name component. Then, connect another output connector of the Distributor1 component to the Clear Text trigger on the Customer Name component. (See Figure 2.24.)

3. Repeat Step 2 for all the Text Field or Text Area components, including Customer Address, Credit Card Number, and Number Of Maps. As you wire these components, you might need to rearrange the components in the Design window in order to track where the connections are going.

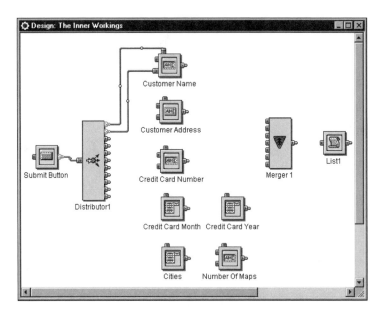

Figure 2.24
Connect two output connectors of the Distributor component to the trigger input connector and the Clears Text input connector of the Customer Name component.

▶Tip

But You Wanted To Build A Bean

Be patient. We'll cover how to express these designs in all their myriad forms in later chapters. Right now, we are focusing on how to build designs. Of course, you can go to the Generate menu and choose to generate the design as an applet, Bean, application, or Packaged Design, as explained in Chapter 1. If you want to make an informed decision about how to best use those features, see the chapters that deal with applets, applications, JavaBeans, and Packaged Designs.

4. Connect the remaining output connectors of the Distributor component to the trigger input connector for the three Choice components.

5. Connect the output connector for each form component to the input connectors of the Merger component.

6. Connect the output connector of the Merger component to the input connector of the List component, as shown in Figure 2.25.

7. From the File menu, choose Save. You will use this design in later chapters.

That's it for this design!

Voila! You Just Built A JS Design

Pretty interesting, isn't it? You've just thrown together an order form, quick-like-a-bunny. You're practically ready to set up the Web site for Hello Indiana, Inc.

Okay, maybe there are a few more elements involved, such as the interface for the form. Chapter 4 takes care of that aspect. But before you create an interface form, Chapter 3 goes into detail on

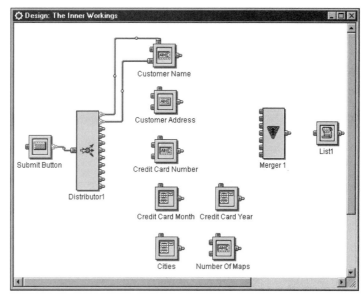

Figure 2.25
Connect the output connector on each form component to an input connector on the Merger component.

some of the decisions made during the design process presented in this chapter. For example, why is your design more complicated than the sample order form in the Java Studio documentation? Read on, and you'll find out.

Chapter 3

Understanding Java Studio Designs Built With The Design Window

If the logic behind the procedures in Chapter 2 seems obvious to you, you might want to skip the details presented in this chapter. On the other hand, if you seek further clarification regarding the two designs you built in Chapter 2, this chapter offers helpful information.

Before we begin looking at the designs you built in Chapter 2, let's clarify some of the basic terminology used in Java Studio. Table 3.1 provides descriptions and illustrations of common Java Studio terms.

Okay, now that we're all on the same page, let's dissect those designs from Chapter 2.

About That Hello World Design

The Hello World design is pretty straightforward, but you might be asking a few questions, such as:

- In the Label Customizer, what's the difference between the Hides And Shows The Label option and the Enables And Disables The Label option?

- What's the difference between the Label component and the Label3D component?

- Why did the Button Caption for the first button need to be True, rather than Show?

The following sections answer each of these questions in short order.

Table 3.1   Java Studio terminology.

Term	Description	Illustration
Component	Building blocks.	
Customizer	Reshapes the building blocks. See Figure 3.1.	
Connectors	The ends for connections; the banana plugs.	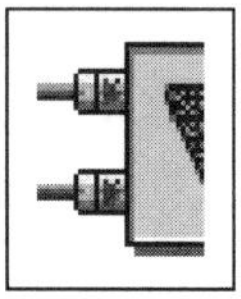
Connections	Ties components together; the wiring.	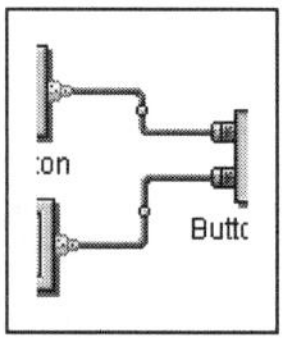

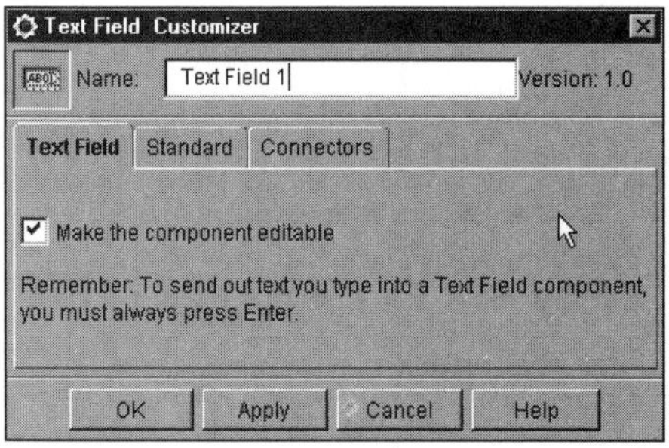

Figure 3.1
Customizers reshape the Java Studio building blocks.

Hides And Shows Vs. Enables And Disables

In the customizer for the Label component, on the Connectors tab (see Figure 3.2), there are two choices that might sound similar—the Hides And Shows The Component option and the Enables And Disables The Label option. While these options seem similar, they create different results.

Chapter 2 briefly explains how hiding a label works. When you send a True message to the connector for hide and show, the

Figure 3.2
The Connectors tab on the Label component has some choices that sound similar.

label appears in the GUI window. When you send a False message, the label does not appear in the GUI window. Therefore, this option controls whether the button appears in the GUI window.

Enabling and disabling can be used to activate or deactivate an option—the button always displays in the GUI window, but it can appear grayed out (deactivated). When a label is enabled, it appears normal. When a label is disabled, it appears grayed out. When you design interfaces, you use graying out to indicate when a choice is currently not valid. Figure 3.3 shows the Hello World label grayed out.

Label Vs. Label3D

You might have noticed that the GUI tab on the tool palette has two components for labels: the Label component and the Label3D component. Use the Label component for simple labels and the Label3D component for labels that appear as buttons (or for a label that has a border). In the customizer for the Label3D component, the Label3D tab allows you to control the kind of visual effects you want applied to the label (see Figure 3.4).

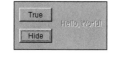

Figure 3.3
This is the Hello World label in the disabled state.

The Label3D Border Style field offers several choices, including IN, OUT, BORDERED, NOT BORDERED, and GRID LABEL. The purpose of the NOT BORDERED and the GRID LABEL choices are unclear. They don't appear to have any visible effect

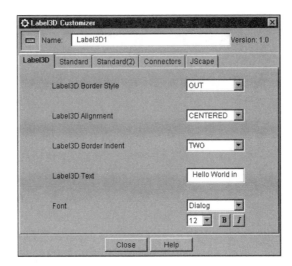

Figure 3.4
Use the Label3D component to create labels that look like buttons.

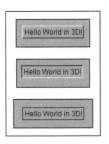

Figure 3.5
Label3D components when the border is specified as OUT, IN, and BORDERED.

on the appearance of the label in the GUI window. Figure 3.5 illustrates how the first three choices affect the label's appearance.

The Button Caption Is True

One odd aspect of the Hello World design is that the buttons are labeled True and Hide, which begs the question, "Shouldn't they be labeled Show and Hide?" Well, they should, and this is an area where Sun Microsystems can improve Java Studio's design. Here is the problem. The connector on the Label component for Hides And Shows The Label needs a value of True for the label to display in the GUI window. Any other message other than True is interpreted to be False, and therefore, any message other than True hides the label.

When a button is pressed, the value of the Button Caption field is sent to the output connector. We hope that when Sun releases the next version of Java Studio the Button component will have two fields in the customizer—Button Caption and Value When Pressed—so that the output string and the label on the button are two distinct items. Because Java Studio allows you to create your own Packaged Designs, Chapter 12 shows you how to create your own components which will allow you to create a customized Button component and specify the Button Caption and the value sent to the output connector.

Now that we've covered the questions concerning the Hello World design, let's turn to the order form design.

▶**Tip**

True, TRUE, Or true

When Java Studio is looking for a True message, it can be any incarnation of the word true. It can be TRUE, true, tRue, or any other combination of upper- and lowercase letters. However, unlike other development environments or languages, it cannot be the digit 1 or the word yes.

Figure 3.6
This is how the Text Field and the Text Area components appear in the Design window.

About That Order Form

Let's open up the order form created in Chapter 2 and take a look inside. This section discusses:

• Text Field and Text Area components

• Choice components

• Distributor and Merger components

• Sun's order form

By the time you're done reading this section, you'll be very well acquainted with the components covered here—practically an expert.

Exploring Text Field And Text Area Components

While working through the order form exercise, you might have wondered how you know when to choose a Text Field component and when to choose a Text Area component. The answer lies in how you want to use the component.

Use a Text Field component when the information you are collecting is a single unit of information. In contrast, use the Text Area component when you need to collect more ambiguous units of information. The Text Area component uses scrollbars, so users can enter as much information as they want. Figures 3.6 and 3.7 show how the Text Field and Text Area components appear in the Design and GUI windows.

Figure 3.7
This is how the Text Field and the Text Area components appear in the GUI window.

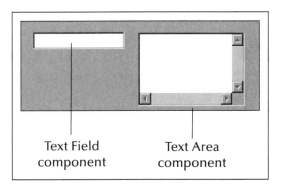

Text Field component   Text Area component

Tip

The Text Area component sends the entered information as a long string. If the user presses Enter or Return between the lines of text, the Enter is included in the string sent to the output connector. When you process the address information, you need to parse the string for the individual items. So, you might decide that you want to collect address information as individual units with Text Fields. For example, you can ask for the customer's city in one Text Field, the state in another Text Field, and the ZIP code in a third Text Field. Text Field components are very flexible, and you can use them for text as well as numbers.

Text Fields For Numbers

As you probably recall, you used a Text Field component for the number of maps ordered instead of a number component. We did this because the only component that can collect numerical information is the (poorly named) Floating Text Field on the GUI tab. Contrary to its name, it doesn't have anything to do with levitating text. Instead, it accepts numbers containing 1 to 20 digits after the decimal point, and it enables you to specify the number of digits before the decimal point. Because users can order maps only in whole number increments, it would be pointless to ask for the number of maps with a Floating Text Field component, as shown in Figure 3.8.

Because Text Fields can accept and send whole numbers, it is a good idea to use Text Field components for any whole number fields. In fact, Text Fields can also accept floating-point numbers, but you cannot control the number of digits before or after the decimal point.

Figure 3.8
The minimum number of digits after the decimal point in a Floating Text Field component is one, which doesn't work when you're working with whole numbers.

The Text Field component always has an output connector and an input connector, and it can have other connectors as well.

Text Field Connectors

By default, the Text Field component has an input connector that allows you to send text that replaces any text in the Text Field. Furthermore, it has an output connector where text is sent when the user presses Enter or when a trigger message is received. In order to receive a trigger message, the Text Field component needs to have a trigger connector. To add a trigger connector to a Text Field component, select the checkbox on the Connectors tab in the Text Field Customizer called Triggers The Component. When you add a trigger connector, it appears on the top of the component in the Design window. Figure 3.9 shows the connectors available for the Text Field component.

Text Area Connectors

The Text Area component, by default, has one connector called Append Text. It allows you to specify text that you want appended to the end of the text in the Text Area. Additional Text Area connectors are similar, but not identical, to the available Text Field connectors. Even the order of the items on the Connectors tab is a little different from the Text Field component (see Figure 3.10).

Text Field And Text Area Connectors In The Order Form Design

In the order form design, you added a Clears Text connector for both the Text Field and Text Area components. The Clears Text connector allows you to clear the fields when a message is received. In the order form, the message is the signal generated when the Submit button is pressed. The Clears Text connector erases the text in the fields when the user presses the Submit button. If this connector is omitted, the text stays in the fields until the user deletes the text manually.

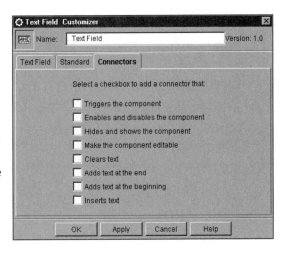

Figure 3.9
By default, the Text Field component has one input connector and one output connector. You can add more connectors using the Connectors tab.

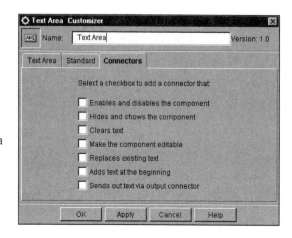

Figure 3.10
By default, the Text Area component has one input connector. You can add more connectors with the Connectors tab.

The other action performed with the Text Field and Text Area components is sending the text to the output connector. The text is sent to the output connector when the user presses Enter within the field or when a trigger message is received. Because it is very unintuitive for users to press Enter at the end of each field on a form, the order form uses the trigger method.

As discussed earlier in this section, in order for the Text Field component to have a trigger connector, you need to select the Triggers The Component checkbox on the Connectors tab. However, the Text Area component does not have a similar checkbox. How do add a trigger component on a Text Area component?

After you select the connector Sends Out Text Via Output Connector, the Text Area component adds an output connector and a trigger connector. You get two connectors for the price of one!

Exploring Choice Components

Another common question is, "When should you use a Choice component instead of a Text Field or Text Area component?" This section addresses how you can tell when you need a Choice component. After you determine that a Choice component will serve your users' needs best, the next step is to thoughtfully create the choices available in your component.

Using Choice Components

Use a Choice component when you want a user to select an item from a predefined list. This restricts the input and makes it clear to your users the type of response you are seeking. However, it might frustrate users if their choice does not appear on the list. So, think carefully about the items to include. Furthermore, a Choice component limits any creativity on the part of the user. The usefulness of a Choice component is left to your judgment.

Choice components function a little differently than Text Field and Text Area components in that they send out their text as soon as the user makes a choice. If you want the text from the Choice component sent out along with the other text, in the correct order, you need to add a trigger component, as shown in Figure 3.11.

In the order form, the items from the Choice components are sent to the display when you select an item from the list. Then, the items are sent again when you press the Submit button. The application that processes the text from the order form should probably discard the Choice items when they are initially received, because users don't actually submit their information until they press the Submit button.

Choices, Choices—Making Your List

After you decide that you want users to select options from a list, you need to specify the contents of the list. You do this on the Choice tab in the Choice customizer, as shown in Figure 3.12.

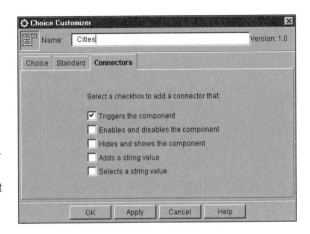

Figure 3.11
Add a trigger connector to a Choice component to control when the text is sent to the output connector.

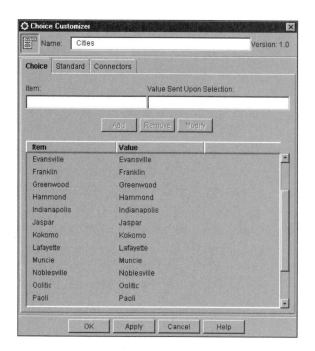

Figure 3.12
Specify the items in the Choice list on the Choice tab.

When you add items to the list, add them in the order you want them to appear in the list. You have some limited methods of rearranging the list, such as modifying and deleting existing items. But you cannot explicitly move items in the list to another location in the list.

The first item in the list, by default, is called Choice. You can delete this item, and you can add an item that helps the user to remember to select an item (or at least to indicate to you when they don't make a selection). The first item could be a choice such as "Choose a month," and you could set the value to be "Default month".

By default, when you add an item, the text you type in the Item field is duplicated in the Value Sent Upon Selection field. You can modify the contents of the Value field. For example, you can list all the months in the Item field. In the Value field, you can abbreviate each month's name to three characters. To modify the contents of the Value field, select the item to modify, change the contents of the Value field, then click Modify. The items listed in the Value column are the actual text strings sent to the output connector when the user selects an item from the list.

Distributor And Merger Components

Distributor and Merger components are two sides of the same coin. One takes one input and sends it to many components, and the other takes many inputs and merges them into one output. For both components, you can add as many inputs (for Merger components) or outputs (for Distributor components) as you like.

As you work with Distributor and Merger components, you will discover that it makes sense to name the connectors consistently. For example, for the Merger component, you can name the added input connectors as Input 3, Input 4, Input 5, and so on. Because it comes with two input connectors called Input 1 and Input 2, the new connectors can carry on the pattern. The same naming convention works for new output connectors on a Distributor component. You can call the connectors Output 3, Output 4, Output 5, and so on.

We have now reviewed the components used in the order form design. With this knowledge in mind, let's review the difference between the order form design and the order form in Sun's documentation for Java Studio.

Why Your Order Form Differs From The Documentation

In Sun's documentation that comes with Java Studio, Chapter 6 is about creating a user information form. As you can see, Sun's order form appears less complicated than yours. As you will see, there is a reason for this. If you want to open Sun's example order form, it's called Basic_Form.vj, and it's stored in the Java-Studio1.0\Js\examples directory. You can also get to the example by going to the Help menu and choosing Help On Java Studio. Click the book next to Tutorials And Examples, then click List Of Additional Examples. The second section is called "How do I do a basic input information form?" Figure 3.13 shows Sun's order form.

The Sun example gets the task done, but it asks a lot of the user. For example, the user is instructed to press Enter after each field. This is the only way the text in the field is collected, so it can be

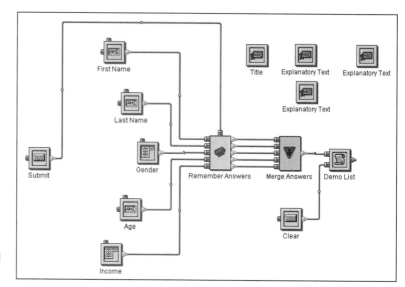

Figure 3.13
Sun's order form uses a
Memory component.
The form requires users
to press Enter at the end
of each field.

sent when the Submit button is pressed. If the user fails to press
Enter at the end of a field, the text will not be sent when the
Submit button is pressed. The other drawback of Sun's sample
form is that the form is not cleared when the Submit button is
pressed. The user has to delete any existing text before entering
new text.

On the other hand, Sun's order form stores all the numbers in a
Memory component until the Submit button is pressed. In this
book's example, the Choice components send their text as soon as
the user selects an item, and then the text is sent again with all of
the Text Field and Text Area components when the Submit
button is pressed.

In your order form, shown in Figure 3.14, you explicitly added
connectors to your components to clear the text, and you added
a Distributor component to distribute the signal from the
Submit button so all the components received the signal at the
same time. The distributed signal both triggers the components
to send their text to their output connectors and sends a message to the Clears Text input connectors. The distributed signal
to each component that triggers sending the text to the output
connectors is the reason your users don't need to press Enter at
the end of each field.

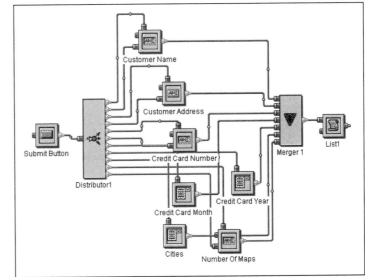

Figure 3.14
Your order form is a bit more complicated than Sun's. Your form clears the field when the user presses the Submit button and doesn't require the user to press Enter after each entry.

The Next Stage

The order form design is a good start, but it's not ready for prime time. There are a few areas you need to address. For example, your users need elements such as labels to tell them how to fill in the fields, and you need to assign the order of the items when the user presses Tab. Not so coincidentally, those topics are covered in the next chapter.

Chapter 4

Building Java Studio Designs Using The GUI Window

Whether we like it or not, appearances matter. In Java Studio, a well-designed GUI window is equivalent to having your hair combed and shirt tucked in. A well-designed GUI window helps you and your users make the most of your design.

In this chapter, you'll work through tasks designed to familiarize you with the GUI window. Then, in Chapter 5, you can learn about the concepts behind the tasks you perform here.

You'll start by working with the design you built in Chapter 2. (Don't worry if you didn't save it. We have one on the CD for you.) You'll spend some time using the GUI window to build the interface to the design. Then we'll discuss tabbing from field to field and how to determine the sequence of fields. We'll end with instructions for adding different colors and backgrounds to your design. If you don't have it running, start Java Studio now.

Start With Your Existing Design

You have a job waiting for you. The design you built in Chapter 2 is in desperate need of an interface facelift. Earlier in this book, you focused on the details of using the Design window—you didn't do squat with the GUI window! Now, here's your chance to focus on the interface. Let's begin with one of the most common interface elements—labels.

Let Them Know What You Want

Your order form needs labels so that your users will know how to fill in the fields. After you add labels, you can use Java Studio's tools to align the order form's elements.

If you have not already done so, open the design you built in Chapter 2. Or, you can open the chapter02_example.vj file stored on this book's companion CD-ROM. After you open the design, perform the following steps:

1. On the GUI tab on the component palette, select the Label component. This time, instead of placing it in the Design window, place it in the GUI window next to the first text field.

2. In the Label Customizer, specify the name of the label as "Customer Name Label". Specify the label text as "Enter your name", as shown in Figure 4.1.

3. Click OK.

4. In the GUI window, notice how the label appears. Do you have enough room to place the labels to the left of the Text Fields and Text Areas? You can increase the size of the GUI window by dragging the width of the window so it is wider, but that's probably not enough. You also need to move the items in the GUI window to the right. To do this, click in the upper left-hand corner of the GUI window and drag to the bottom right-hand corner. When you let go, all the items within the rectangle you have drawn should be selected, as shown in Figure 4.2.

5. After all the items are selected, click and hold on the perimeter of one of the selection rectangles. Then, drag the group

▶**Tip**

Missed Some Items?

If your click-and-drag action missed some of the items in the GUI window, you can add them without starting over. Press and hold the Ctrl key, and then select your missing item. If you still don't have all the items selected, continue to hold the Ctrl key and select the missing items. Then, you can release the Ctrl key. Or, simply click and drag again.

Figure 4.1
Specify the name of the component and the caption on the button in the Label Customizer.

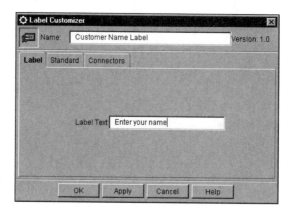

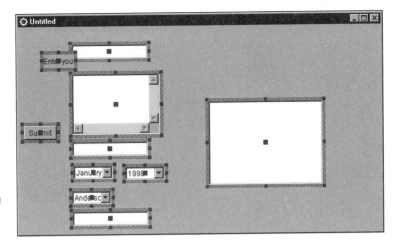

Figure 4.2
Select all the items in the GUI window so you can move them as a group.

to the right. Now, you should have room to add your labels on the left-hand side.

6. Move the label for the Customer Name field so you have room to enlarge the label enough to display the label's text. Then, click and drag the width of the label so the *Enter your name* text displays, as shown in Figure 4.3.

7. Now, add a label for the Customer Address Text Area. Specify the name of the component as Customer Address Label, and specify the label text as "Enter your address", as shown in Figure 4.4.

8. Resize the label in the GUI window so that the label text displays completely, as shown in Figure 4.5. For now, don't worry about the exact placement of the label. You'll take care of the alignment issues later in this chapter.

9. Did you already move the Submit button out of the way? If not, go ahead and select it, and then move it to the bottom of the GUI window, as shown in Figure 4.6.

10. Add a label for the Credit Card Number Text Field. Specify the name of the component as Credit Card Label, and specify the label text as "Enter your credit card number". Resize the

Figure 4.3
Adjust the position and size of the label component in the GUI window so the label text displays completely.

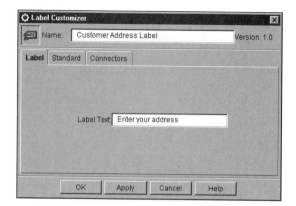

Figure 4.4
Add a label for the
Customer Address Text
Area.

Figure 4.5
Resize the label box in
the GUI window so the
label text displays
completely.

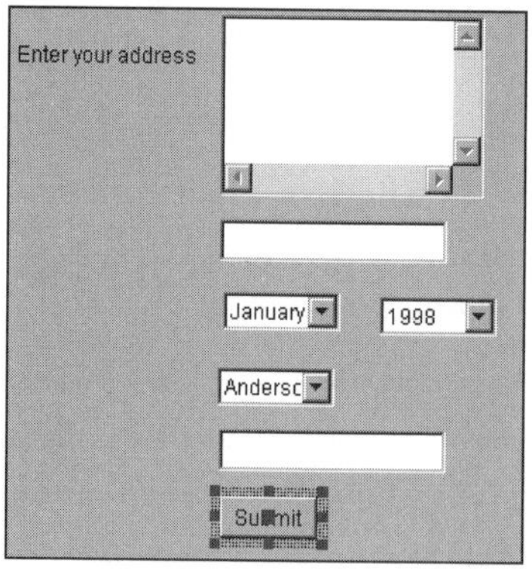

Figure 4.6
Move the Submit button
to the bottom of the GUI
window.

label in the GUI window so that the label text displays
completely, as shown in Figure 4.7.

11. The Label component doesn't allow you to split label text
across multiple lines, so the label for the credit card expiration date should probably be in two Label components. Name
the first one Credit Card Exp1, and name the second one
Credit Card Exp2. Specify the label text for the first one as
"Select your credit card's", and specify the text for the second
one as "expiration date", as shown in Figure 4.8.

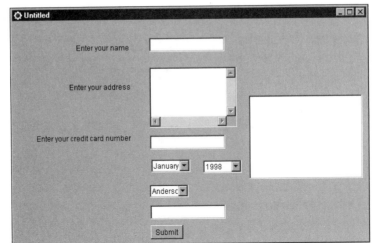

Figure 4.7
Add a label for the Credit Card Number Text Field, and resize it so the label text displays completely.

Figure 4.8
Add two Label components for the credit card expiration date.

12. Add text labels to instruct the user to select the city of the map he or she is ordering, and to specify the quantity of that map. Name the components Map City Label and Number Of Maps Label, and specify the label text as "Select the city for the map" and "Enter the number of maps", as shown in Figure 4.9.

Now all your labels are in the GUI window. Your next task is to resize the Text Field and Text Area components so the user has enough—but not too much—space to type.

Give Them Room

To determine how much room is necessary for each Text Field and Text Area, type sample text that nears the large end of what would be typical. For example, see Figure 4.10.

Of course, you could use each component's customizer and specify the width and height of each item using the Standard tab. But, it's easier to just resize the components in the GUI window. Now that everything should be approximately the right size, let's look at the aesthetics.

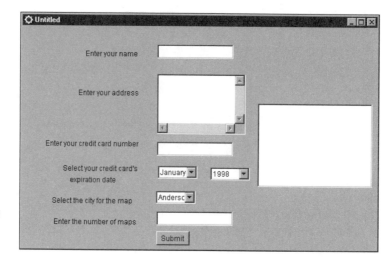

Figure 4.9
Add text labels for the city of the map and the number of maps the user wants to order.

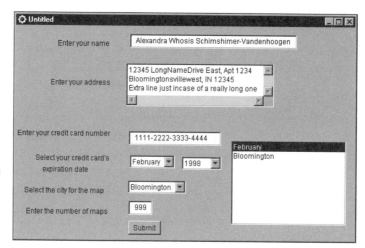

Figure 4.10
Type sample text in each field. Make up long samples, and resize the components in the GUI window as necessary.

Figure 4.11
The Layout menu offers several functions to improve the design of the ordering form.

Make It Nice

In this section, you're going to use the functions available on the Layout menu to improve the design of the ordering form. Figure 4.11 shows the Layout menu.

Java Studio uses a *design grid*, a grid of equally spaced dots that you can use to help you place objects. Or, you can use the design grid for Java Studio's Snap To Grid function. To turn on the grid, go to the Layout menu, and then choose Show Grid. The grid displays. The default setting on the grid is a medium density, as shown in Figure 4.12.

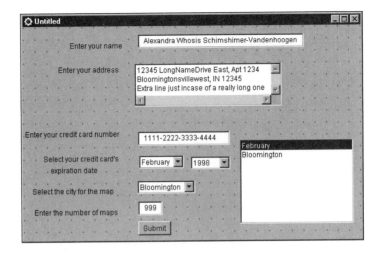

Figure 4.12
The default setting on the design grid is a medium density.

You do not have to use medium density—you can choose small or large density, as well. In this example, let's say you want to work with a smaller granularity right now. Go to the Layout menu, choose Set Grid Size, and choose Small. Now you can take advantage of the grid, so go to the Layout menu and choose Snap To Grid. These settings ensure that every time you move an item in the GUI window, it snaps to one of the design grid points.

You're now set to use the Align and Equalize functions of the Layout menu.

Aligning Items

Unfortunately, Java Studio's Layout menu does not offer the equivalent of a Group function. This means that you need to pay attention to certain items, such as the two text labels for the credit card expiration date, when you align a set of components. Take care not to align items on top of each other in the following steps:

1. Select each component with its label, and align them by their tops. Select the text label *Enter your name* and the Customer Name Text Field. From the Layout menu, choose Align, and then choose Top, as shown in Figure 4.13. When you align the text labels for the credit card expiration date, make sure that you only select the top text. Otherwise, you'll end up stacking both text labels on top of each other.

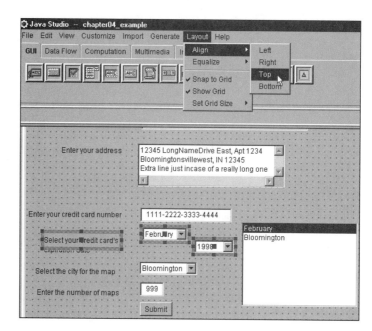

Figure 4.13
Align each text label to the top of the component it labels.

It's Not Quite At The Top

If you feel like the label text doesn't really line up to the top of the component, then be aware that the Align function aligns the label's box, not the label's text, to the top of the other items selected. You can modify the height of the Label component more precisely with the Standard tab on the Label Customizer. If you are using the default font for the text (Dialog, plain, 12 point), then you can set the height to 15. Then, align the label and the Text Field component again.

2. Select all the text labels, and align them to the left, as shown in Figure 4.14.

3. Select the Text Field, Text Area, Choice, and Button components, and align them to the left (but don't select the Choice component with the year, and don't select the List area that you're using to see the text sent to the output connectors). Figure 4.15 displays the selected components.

4. The order form has three main groups: the customer name and address, the credit card information, and the map information. Select the label-and-component groups, and move them so you can create more space between the groups. When you're done, turn off the grid display so you can better see the overall effect. Your form should look similar to the form shown in Figure 4.16.

You're almost done arranging items for this design. The next task involves the Design window.

Design Window? This Is The GUI Chapter

Yes, this is the GUI chapter, but take a look at the Design window. While you were merrily adding Label components, you were

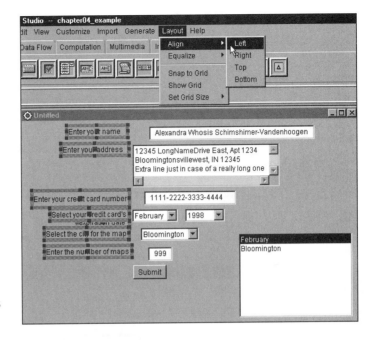

Figure 4.14
Align all the text labels to the left.

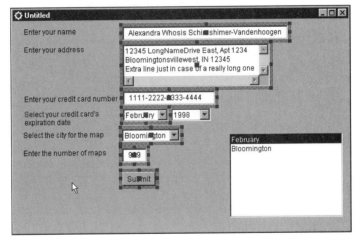

Figure 4.15
Align all of the other components to the left (except for the year and the List component).

also adding components to the Design window, and now, as you can see in Figure 4.17, it's sort of a mess.

The functions of the Layout menu only apply to the items in the GUI window. If you select several components in the Design window and choose to Align Top, then the corresponding components in the GUI window obligingly align.

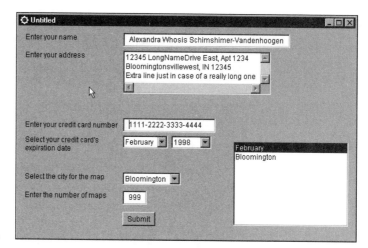

Figure 4.16
Group the related items.

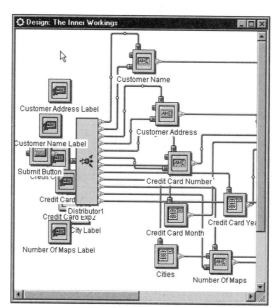

Figure 4.17
The Design window is rather unkempt with all the Label components added.

So, you have to align components in the Design window the old-fashioned way—manually. Let's line up the Label components neatly on the left-hand side or along the bottom. To make some room, maximize the Design window. Click and drag to draw a selection rectangle around most of the functional components of the design. Note that if any part of a component is in the selection rectangle, then it is selected. Also, note that you can Ctrl+click to add items to the selection, but you cannot Ctrl+click to remove items from the selection.

▶Tip

Grid On Or Grid Off?

Should you work with the grid display turned on or off? It's really up to you. The grid points don't affect alignment. The grid helps when you are trying to place items at precise intervals. If placement doesn't matter that much, or if you would rather eyeball it, go ahead and turn off the grid display. Either way, when you're done arranging your items, turn off the grid display so you can see how the interface appears to your users.

After you have selected the functional components of the design, move them to the right. Then, take each Label component and move it so they all line up on the left-hand side of the screen, as shown in Figure 4.18.

You might ask why you're going through this process. The reason is that you need to maintain the function of the design in the Design window. If the Design window isn't organized, then your maintenance job becomes more difficult.

Equalizing Items

One way to improve the interface's design is to maintain consistent distances between items. The Layout menu offers an Equalize function; however, Equalize is not what you want. You use Equalize to change the height or width of a component to match another component.

To use the Equalize function, select the items you want to equalize. Then, go to the Layout menu, and choose Equalize. You can choose to equalize the height, width, or both of the selected components. The Equalize function looks for the component with

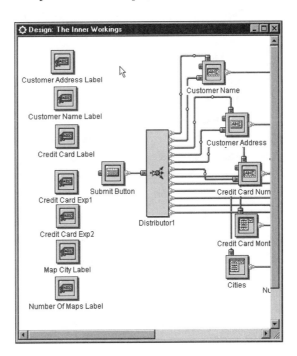

Figure 4.18
Line up the Label components in the Design window.

Figure 4.19
The Equalize function takes the smallest parameter and changes all of the selected components to match.

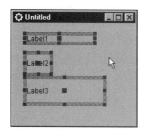 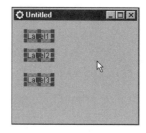

the smallest height, or the smallest width, or both, and then changes all the selected components to match (see Figure 4.19).

We have now covered the fundamentals of the GUI window. You know how to fine-tune, arrange, align, and equalize components in the GUI window. You could sail on to greater glory in interface design (after carefully reading Chapter 5, of course), but there are two more topics we would like to discuss. The first topic is how to determine the sequence of the fields in the GUI window, and the second topic is how to add eye candy to your interface.

Determine The Sequence

Sequence is a topic that you've probably been looking for—how do you control the order of the text fields when the user tabs from field to field?

Bottom line—you don't, at least not easily. It's not a predictable phenomenon. You can guess that it goes in the sequence in which you added the components, but no. Possibly it goes in alphabetical order by the name of the component, or maybe it relies on the order that the components are connected through their input connectors. None of these are the answer. It is highly frustrating that this version of Java Studio does not allow you to dictate the tabbing sequence of your components.

However, the Validation Text Field component, which is used for database applications in Java Studio, does use a predictable order. For more information, see Chapter 16.

You might be able to control the order of Text Fields, Text Areas, and Choice components by creating some custom beans, and perhaps someone in the Java Studio developers community will post one in the comp.lang.java.beans newsgroup. Of course, that's not a great answer right now, but it's the only answer we have.

Finally—if you're feeling ambitious—here's some optional work for you. Java Studio enables you to customize your GUI window's background, and the next section shows you how.

Add Eye Candy

Java Studio allows you to specify wallpaper and background colors for the GUI window. You can also specify the title that appears in the title bar of the GUI window, but your users won't actually see the title bar unless you generate your design as an applet that appears in its own window or as an application. To customize the GUI window, go to the Customize menu and choose GUI Window. Figure 4.20 shows the GUI Window Customizer.

When you open the GUI Window Customizer, the GUI window's width and height are displayed with the current settings. While

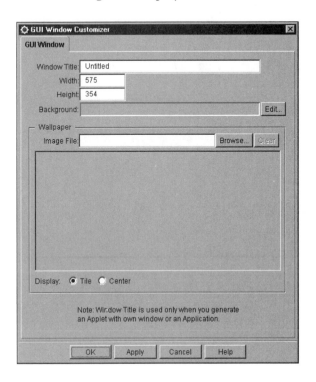

Figure 4.20
The Customize menu offers the GUI Window Customizer.

you're here, specify the name of your design as the Hello, Indiana! Order Form. Now, let's add some wallpaper.

Adding Wallpaper

When you add wallpaper to a design, use caution. If the wallpaper adds to the value of your design and it pleases your users, then go ahead and use it. But, if it's added only to please yourself, then consider avoiding burdening your users with the visual clutter. For the sake of learning how to do it, let's add wallpaper to your order form design. Follow these steps:

1. On the Customize menu, choose GUI Window.

2. In the Wallpaper area, look for the Image File field. Look on the right-hand side for the Browse button. Click Browse, and look for the file indiana.jpg on the CD-ROM that accompanies this book. Select it.

3. Look below the area that displays the wallpaper image at the Display choices. If it's not already selected, select Tile. The results are shown in Figure 4.21. The results aren't pretty. Remember, you need to be cautious about adding wallpaper.

4. Click OK.

Figure 4.21
Add a tiled image as wallpaper to the design.

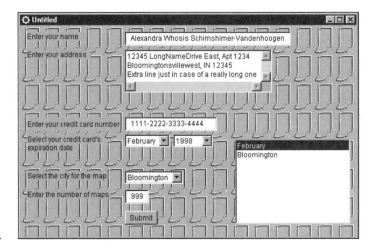

Figure 4.22
The Color Chooser offers a variety of background colors, but choose carefully to avoid annoying your users.

Adding Background Color

Adding background color, depending on your choice of colors, can be a little less intrusive than wallpaper for your users. To customize the background color, go to the Customize menu, and choose GUI Window. Look at the Background field, and click Edit. The Color Chooser displays as shown in Figure 4.22. You can choose from many interesting background colors.

The colors include choices such as:

- aliceblue
- antique white
- aquamarine
- azure
- beige
- bisque

as well as 58 shades of gray and a number of other colors.

Tell Me More, Tell Me More

You've done the grunt work—now it's time for some practical theory. If you want to know more about using the GUI window or if you just want to get into more detail about interface design, dive into Chapter 5.

Chapter 5

Understanding Java Studio Designs Using The GUI Window

Here's your opportunity to explore the details of using the GUI window. This chapter discusses the concepts presented in Chapter 4 that you used to clean up your order form.

In this chapter, you'll look at some of the details that can make you more proficient in using the GUI window. Then, we'll cover some user-interface design basics that you can apply to the techniques you learned.

Why Start With Your Existing Design?

Why did you start the design process in Chapter 4 with the order form design that you created in Chapter 2? For two reasons:

- It sorely needed the work.

- If you used only the GUI window to create a design, you wouldn't have much functionality at the end. You can add components that have a visual component, but you can't connect them, distribute their input, or do much more than change how they look.

Which brings us to an interesting point. Which components have a visual representation in the GUI window? Actually, if you try to add a component to the GUI window that does not have a visual representation, Java Studio lets you know, as shown in Figure 5.1. Java Studio's visual components are shown in Figures 5.2 and 5.3.

Appendix A presents a complete list of Java Studio components. Each description in Appendix A includes how the

Figure 5.1
Java Studio warns you
when you try to add a
nonvisual component to
the GUI window.

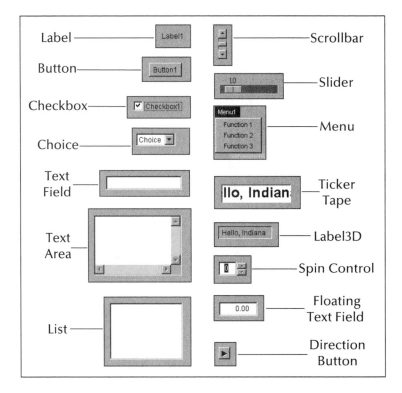

Figure 5.2
Visual components on
the GUI tab, as they
appear in the GUI
window.

component appears in the GUI window and how it appears in
the Design window.

Let's get down to the nitty-gritty of using the GUI window. First,
let's look at how to resize the GUI window and some hints on
manipulating the GUI window. Then we'll look at how to resize
Java Studio components.

Resizing The GUI Window

You can increase the size of the GUI window by dragging the
edges of the window so it is wider, but this might not solve your

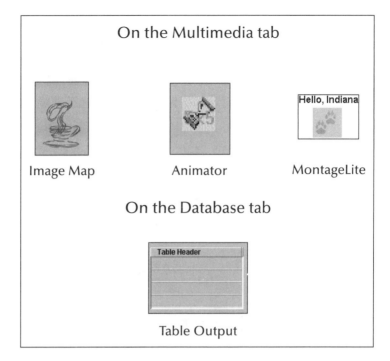

On the Multimedia tab

Image Map   Animator   MontageLite

On the Database tab

Table Output

Figure 5.3
Visual component s on the Multimedia and Database tabs, as they appear in the GUI window.

Figure 5.4
This GUI window needs more room, both horizontally and vertically.

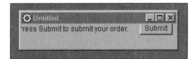

problem if your design is too far to the left or too close to the top. Figure 5.4 illustrates a sample GUI window. Note that you do not receive any feedback (such as scrollbars) from Java Studio indicating that the GUI window is too small.

For some reason, when you drag the left side of the window, you get more space on the right-hand side. When you drag the right side of the window, you get more space on the right-hand side. Figure 5.5 illustrates resizing the GUI window by dragging the left side of the window and by dragging the right side of the window. Figure 5.6 illustrates the problem when the design is too close to the top. Dragging either the top of the window or the bottom of the window gives you more space on the bottom.

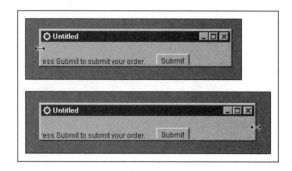

Figure 5.5
Neither stretching the left edge nor stretching the right edge fixes the GUI window.

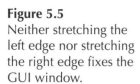

Figure 5.6
Neither stretching the top edge nor stretching the bottom edge fixes the GUI window.

Solving The GUI Window Sizing Dilemma

Fortunately, there's a workaround to sizing the GUI window. The following steps present a technique that makes it a little easier to arrange components in the GUI window:

1. Maximize the GUI window by clicking the maximize icon in the upper-right corner of the window.

2. Select all the components in the GUI window. (For more details on selecting components in the GUI window, refer to the tip regarding selecting components later in this chapter.)

3. Move the components as a group to the upper-left corner of the GUI window so that all the components appear in the window.

4. Restore the size of the GUI window by clicking the Restore icon in the upper-right corner.

5. Now, you can resize the window by dragging the edges to make it the proper size, as shown in Figure 5.7.

Figure 5.7
Now the GUI window is the proper size, and the components are in the correct place.

Resizing Components—Larger Is Easier Than Smaller

Let's say the Label component is not big enough to display the label text completely. You can smile confidently, and smoothly drag the side of the component so that it is big enough. But, later, when you realize that the component needs to be smaller, that confident smile is nowhere to be found. Unfortunately, when you resize a component in the GUI window, you don't receive visual feedback that tells you the size of the rectangle as it gets smaller.

All Together Now! Selecting Components

Did you have problems selecting all the components in the GUI window in the preceding section? If so, here are a few hints to help make selecting easier:

- To add items to a group of selected items, press and hold the Control key, and click the item to add to the selection.

- You cannot Ctrl+click to subtract items from a selection. If you selected too many items, you need to click outside of the selection to deselect everything, and start over.

- If you are having problems because one component is in the way (one you don't want to select), just cut the component and paste it on another area. Make your selection. Later, cut and paste the component back to its original location.

- When you click and drag to create a selection rectangle, if any part of a component is in the rectangle, it is included in the selection. Figure 5.8 illustrates a selection rectangle that selects both components.

Figure 5.8
If any part of a component is in the selection rectangle, the component is included in the selection.

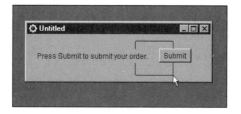

Figure 5.9
When you make a
component larger, you
see an indication of the
newly proposed size.
When you make it
smaller, you're just
guessing.

On the other hand, you do get feedback when you make a component larger. Figure 5.9 illustrates the problem.

When you're making a component smaller, plan on doing it with multiple attempts. You need to wait until you apply your changes before seeing the actual size. Then just try again. It's not elegant, but it's all we have in this version of Java Studio.

Sizing A Component Precisely

Each component that appears in the GUI window has a Standard tab in its customizer that allows you to specify the height and width of the component as it appears in the GUI window. The numbers you specify for the height and width are pixels, just like the specifications for your monitor display. Figure 5.10 illustrates the size of various buttons, as specified in pixels.

We've covered just about everything there is to know about using the GUI window. Now, we'll review some principles of user-interface design so you know what to do with your newfound techniques.

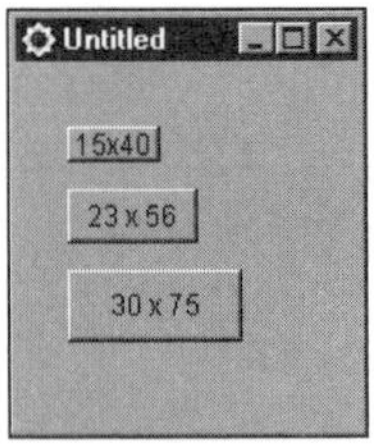

Figure 5.10
The default size for a
Button component is 23
by 56 pixels.

A Quick Tutorial On Interface Design

At this point, you should feel like you have the technical know-how to design an interface. Now, you need to look at some interface design basics. Knowing about interface design enables you to intelligently and thoughtfully arrange text fields and labels and to choose colors and wallpaper with an eye toward helping your users rather than pleasing yourself.

In this section, you'll learn the most important rule to keep near and dear to your heart when considering the interface of your design. We'll also discuss ways you can use the Label3D component to your advantage, review the principles of arranging items, and list some basics about choosing colors for your design.

The Number One Rule

Users won't tolerate a sluggish design—no matter how elegant the interface. How slow does a design have to be to be ranked as sluggish? Standard interface design methodologies say that for items to appear connected, the response time needs to be 200 milliseconds or less. The actual response time might not be totally under your control, but keep this number in mind.

The next number you need to keep in mind is 10 seconds. That's how long you have (if you're lucky) before a user reboots the machine, in the absence of any sort of feedback. So, when the user presses the Submit button, immediately display a message such as "Processing order. Please wait…" to acknowledge the user's action. Providing a message buys some time as the order processes.

A very close second to the Rule Of Speed is the Rule Of Spell Check. It's careless not to check your spelling. Misspellings distract users from the message of your Web site. Even though a spell check is easy to do, it's forgotten often enough to bring it up here.

Leveraging The Label3D Component

You can use the Label3D component to add life to your design. For example, you can use Label3D components to create navigational aids. As you might remember from Chapter 3, the Label3D component allows you to choose several effects, including the appearance of a pressed-in button.

You can use the components as buttons to show the main elements of a Web site, as shown in Figure 5.11. Then, when the user

Figure 5.11
Use the Label3D component to identify the main sections of a Web site.

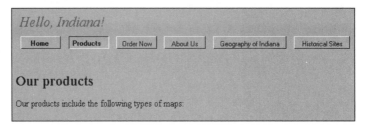

Figure 5.12
A Label3D component, with the Label3D Border Style set to IN, tells users which area of the Web site they are visiting.

 Tip

Matching Colors

You can set the background color of your Web site to be the same as the default color of the GUI window, called lightgray. To do so, change the <BODY> tag in your HTML file to: <BODY BGCOLOR="#C0C0C0">.

is in one of the Web site's main sections, you can change the appropriate component so that it has a pressed-in appearance, as shown in Figure 5.12.

The Art And Science Of Arranging Items

In addition to the concepts presented in this chapter, there are a number of design issues you should be aware of. To help you get a jump start on good design, here's a 60-second tutorial in layout issues:

- Place the OK button on the bottom left and place the Cancel button on the bottom right.

- If you are building a design for a primarily English-speaking audience, arrange items as they would read them—from top to bottom and from left to right. If you are designing for non-English speakers, follow the standard pattern for the dominant language.

- Match field sizes to the expected input. If the field is much larger or smaller than the user's input, the user might be a little unsure about what to type.

- Left-justify items.

- Consistency is good, but it's not the ultimate rule. Try to make the buttons on all your screens similar in size, but if you need to conserve space, it's okay to modify a button to be a little smaller.

- Make it easy for your users to do the right thing. If the next step is to click the OK button, make the button big enough so that the user doesn't have to work hard to find and click the button.

- To avoid cluttering the screen, group related items, and leave space between the groups.

- Avoid displaying labels or instructions in all capital letters, unless you're a font designer and have a beautiful all-caps font and know what you're doing. All capitals are hard to read, and of course, many people familiar with email and newsgroups consider text displayed in all capital letters to be the same as shouting. (Take a look at the choices in the customizer for the Label3D component. Do you like reading the capital letters?)

The Art And Science Of Color

Color plays an enormous role in good design. Therefore, in addition to the preceding 60-second tutorial on good design, here's a bonus 30-second lesson on using color in your design:

- First, complete your design in black and white. Make sure the information is complete and understandable without color. Then, go back and add color where it enhances information retrieval, comprehension, and the visual appeal of your site.

- Avoid burdening your users with more than six colors on a screen.

- Build on the meanings associated with color. For example, red often equals danger, error, fast, down (ever notice that the down button for elevators are red?); green equals good, go ahead, up, environmental; orange equals safety; and dark blue indicates stability and tradition. You can find many resources in bookstores, on the Web, and at your local library discussing meanings associated with colors.

- Make sure that your text color displays in high contrast to your background color. For example, yellow text on a white screen is unreadable, just as red or blue text on a black screen is unreadable. One of the reasons why black text on white screens is so common is that it provides high contrast. If you want more variety than black text on white backgrounds, experiment with dark colors, such as dark blue or dark gray, on light backgrounds, such as pale yellow or cream.

- Be very cautious of using white text. It's hard to use without losing legibility.

Chapter 6

Building An Applet With Java Studio

"Bouncing is what Tiggers do best," said Tigger. Well, applets are what Java Studio does best. Applets tend to be small, which is better suited for Java Studio, and Java Studio automates some of the tasks involved in adding an applet to your Web site.

In this chapter, we discuss a few general points about applets, plan to build an applet, and then build a Java Studio design. Once the design is complete, we'll use Java Studio to generate an applet from the design, and finally we'll test the newly generated applet.

About Applets

As you know, the difference between applets and applications is that applets run in a Web browser. This means that when you are developing applets, you need to keep a couple techniques in mind:

- *When you're done building the applet, test it with both Microsoft Internet Explorer and Netscape Navigator.* If at all possible, test it using several versions of these browsers. Of course, if you're building this applet for an intranet, you might be able to narrow down the number of browsers that will be used to view your applet and save yourself some testing time.

- *Aggressively conserve your user's time and screen real estate.* Many forces are working against you in terms of time, and as discussed in Chapter 5, time is a prime consideration in good interface design.

Now that your senses and sensitivities are primed for applets, let's take a look at the applet we're going to build.

Planning The Applet

Being informed designers, we'll spend some time planning this applet before building it. We'll discuss the goal, build the design, and then test it. First, let's talk about this applet.

Goal: Calculate Monthly Mortgage Payments

We're going to create an applet that calculates monthly mortgage payments. Are you well versed in the six functions of a dollar? What about the sinking fund factor? Fortunately, we don't need to have the details of these functions committed to memory, because we happen to have the formula for computing a monthly mortgage payment. Therefore, we can skip over the gory details of how one derives the function and leave that to the mortgage wonks.

Our applet makes use of some of the components from the Computation tab to calculate a monthly mortgage payment. Users will only need to provide the interest rate, loan term, and loan amount. The formula for computing a monthly payment is shown in Figure 6.1. In Figure 6.1, *intrate* is the annual interest rate (such as 7.5 percent), *years* is the number of years of the loan (such as 30 years), *principal* is the amount of the loan (such as $150,000), and *monthly payment* is equal to the amount you pay each month for the principal and interest.

Of course, when you write that monthly check, it normally includes money for property taxes, private mortgage insurance, and insurance. Our applet just focuses on the amounts for principal and interest. Adding the other amounts is left as an exercise for the overachievers (or for those who want to add this applet to their Web site for real).

Ready to dive in?

Figure 6.1
The equation for a mortgage payment uses the interest rate, loan term, and loan amount.

$$\left(\frac{intrate}{12} + \frac{\frac{intrate}{12}}{\left(1 + \frac{intrate}{12}\right)^{years \times 12} - 1} \right) \times \; principal \; = \; monthly\ payment$$

Building The Applet

Before we have an applet, we need a Java Studio design. We are going to divide this task of creating the design into three parts: build the text fields, build the labels for the interface, and build the functional part where the numbers are calculated. After the design is complete, we'll generate an applet.

▶Tip

Again With The Triggers?

We need to add triggers to each component that collects data. Otherwise, the user must press Enter at the end of each field in order for the data to be sent through the design for processing. In the examples in Java Studio's documentation, this technique is not used. We favor adding triggers because we believe that users are unlikely to press Return at the end of each field without being harangued.

Build The Text Fields

If you haven't already done so, start Java Studio. If you still have Java Studio running from earlier chapters, save your current design, open the File menu, and choose New.

Our applet will require three input fields—interest rate, the number of years of the loan, and the amount of the loan. We will add these fields to the Design window, about a third of the way from the left. Follow these steps to create the input fields:

1. On the GUI tab, select the Text Field component, and click in the Design window. Name it Interest Rate Text Field, and add two connectors to trigger the component and to clear text, as shown in Figure 6.2.

2. Click OK.

3. On the GUI tab, select the Choice component, and click in the Design window. Name it "Number of Years Choice". On

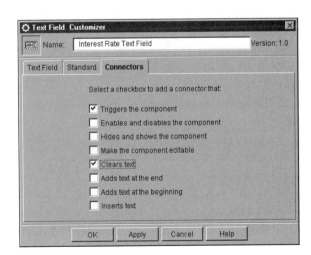

Figure 6.2
Use the customizer to add two connectors to the Interest Rate Text Field component.

the Choice tab, first modify the default item Choice so it reads "Choose".

4. Add three more items to the Choice tab named 15 Years, 20 Years, and 30 Years, as shown in Figure 6.3.

5. Click the Connectors tab and select the Triggers The Component option.

6. Click OK.

7. From the GUI tab, select the Text Field component, and click in the Design window. Name it "Principal Text Field", and select the Triggers The Component and the Clears Text options on the Connectors tab.

8. Click OK.

9. Tidy up the components in the Design window by manually lining them up, as shown in Figure 6.4.

10. Tidy up the components in the GUI window by manually moving them closer to each other, and then by left aligning them, as shown in Figure 6.5. If you like, go ahead and widen the Choice component a bit.

   Now, we are going to add text fields to the GUI window. We'll add four text fields that will be used to gather mortgage information, as shown in Figure 6.6.

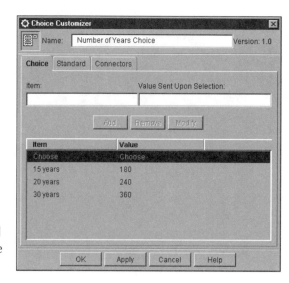

Figure 6.3
Add a Number of Years Choice component, and add items on the Choice tab.

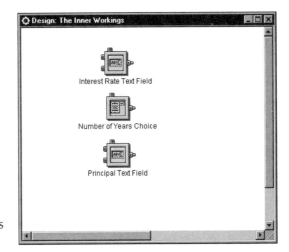

Figure 6.4
Tidy up the components in the Design window.

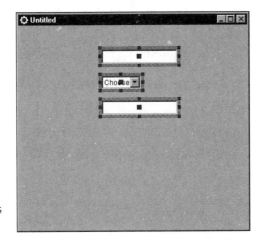

Figure 6.5
Tidy up the components in the GUI window.

11. Add a Text Field component named Interest Rate Text Field Display to the Design window and make it smaller, as shown in Figure 6.6. Plan on the text field displaying a maximum of 3 or 4 digits and a decimal point, such as 7.25. Change the size of the text field so that the number displays entirely but without too much extra space. In our example, the width of the text field is 38 pixels.

12. Add a Text Field component below the Interest Rate Text Field Display component. Name the new text field "Number of Years Text Field Display".

13. Make the Interest Rate Text Field and the Number of Years Text Field components the same width. Select the Interest Rate Text Field Display component, press Shift, click the Number of Years Text Field Display component, and release the Shift key. With the components selected, open the Layout menu, and choose Equalize|Width.

14. Add a Text Field component named Principal Text Field Display below the Number of Years Text Field Display, as shown in Figure 6.6.

15. Add a Text Field component named Payment Text Field Display below the Principal Text Field Display, as shown in Figure 6.6.

16. Align the four Text Field display components along their left edges, as shown in Figure 6.7.

17. Add a button between the input text fields and the display text fields. Name it "Submit Button", and specify a button label of Submit, as shown in Figure 6.8.

18. Go ahead and spend a little time tidying up the Design window. Place the Submit button on the far left side, and spread the display text fields along the bottom of the window, as shown in Figure 6.9.

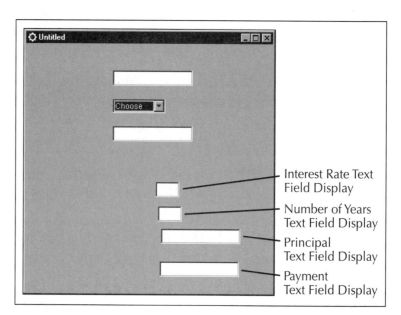

Figure 6.6
Add four Text Field components in the GUI window.

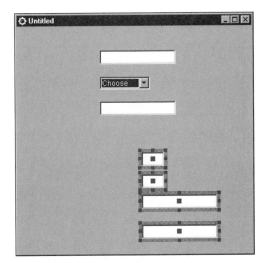

Figure 6.7
Align the Text Field display components along their left edges.

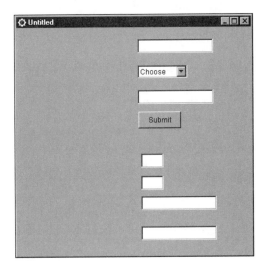

Figure 6.8
Add a Submit button between the input text fields and the display text fields.

Now, we can add the labels to the GUI window.

Build The Labels

As we add a label, we'll align it to the item it is documenting. After a group of labels is added, we'll left-align them. Follow these steps to build the labels:

1. Add a Label component named Interest Rate Label. Specify the label text as "Enter the interest rate:"; then resize its height to 10 pixels. Add another label directly below it, and

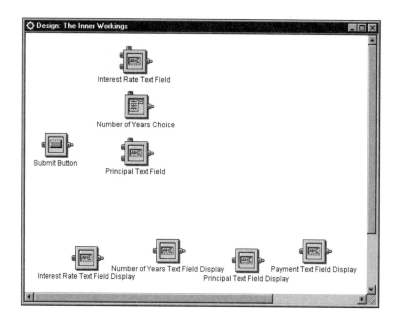

Figure 6.9
Invest some time in rearranging the Design window.

name it Interest Rate Label 2. Specify the label text as "(Example: 8.5)", and resize its height to 15 pixels, as shown in Figure 6.10.

2. Align the top Label component with the Interest Rate Text Field component, as shown in Figure 6.11. Don't worry about left-aligning the two Label components yet. We'll do that after all the labels for this section have been added.

3. Add a Label component named Number of Years Label. Specify the label text as "Choose the term of the loan:" as shown in Figure 6.12.

4. Align the top edges of the Number of Years Label component and the Number of Years Choice component.

Figure 6.10
Add labels for the interest rate.

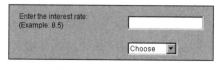

Figure 6.11
Align the first label with the Interest Rate Text Field.

Figure 6.12
Add labels for the Number of Years and Principal Text Field components.

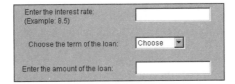

5. Add a Label component named Principal Label. Specify the label text as "Enter the amount of the loan:" as shown in Figure 6.12.

6. Align the top edges of the Principal Label component and the Principal Text Field component.

7. Select all the labels and left-align them, as shown in Figure 6.13. If you like, move all the labels a bit closer to the input fields.

   Now, we're going to add the labels for the display area.

8. Add a Label component named Interest Rate Display Label, and specify the label text as "Interest rate =" as shown in Figure 6.14.

9. Align the top edges of the Interest Rate Display Label and the Interest Rate Text Field Display component.

Figure 6.13
Align the Label components along their left edges.

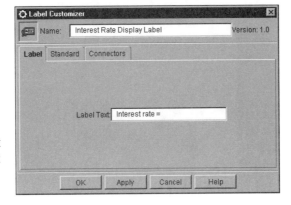

Figure 6.14
Add a Label component for the Interest Rate Text Field Display component.

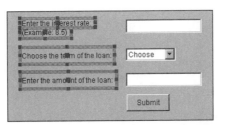

10. Add a Label component named Number of Years Display Label, and specify the label text as "Term of the loan =".

11. Align the top edges of the Number of Years Display Label and the Number of Years Text Field Display component. Now, both labels in the display area should be aligned with the fields they are documenting, as shown in Figure 6.15.

12. Add a Label component named Principal Text Field Display Label, and specify the label text as "Amount of the loan =".

13. Align the top edges of the Principal Text Field Display Label and the Principal Text Field Display component.

14. Add a Label component named Payment Text Field Display Label, and specify the label text as "Your monthly payment =".

15. Align the top edges of the Payment Text Field Display Label and the Payment Text Field Display component.

16. Now, select all of the labels in the display area and align them along their left edges, as shown in Figure 6.16.

17. Whew. Now, we can spend just a minute or two straightening up the Design window, then we're ready to build the functional part of this applet. Move all the Label components to the bottom of the Design window, as shown in Figure 6.17.

Now, we can build the part where the all the action happens.

Figure 6.15
Both labels in the display area are aligned with the text fields they are documenting.

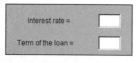

Figure 6.16
Align the Label components in the display area along their left edges.

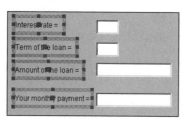

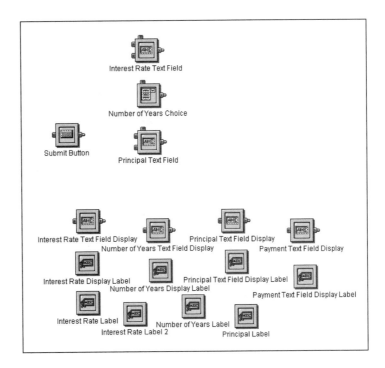

Figure 6.17
Move all the Label components to the bottom of the Design window.

Build The Functional Part

We have three components at our disposal for doing some number crunching—the Arithmetic component, the Math component, and the Expression Evaluator component. The details of these components are explained in Chapter 7. For now, just say, Build!

First, quickly review the formula for computing the mortgage payment, as shown earlier in this chapter in Figure 6.1. Then, follow these steps to build the functional part of your site:

1. On the Computation tab, select the Expression Evaluator component and place it in the Design window. Name the component "Payment ExpEval", and enter the following formula in the Expression To Evaluate field (see Figure 6.18):

   $(a/1200 + (a/12)/(b-1)) * c$

   Note that the variable **b** represents a portion of the original formula, as shown in Figure 6.19.

2. On the Computation tab, select the Expression Evaluator component, and place it to the right of the Interest Rate

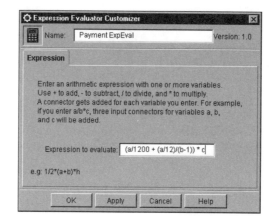

Figure 6.18
Insert an Expression
Evaluator component
and specify the
expression.

Figure 6.19
This part of the original
formula is represented
by the variable **b** in the
component Payment
ExpEval.

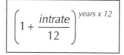

$$\left(1 + \frac{intrate}{12}\right)^{years \, x \, 12}$$

Text Field component in the Design window, as shown in Figure 6.20.

3. Name the component B ExpEval, specify the formula **1 + (a/12)**, and click OK.

4. On the Computation tab, select the Math component, and click in the Design window to the right of the B ExpEval component, as shown in Figure 6.21.

5. Name the component "B Power Math", choose **pow(x,y)** from in the Function drop-down list, and click OK.

6. Now, we need some Distributor components. (If you want a preview of where the Distributor components are placed, take

Figure 6.20
Place the new
Expression Evaluator
component to the right
of the Interest Rate Text
Field component.

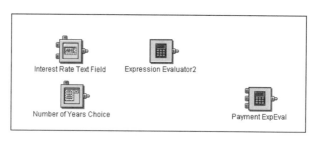

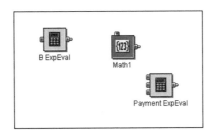

Figure 6.21
Place the new Math
component to the right
of the B ExpEval
component.

a peek at Figure 6.23.) On the Data Flow tab, select the
Distributor component, and place one between the Submit
button and the input text fields. Use the default name for the
component, and make sure it has a total of five output connectors, as shown in Figure 6.22.

7. Add another Distributor component to the right of the
   Interest Rate Text Field. Leave the default name, and add one
   more output connector to the two default output connectors.

8. Add another Distributor component to the right of the
   Number of Years Choice component. Leave the default name
   and the default two output connectors.

9. Add another Distributor component to the right of the
   Principal Text Field. Leave the default name and the default
   two output connectors. Your Design window should now look
   similar to Figure 6.23.

10. From the Computation tab, select an Arithmetic component,
    and add it above the Number of Years Text Field Display

Figure 6.22
Add a Distributor
component, and add
three more output
connectors.

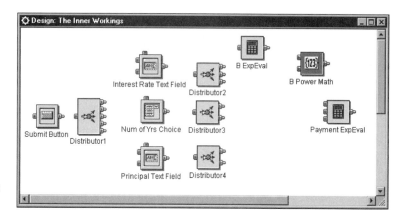

Figure 6.23
Add three more
Distributor components
to the design.

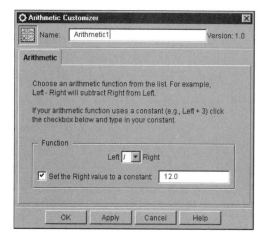

Figure 6.24
Add an Arithmetic
component to process
the data for the Number
of Years Text Field
Display.

component near the bottom of the screen. Leave the default
name, and choose to divide the input by 12, as shown in
Figure 6.24.

Wire Components Together

With all the components in place, we can now wire them together. This is the last step in building this design. Follow these
steps to connect the components:

1. Connect the Submit button to Distributor1.

2. Connect the first two output connectors on Distributor1 to
   the Trigger and Clear Text connectors on the Interest Rate
   Text Field component.

3. Connect the next output connector on Distributor1 to the Trigger connector on the Number of Years Choice component.

4. Connect the next two output connectors on Distributor1 to the Trigger and Clear Text connectors on the Principal Text Field component. You now have used all the output connectors on Distributor1, and your Design window should appear similar to Figure 6.25.

5. Connect the Interest Rate Text Field and the Distributor2 components.

6. Connect one output connector on Disbtributor2 to the B ExpEval component, one to the first input connector of the Payment ExpEval component, and one to the Interest Rate Text Field Display at the bottom of the screen, as shown in Figure 6.26.

7. Connect the output connector of the B ExpEval component to the top input connector of the B Power Math component.

8. Connect the Number of Years Choice component to the Distributor3 component. Then connect the first Distributor3 output connector to the second input connector of the B Power Math component, and connect the second Distributor3 output connector to the input connector for the Arithmetic1 component, as shown in Figure 6.26.

9. Connect the output connector of the B Power Math component to the second input connector of the Payment ExpEval component, as shown in Figure 6.27.

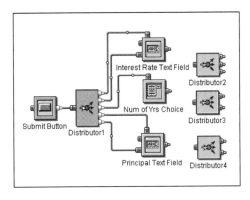

Figure 6.25
Wire all of the Distributor1 output connectors.

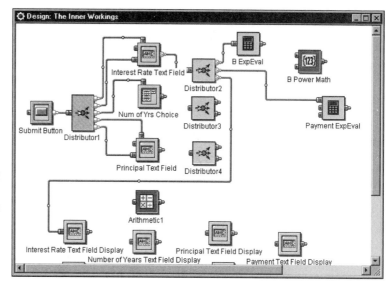

Figure 6.26
Connect the Distributor2 output connectors. Also, Connect the Distributor3 output connectors, and connect the input connectors of the B Power Math component.

10. Connect the Principal Text Field component to the Distributor4 component. Then, connect the first Distributor4 component to the third input connector of the Payment ExpEval component, and connect the second Distributor4 component to the Principal Text Field Display component, as shown in Figure 6.27.

11. Connect the Payment ExpEval component to the Payment Text Field Display component near the bottom of the screen. Okay, at this point, your design is complete and should appear as shown in Figure 6.27.

It's time for a celebration dance—or at least a little jig. Let's save the big dance until the applet is successfully running on a Web site. So, let's get to it—the design is complete and ready for testing.

Generating The Applet

We are ready to generate our applet and test it. First, we need to clear out the values in the fields before we generate. Otherwise, the applet starts with these values. Fields cleared? Okay, let's generate the applet. Follow these steps to generate the applet:

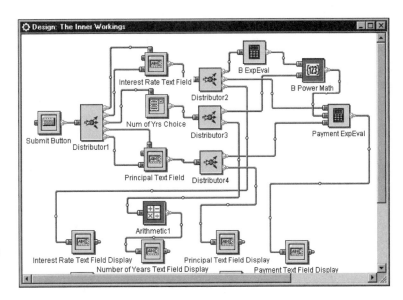

Figure 6.27
Connect the Distributor4 output connectors. Also, connect the remaining input connectors of the Payment ExpEval component.

1. From the Generate menu, choose Applet. Note the directory the file is stored in as well as the name of the file. Continue to click Next until Next is grayed out and then click Finish.

2. Review the applet in the Java Studio browser window. Test it a few times. Does it work the way you expected it to? Let's examine exactly what was generated.

Java Studio used the name you specified in the Generate sequence to create an HTML file. To view the HTML file, open Notepad or your favorite text editor. An example of the HTML file is shown in Listing 6.1.

Listing 6.1   When you generate an applet, Java Studio creates an HTML file with the <APPLET> tag.

```
<APPLET
  NAME="chapter06_example"
  CODE="VJad22ecc93bc"
  CODEBASE="classes"
  ARCHIVE="chapter06_example.zip"
  WIDTH="403"
  HEIGHT="378">
</APPLET>
```

As you know, the **NAME** parameter specifies the name that appears in the status bar of the browser window when the applet is

Figure 6.28
The name of the applet, as specified by the **NAME** parameter in the <**APPLET**> tag, appears in the status bar.

running, as shown in Figure 6.28. The **CODE** parameter specifies the name of the class file containing Java bytecodes. In Listing 6.1, the class file is **Vjad22ecc93bc.class**. (The **CODE** parameter assumes the file you specify has a .class extension.) The **CODEBASE** parameter specifies the relative directory where the class file resides.

We now need to upload the CLASS file to the Web site. To do this, look for the CLASS file as specified by the **CODE** parameter, in the subdirectory specified by the **CODEBASE** parameter. When you find it, upload the CLASS file and the DAT file to your Web site. Make sure you create a classes subdirectory on your Web site, and store the CLASS file and the DAT file in the classes subdirectory.

Leverage the help Java Studio provides by copying the contents of the generated HTML file into the HTML file on your Web site. When we did this, our hard returns and spaces turned a little funky and appeared in the HTML file, as shown in Figure 6.29.

If this happens to you, simply edit the uploaded HTML file, and delete the black blocks. Save the file, and now we're ready to test.

Testing The Applet

Testing comes in two phases: local testing on your PC and testing after the applet is running on your Web site. If you plan to use an applet like this on a public Web site, you need to test the applet using both Internet Explorer and Netscape Navigator.

Test Locally, Think Globally

The function of the applet is relatively simple, so your previous testing may be adequate. First, ask yourself these questions:

- What happens when you don't enter any data, and you press the Submit button?

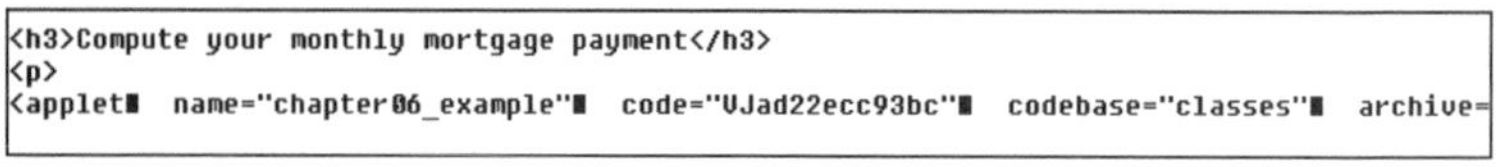

Figure 6.29
The uploaded HTML file had hard returns and spaces that looked a little funky.

```
<h3>Compute your monthly mortgage payment</h3>
<p>
<applet  name="chapter06_example"  code="VJad22ecc93bc"  codebase="classes"  archive=
```

- What happens when you enter a ridiculous percentage, such as 2,000 percent?
- What happens when you enter negative data?
- What happens if you don't have the money to make this kind of mortgage payment?

Fortunately, our applet feeds back the data, so the user can easily see if the data was mistyped. As far as coming up with the money for the mortgage payment, you'll have to consult the lending practices of The Bank of Dad, but beware of that lender's lecture requirements.

Upload, Then Test Again

After you have uploaded the files, point your browser to the HTML file that contains the **<APPLET>** tag. When we told Netscape Navigator to load the HTML file, we received an error message, as shown in Figure 6.30.

What's wrong? Well, we uploaded our applet, but we didn't upload any of the other classes needed by the applet. Go back and look at your development directory. Look for three subdirectories in the classes directory called com, connect, and sunw. You could upload these subdirectories, and all of their contents, to your Web site. However, Java Studio has made it even easier for you by putting all the classes into an archive file, called a ZIP file. Look on your hard drive where you found the generated HTML file, the CLASS file, and the DAT file. You'll also find a ZIP file. Upload the ZIP file and try this again.

Point your browser to the HTML file again, and click the Reload button. This time, we received the error message, as shown in Figure 6.31.

Figure 6.30
Our applet tried to run, but it can't find the basic Java class.

Applet VJad22ecc93bc can't start: error: java.lang.NoClassDefFoundError: com/sun/jpro/vj

Figure 6.31
Now our applet is complaining that some classes are already loaded.

Applet VJad22ecc93bc can't start: error: java.lang.ClassFormatError: Class already loaded

Some browsers aren't very good about letting go of loaded classes, so pressing the Reload button doesn't produce reliable results. If you receive this error, close your browser, and restart it. Then, point your browser to the HTML file again. This time, we saw our applet, as shown in Figure 6.32.

Of course, we didn't set the background color of the Web site to match the background color of the applet, as we discussed in Chapter 5. But that's an exercise that you can complete on your own.

Finally!

Now it's time for our celebration dance. The applet is done!

Curious about some of the details? Then, move on to Chapter 7, where we will regale you with torrid tales from this chapter. Or something like that.

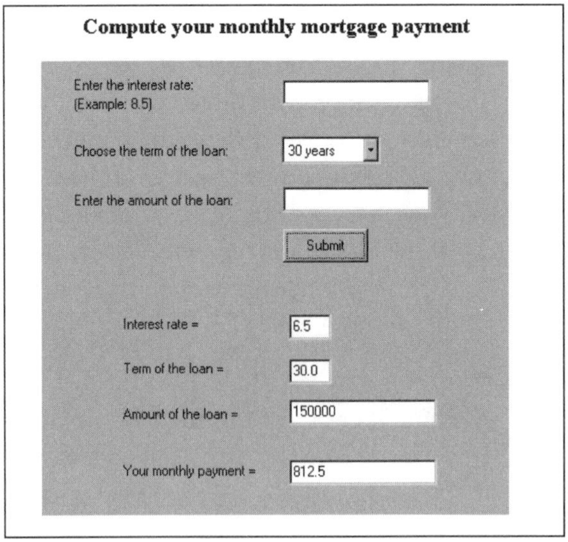

Figure 6.32
The applet runs!

Chapter 7

Understanding Applets Built With Java Studio

According to the children's song, Tiggers are made of rubber and springs. So, what are Java Studio applets made of? Simply put, Java Studio applets are made of components and common sense. Let's take a look.

In this chapter, we examine the applet we built in Chapter 6. Then, we review the interface structure and explore some of the decisions we made concerning the appearance in the GUI window.

About The Applet

Consider this question: When should you put something in an applet, and when should you just do it in HTML? In short, whenever you can do something in HTML, do it. HTML is much more efficient and downloads quicker.

Did you notice that we didn't add a big title at the top of the applet? We coded it in HTML. Besides being faster, it allows your users to know what is happening because it displays right away. When you go to a Web page that contains a Java applet, you see a gray box while the applet loads. By displaying the title before the applet is called, you let your users know that something is indeed happening.

Of course, a better choice would be to provide an hourglass animation or a progress bar that helps your users visually understand that the task will soon be complete. Listing 7.1 shows an hourglass animation.

▶Tip

Remind Me. What's An Applet Again?

When most people use the word applet, *they are referring to a small application that runs inside a browser window; it cannot run without the browser window. If it could, it would be an application. The word* applet *also implies that it is written in Java. Applets, running in Web browsers, have their own set of security rules to follow. For more information, see Chapter 18.*

Listing 7.1   Polite Web designers help their users know that an applet is loading.

```
<HTML>
<HEAD>
<TITLE>Compute your monthly mortgage payment</TITLE>
</HEAD>
<BODY>

<H2>Compute your monthly mortgage payment</H2>
<IMG SRC="hourglass.gif" ALIGN=left>
<P>Please wait while the applet loads...</P>
<APPLET
  name="chapter06_example"
  code="VJad22ecc93bc"
  codebase="classes"
  archive="chapter06_example.zip"
  width="403"
  height="378">
</APPLET>
</BODY>
</HTML>
```

While we're discussing HTML, let's take care of our users who do not use Java-aware browsers.

Accommodating Older Browsers

We all know that if you are publishing an applet publicly (that is, not on an intranet), then you are going to have a variety of browsers accessing the applet. The good news is that browsers that are not Java-aware will ignore the contents of the **<APPLET>** tag and interpret any HTML text between the **<APPLET>** and **</APPLET>** tags. On the flip side, Java-aware browsers ignore the HTML between the **<APPLET>** tags. So, the best way to accommodate older browsers is to provide alternative HTML between the **<APPLET>** tags.

For example, you can do something like the Web page shown in Listing 7.2.

Listing 7.2   Accommodate older browsers with alternate HTML between the <APPLET> tags.

```
<HTML>
<HEAD>
<TITLE>Compute your monthly mortgage payment</TITLE>
```

```
</HEAD>
<BODY>

<H2>Compute your monthly mortgage payment</H2>
<IMG SRC="hourglass.gif" ALIGN=left>
<P>Please wait while the applet loads...</P>
<APPLET
  name="chapter06_example"
  code="VJad22ecc93bc"
  codebase="classes"
  archive="chapter06_example.zip"
  width="403"
  height="378">
<P>This applet computes a monthly mortgage payment,
if you specify the interest rate, the term of the loan,
and the amount of the loan. I'm sorry, but your browser
does not understand applets, so you won't be able to use
this applet.</P>
</APPLET>
</BODY>
</HTML>
```

At this point, you might be wondering which browsers are unable to understand applets. Table 7.1 lists the main browsers affected.

It's clear that you can take another step to accommodate older browsers. Namely, you can upload the class directories and files, in case viewers are using browsers that don't understand the **ARCHIVE** attribute.

Table 7.1   Some browsers and their abilities to understand relevant HTML.

Browser	Issue
Microsoft Internet Explorer 2	Doesn't understand the **<APPLET>** tag.
Microsoft Internet Explorer 3	Doesn't understand the **ARCHIVE** attribute, so you need to upload all the subdirectories of the classes directory; otherwise, your users won't be able to use the applet.
Microsoft Internet Explorer 4	Understands the **<APPLET>** tag and the **ARCHIVE** attribute.
Netscape Navigator 2	Doesn't understand the **ARCHIVE** attribute. See the comments for Microsoft Internet Explorer 3.
Netscape Navigator 3	Understands the **<APPLET>** tag and the **ARCHIVE** attribute.

About The ARCHIVE Attribute

What exactly is the role of the **ARCHIVE** attribute in the **<APPLET>** tag? **ARCHIVE** allows you to specify an archive file, which contains all the necessary classes, sounds, and image files required by the specified applet to run. By putting all the needed files into one archive file, the applet loads faster because only one connection is made by the HTTP transfer protocol to download the archive file. If, for example, the user is using Navigator 2, multiple connections are made to separately download each necessary class file.

If you use an archive file, more time is needed when the applet initially loads, but then it runs quickly and without pauses. If you don't use an archive file, the applet loads more quickly, because it only loads the first class file. But the time necessary to run the applet increases, because the applet pauses as it reaches each class file to download.

As you have already seen, Java Studio automatically creates a ZIP file for you, and the generated HTML code specifies the ZIP file on the **ARCHIVE** attribute.

Netscape Communicator 4 and Microsoft Internet Explorer 4 both support using a JAR file on the **ARCHIVE** attribute. A JAR file is a Java archive. It's similar to a ZIP file, except that it is compressed and therefore downloads more quickly. A JAR file can also contain a digital signature, which gives a user assurance about the applet's intent.

Now you know how to make sure your users see your applet. But once they see it, will they like what they see? Let's review our applet's interface design.

Designing The Interface

In this section, we discuss the input, output, layout, and functionality of the applet we created in Chapter 6. In the applet, users need to specify three items: the interest rate, the number of years of the loan, and the amount of the loan, as shown in Figure 7.1. In the figure, *intrate* is the annual interest rate (such as 7.5

Figure 7.1
The formula for a monthly mortgage payment has three variables.

$$\left(\frac{intrate}{12} + \frac{\dfrac{intrate}{12}}{\left(1 + \dfrac{intrate}{12}\right)^{years \times 12} - 1} \right) \times \; principal \; = \; monthly \; payment$$

percent), *years* is the number of years of the loan (such as 30 years), *principal* is the amount of the loan (such as $150,000), and *monthly payment* is equal to the amount you pay each month for the principal and interest.

Input

Each of the three variables are specified by the user in Text Field components. Let's review each input field.

Interest Rate

If you ask someone, "Hey, Bob! What interest rate did you get on that mortgage?" Bob would answer "6 and a quarter!" Bob would not say, "0.0625." So, plan on users entering the interest rate as a whole number rather than as the actual decimal. For example, our friend Bob would enter 6.25, not 0.0625. We can easily convert the number to a percentage by dividing it by 100 with an Arithmetic or Expression Evaluator component.

In the formula, the interest rate is divided by 12. Because we are computing a monthly mortgage payment, you only pay one-twelfth of the interest due on the principal each month. Interest rates are specified in terms of one year, so it's easier on users if we just divide the interest rate by 12.

Loan Term

Let the users choose the term of the loan from a list, because mortgages come in a fairly finite set of lengths. This also makes it easy for us to do some pre-calculations, because the Choice component lets us specify the value to send to the output connector.

Because we are computing a monthly payment, we need to multiply the number of years of the loan by 12 months. That's why the value sent out for each Choice item is multiplied by 12, and why the value is divided by 12 before it is displayed at the bottom.

Loan Amount

Ideally, we would like the user to input a number for the principal, such as 150000, and we could display it as $150,000. We could use a combination of the String components, but it is beyond the scope of this particular example. But look for this as an exercise in Chapter 12, when we work with Packaged Designs.

Output

In Chapter 6, we created the applet so that the input fields clear when users press the Submit button. We also designed the applet to feed back the input so users can print the screen and have the data handy. Otherwise, the user would end up seeing results like those shown in Figure 7.2.

The other choice would be to not clear the input fields when users press the Submit button, but then the user would have to delete the data before experimenting with a different set of numbers.

Layout

When fiddling with the layout in the GUI window, we specified the exact height of the labels for the Interest Rate Text Field component, as shown in Figure 7.3.

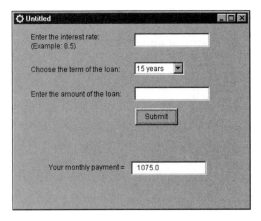

Figure 7.2
If we didn't provide feedback about the input, the user wouldn't have very much information after pressing the Submit button.

Figure 7.3
The labels for the Interest Rate Text Field component needed some special handling.

For the first label, we set the height to be 10 pixels, and we set the second label to be 15 pixels tall. The reason why we went through these hoops is because these two labels go together, and the default height for the Label component puts too much space between the labels for them to appear to belong together.

The second label needed to be a bit taller than the first one because the second label contained a character with a *descender* (a descender is the part of a character that falls below the baseline—in this case, it's the letter *p* in *Example*).

Functionality

We have three components at our disposal for doing some number crunching: the Arithmetic component, the Math component, and the Expression Evaluator component. Of course, all three components are on the Computation tab. Table 7.2 describes each component's capabilities and limitations.

Table 7.2   Three components and their capabilities and limitations.

Component	Capabilities And Limitations	As They Appear On The Tool Palette
Arithmetic	Evaluates two inputs, and only with the following operands: +, -, *, /. Can set one side of the expression to a constant.	
Math	Performs one of the following math functions: abs(x), acos(x), asin(x), atan(x), atan2(x), ceil(x), cos(x), E(), exp(x), floor(x), ieeeRemainder(x,y), log(x), max(x,y), min(x,y), pow(x,y), PI(), random(), rind(x), round(x), sin(x), sqrt(x), and tan(x). The function selected determines how many input connectors it has.	
Expression Evaluator	Evaluates a whole expression, with as many inputs as you want to specify. The only allowed operands are +, -, *, /. The number of variables you put into the expression determines the number of input connectors.	

More Fun And Excitement

Ready for a bigger challenge? Then, you're looking for Chapter 8, where we'll build a real live application.

Chapter 8

Building An Application With Java Studio

You probably don't want to use Java Studio to build a prime-time application, but it's fine for small home-grown use. It's not quite rich enough with features for building a full application, but we can certainly complete some interesting projects without a lot of effort.

After you build a Java application, you run the application from your DOS prompt. If you are using a flavor of Windows, you run a BAT file; if you're using a flavor of Unix, you run a SH script. Java Studio builds a BAT file and a SH file for you when it compiles your Java application. However, building the application is up to you.

Planning An Application

The design we build in this chapter will help you estimate the cost for building a simple Web site. It's very possible that you don't want to share your estimating methodology or your prices with any competitors, so we figure this is a good example to use for an application. But before we get around to planning the application, we need to make sure your environment is set up to generate and run Java applications.

Preparing To Generate And Run Java Applications

When you generate an application in Java Studio, you are warned to make sure that the Java Development Kit (JDK) is in your path. But it takes a little more than that for this project to be successful. You also need to have the Java interpreter in your path. Not quite sure how to go about doing all this? Don't worry—that's what the rest of this section is about.

Run the MS-DOS prompt utility. If you aren't sure where it is, look for it in the Accessories folder or in a folder called Microsoft Stuff. Or click the Start button, and choose Find|Files Or Folders. Search for the file command.com, and then open the file.

At the MS-DOS prompt, type the **PATH** command, as shown in Figure 8.1.

You need to have the location of the Java interpreter in your path, as well as the JDK. Are you unsure where the Java interpreter is residing at the moment? No problem. Go to the Start button, and choose Find|Files Or Folders. Look for the file java.exe. It might be in the directory Java-Studio1.0\Jdk\bin or in a similar directory. Wherever it is, edit your autoexec.bat file, and add the directory to your path. You also need to add the JDK directory to your path.

To edit your autoexec.bat file, use the Windows Explorer to view the contents of your root directory (C:). Find the file called autoexec.bat, and right-click it. Choose Edit. Then, add the **SET PATH** statement, as shown in Figure 8.2.

Now, we're set up to run the Java interpreter and, therefore, to run our Java application after we build it. So, let's take a look at the goals, interface, and functionality of our application.

Figure 8.1
Use the **PATH** command at the MS-DOS prompt to determine the current state of your **PATH** environment variable.

Figure 8.2
Add the **SET PATH** statement to your autoexec.bat file to add the Java interpreter and the JDK to your path.

About The Application

This application computes the estimated cost for building a simple Web site. Be forewarned—we are not advocating this methodology as the ultimate tool for estimating this kind of work. It is merely a logical way to approach an estimate, and we leave the refinement (or total revamping) of this methodology as an exercise for you.

In this chapter, we are focusing on building the design. For a discussion of the methodology, see Chapter 9.

Here's the premise. You can usually scope out a project using the following parameters:

• How many levels of hierarchy does the Web site have? (Assume the home page is one level, any child pages of the home page constitute a second level, and so on.)

• How many pages of text are on the Web site? (Use a hardcopy page as your measurement for how much content equates to one page, because a lot of clients start a Web site by throwing existing hardcopy material onto a site.)

• Of those pages of text, how many need to be written?

• Of the pages of text that already exist, how many are already in electronic format and converted to HTML?

• How many photographs need to be scanned and prepared for the Web site?

• How many icons need to be designed and drawn for the Web site?

• How many other graphics need to be designed and drawn for the Web site?

Figure 8.3 illustrates the completed application.

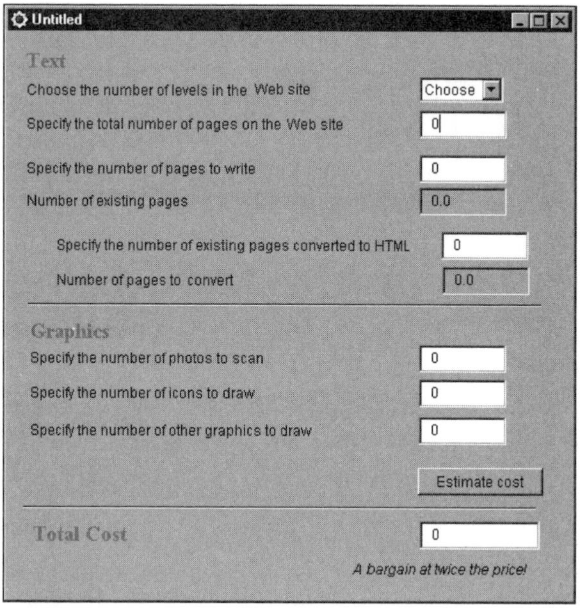

Figure 8.3
The completed application is ready to use to estimate Web site development costs.

We all know there are more factors and levels of complexity when providing an estimate than we can present in this chapter, but this application provides a good foundation for refining the estimation process.

Interface Design

The input for this application can be divided into two groups: textual content and graphics services. Textual content is the actual text the Web site displays. Depending on the nature of the Web site, it can include items such as press releases, articles, white papers, investor information, and a cheery "Welcome to our Web site" introduction. Graphics services include any graphics that need to be developed for the Web site. For example, the client may want an icon to represent each of the major areas of the site. Or the client may want a beautifully rendered drawing of the company's best-selling product to use as a background image on the site.

The output of the application is the total cost for the Web site development. With two sections of input, and one for output, we will visually divide the GUI window into three areas. Review

Tip

Save Often

As you may have noticed, Java Studio crashes. Even when you haven't done anything to deserve it—it crashes. So make sure that you save your design frequently, especially when you start building more complex designs like we'll do in this chapter.

Figure 8.3, and you can see the three sections indicated by the three headings: Text, Graphics, and Total Cost.

Functionality

As we discussed in the previous section, we need to define a variety of parameters in order to do the estimate. For example, after we know the total number of pages for the Web site and the number of new pages needed, then we can determine the number of existing pages. Of the existing pages of text, after we know the number of pages that are already converted to HTML, then we can determine the number of existing pages that need to be converted to HTML.

For a complete discussion of the formula we use for this estimate, see Chapter 9.

Ready to build? Let's get started.

Building The Application

If you have not already done so, start Java Studio. If you already have Java Studio running, then save your current design, open the File menu, and choose New.

We will start in the GUI window, build the text area, and then build the graphics area. As we build, we will periodically take breaks to clean up the Design window. After all the visual components are in place, we will switch to the Design window and finish building the functionality.

Build The Text Area Labels

The text area is the first section of the application, identified by the heading in Figure 8.3 called Text. The text area labels include the heading and the labels for each of the six fields. Build the labels by following these steps:

1. Let's get started with that colorful label that identifies the text area. On the GUI tab, select the Label component. Click in the upper-left corner of the GUI window. Name the

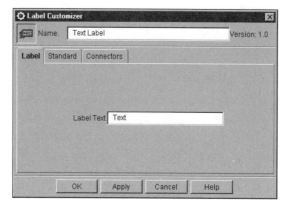

Figure 8.4
Add a Label component, and name it Text Label.

component Text Label, and specify the label text as "Text", as shown in Figure 8.4.

2. Click the Standard tab. Change the Foreground color by clicking the button with the ellipsis to the right of the Foreground field. This displays the Color Chooser window. To select a color for the label's text, scroll through the items in the list, and choose something you like. In the example, we chose blueviolet, as shown in Figure 8.5. After selecting a color, click OK to close the Color Chooser window.

3. Change the font family by clicking the button to the right of the Font field. Select the Times Roman font, the Bold style, and 18 point font size, as shown in Figure 8.6.

4. Click OK.

Figure 8.5
Choose a color for the label's text.

5. Add another Label component. It doesn't really matter where you place it right now, because we will arrange items in the GUI window later. Name it Num Levels Choice Label, and specify the label text as "Choose the number of levels in the Web site". After you click OK, adjust the width of the label in the Design window so the label text appears.

6. Add a Label component beneath the Num Levels Choice Label component. Name this one Total Pgs Label, and specify the label text as "Specify the total number of pages on the Web site". After you click OK, adjust the width of the label so all the label text appears, as shown in Figure 8.7.

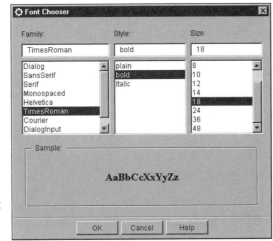

Figure 8.6
Change the characteristics of the text for the Text Label component.

7. Add two more Label components. Name the first one Pgs To Write Label, and specify the label text as "Specify the number of pages to write". Name the second component Pgs Existing Label, and specify the label text as "Number of existing pages".

8. Add the last two Label components for the text area. Name the first one Pgs Converted Label, and specify the label text as "Specify the number of existing pages converted to HTML". Name the second one Pgs Converted Label, and specify the label text as "Number of pages to convert".

9. Arrange the labels in the GUI window so the first four labels are left-aligned. Arrange the last two labels so they are indented, as shown in Figure 8.7.

Now, we can add the text fields associated with the labels.

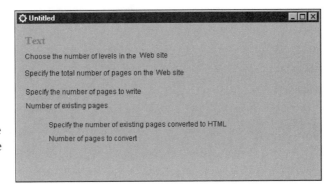

Figure 8.7
Arrange the labels in the GUI window so they are left-aligned, and indent the last two labels.

Build The Text Area Fields

The text area fields appear in the first section of the application. They include a Choice component and five Text Field components. Build the text area fields by following these steps:

1. On the GUI tab, select the Choice component. Click to the right of the first label. Name the Choice component Num Levels Choice, and add the items as shown in Figure 8.8. Also, add a connector to trigger the component.

2. Top-align the Choice component with the Label component.

3. Add a Text Field component for the second label. Name it Total Pgs TF, and add a connector to trigger the component.

4. Resize the width of the Total Pgs TF component so it is smaller, and top-align it with the Label component.

5. Add a Text Field component for the third label. Name it Pgs To Write TF, and add a connector to trigger the component.

6. Top-align the Pgs To Write TF component with the Label component. Don't worry about resizing the width right now. In a moment, we'll resize all the Text Field components to match the first one. Besides, keeping the components small helps with organization in these early stages.

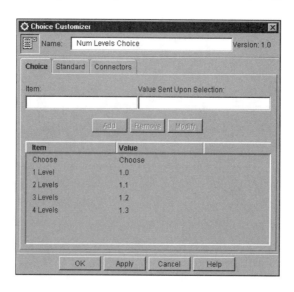

Figure 8.8
Add a Choice component for the first text label.

7. Add a Text Field component for the fourth label. Name it Pgs Existing TF, and deselect the checkbox on the Text Field tab that states Make The Component Editable as shown in Figure 8.9. (We'll review the purpose of this checkbox in Chapter 9.) Click the Connectors tab, and add a connector to trigger the component.

8. Top-align the Pgs Existing TF component with the Label component.

9. Add a Text Field component for the Specify The Number Of Existing Pages… label. Name it Pgs Converted TF, and add a connector to trigger the component.

10. Top-align the Pgs Converted TF component with the Label component.

11. Add a Text Field component for the last label in the text area. Name it Pgs To Convert TF, and deselect the checkbox on the Text Field tab that states Make The Component Editable. Then, click the Connectors tab, and add a connector to trigger the component.

12. Now, in one fell swoop, let's fix the width of most of the Text Field components. Select the Text Field components. Open the Layout menu, and choose Equalize|Width, as shown in Figure 8.10.

Figure 8.9
Add a Text Field component for the number of existing pages, and deselect the checkbox so it's not editable.

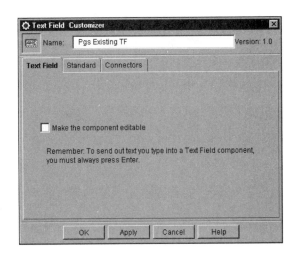

13. Left-align the Choice component and the first three Text Field components. Then, left-align the last two Text Field components indented from the rest of the Text Fields, as shown in Figure 8.11.

14. Left-align all the Label components except for the last two. Indent the last two Label components.

With the GUI window in order, we can turn our attention to the Design window.

Clean Up The Design Window

The Design window is a mess, probably looking similar to Figure 8.12. Let's take a few minutes to straighten things up.

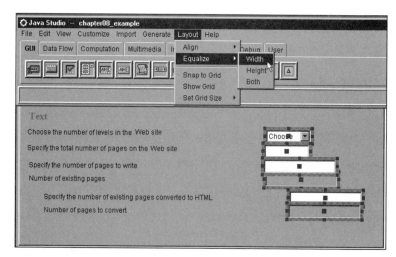

Figure 8.10
Equalize the width of all the Text Field components.

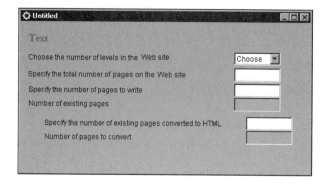

Figure 8.11
Left-align the fields in the text area.

Move the Label components out of the way. As you know, we prefer to stack them along the bottom of the Design window, alternating the level of each Label component to fit more into the space and still read each component's name, as shown in Figure 8.13.

For the rest of this chapter, we're going to change the Design window so we don't even see the Label components. Just be aware that they're down there. Rearrange the Text Field components and the Choice component so your Design window appears similar to Figure 8.14. With the text area taken care of, we can build the design for the graphics area.

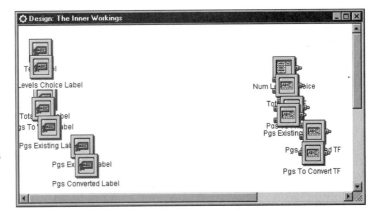

Figure 8.12
The Design window has a lot of components stacked up on top of each other.

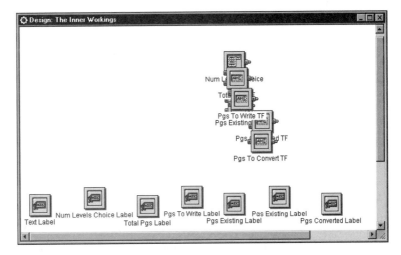

Figure 8.13
Move the Label components out of the way.

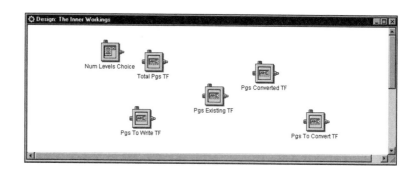

Figure 8.14
Move the Text Field components and the Choice component so they have some space and order.

Build The Graphics Area

The graphics area is shorter and simpler, with only three labels and three Text Field components. Start by adding a label to identify this as the graphics area. Follow these steps:

1. The label identifying the graphics area needs to match the look and style of the label for the text area. On the GUI tab, select the Label component. Click in the middle of the GUI window below the text area. Name the component Graphics Label, and specify the label text as "Graphics".

2. Click the Standard tab. Change the foreground color to blueviolet (or whatever you chose for the text color for the Text Label component) as was shown in Figure 8.5.

3. Click OK.

4. Change the font family to the Times Roman font, the Bold style, and 18 point font size, as was shown in Figure 8.6.

5. Click OK. You probably need to resize the width of the Label component so all the text appears.

6. Add three label components. Use Table 8.1 to determine the names and characteristics of the components. Figure 8.15

Table 8.1   The names and label text for the Label components.

Component Name	Label Text
Pix TF Label	Specify the number of photos to scan
Icons TF Label	Specify the number of icons to draw
Other Graphics TF Label	Specify the number of other graphics to draw

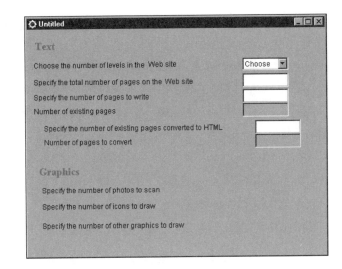

Figure 8.15
Add three Label components for the graphics area.

Tip

Alignment Out Of Whack?

If your alignment didn't work the way you expected it to, you may have your unaligned fields further to the left than your aligned fields. When you choose Align|Left, Java Studio aligns all selected components to the leftmost item. To fix the problem, move your unaligned component further to the right, and try aligning again.

displays the GUI window after the three Label components have been added and resized.

7. Add the three Text Field components. Use Table 8.2 to determine the names and characteristics of the Text Field components. Figure 8.16 displays the GUI window after the three Text Field components have been added.

8. Select the first Text Field component in the graphics area, and one of the Text Field components in the text area that is not indented. From the Layout menu, choose Equalize|Width.

9. With the two Text Fields still selected, open the Layout menu, and choose Align|Left.

10. Select all three of the Text Field components in the graphics area. On the Layout menu, choose Equalize|Width.

11. With all three Text Field components in the graphics area still selected, open the Layout menu, and choose Align|Left.

Table 8.2   The names and characteristics for the Text Field components

Component Name	Connector To Add
Pix TF	Triggers the component
Icons TF	Triggers the component
Other Graphics TF	Triggers the component

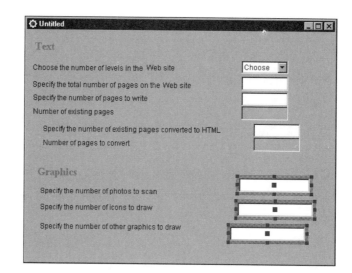

Figure 8.16
Add three Text Field components for the graphics area.

12. Top-align each label in the graphics area to its associated text field. Figure 8.17 displays the GUI window after the width and alignment processes have been applied.

All the items for the graphics are added. Now, it's time to take a break and clean up the Design window again.

Clean Up The Design Window Again

In your Design window, move the Label components out of the way. Earlier, we resized the Design window so we wouldn't see the labels any more—you'll need to resize the window now so they are visible once again. The stacked Label components are shown in Figure 8.18.

Rearrange the Text Field components so your Design window appears similar to Figure 8.19.

With the graphics area complete, we have just one more section before finishing our work in the GUI window.

Build The Button And Output

Our remaining tasks are to add a button to trigger the estimate and add a section for the output. Follow these steps:

1. On the GUI tab, select the Button component. Click in the GUI window in the bottom-right corner, below the

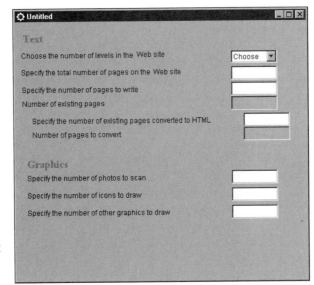

Figure 8.17
Align the labels and text fields in the graphics area.

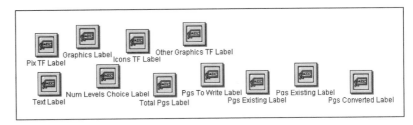

Figure 8.18
Move the Label components out of the way.

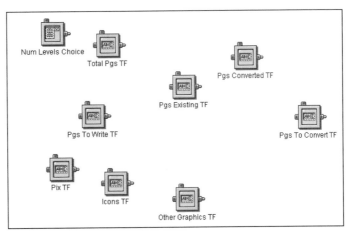

Figure 8.19
Move the Text Field components.

graphics area. Name the Button component Estimate Button, and specify the button text as "Estimate cost" as shown in Figure 8.20.

2. Add a label to identify the output area. On the GUI tab, select the Label component. Click in the GUI window in the bottom-left corner. Name the component Cost Label, and specify the label text as "Total Cost". Change the characteristics of the text color, font, and size as we did for the Text and Graphics labels earlier in this project. Then, left-align it with the other labels in the GUI window. Figure 8.20 displays the new label.

3. Add a Text Field component to display the estimated cost. On the GUI tab, select the Text Field component. Click in the GUI window below the Estimate Cost button. Name the component Cost TF. You don't need to add a connector to trigger this component.

All the components for the GUI window are now in place. Let's switch to the Design window and build the guts of this design.

Build The Functionality

First, we'll add the components to distribute messages and perform the calculations. Then, we'll wire everything together. Follow these steps:

1. Switch to the Design window. Move the Estimate Button component to the far left side of the Design window, and move the Cost TF component to the far right side of the Design window. You might also want to move the Cost label down to the bottom with the other labels.

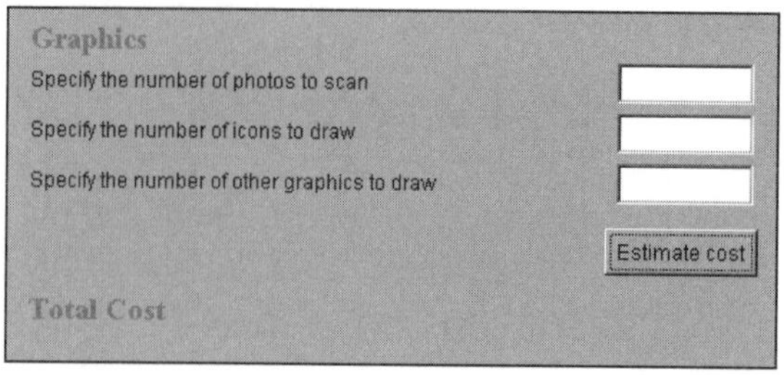

Figure 8.20
Add a label identifying the output area.

2. Click the Data Flow tab, and add a Distributor component to the right of the Estimate button. Leave the default name for the Distributor component, and add seven more connectors for a total of nine output connectors, as shown in Figure 8.21. With this many connectors, it's not a bad idea to name the added connectors sequentially, as in Connector 3, Connector 4, Connector 5, and so on. This naming convention might prove useful when your eyes are tired and you're trying to figure out exactly how many output connectors you have.

3. Add a Distributor component to the right of the Pgs To Write TF component. Leave the default name for the Distributor, and leave the two default output connectors, as shown in Figure 8.22.

4. Add a Distributor component to the right of the Pgs Converted TF component. Leave the default name for the Distributor, and leave the two default output connectors, as shown in Figure 8.23.

5. We need two Arithmetic components to calculate the derived fields: the Pgs Existing TF component and the Pgs To Convert TF component. The first Arithmetic component takes the Total Pgs TF and subtracts the Pgs To Write TF. Click the Computation tab and add an Arithmetic component to the right of the Total Pgs TF component. Name the Arithmetic component Pgs Existing Arith, and choose the minus operand, as shown in Figure 8.24.

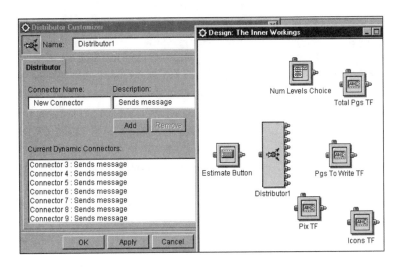

Figure 8.21
Add a Distributor component with nine output connectors.

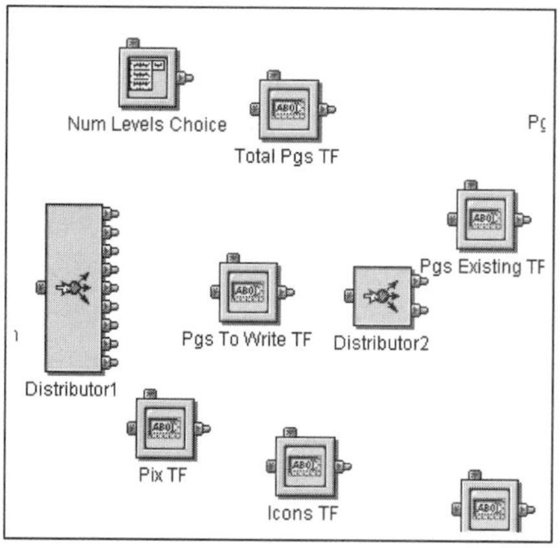

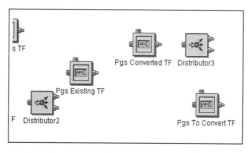

Figure 8.22
Add a Distributor component to the right of the Pgs To Write TF component.

Figure 8.23
Add a Distributor component to the right of the Pgs Converted TF component.

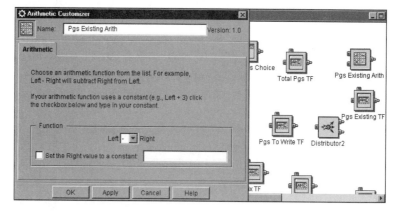

Figure 8.24
Add an Arithmetic component to compute the number of existing pages using the Pgs Existing TF and the Pages To Write TF components.

6. The second Arithmetic component takes the Pgs Existing TF and subtracts the Pgs Converted TF. Add an Arithmetic component beneath the Pgs Converted TF component. Name the Arithmetic component Pgs To Cvt Arith, and choose the minus operand, as shown in Figure 8.25.

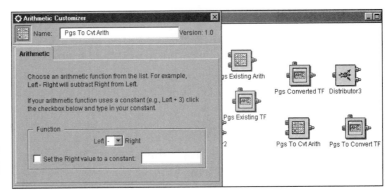

Figure 8.25
Add an Arithmetic component to compute the number of existing pages that need to be converted to HTML, using the Pgs Existing TF and the Pages Converted TF components.

7. The last component to add is an Expression Evaluator component that does most of the work. On the Computation tab, select the Expression Evaluator component, and click in the Design window on the far right side, above the Cost TF component. Specify the following expression:

$(a*(2*b + .25*c + 1*d))*50 + (.5*e + 3*f + 5*g)*40$

The field for the expression can't display the whole expression, but just keep typing. Figure 8.26 displays what can be seen in the customizer for the Expression Evaluator.

All the components are now present. It's time to connect them.

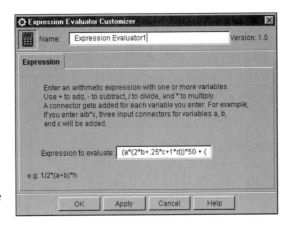

Figure 8.26
Add an Expression Evalutor component, and specify the expression $(a*(2*b + .25*c + 1*d))*50 + (.5*e + 3*f + 5*g)*40$.

Wiring The Design

The connections in this design end up looking pretty complicated, which makes it hard to follow. If you need to, rearrange the components in the Design window while you work, to simplify the look (but be aware that your Design window won't match ours anymore if you rearrange your components). Follow these steps to wire the design:

1. Connect the Estimate Button component and the Distributor1 components, as shown in Figure 8.27.

2. Connect the Distributor1 output connectors to the Trigger connector on each of the nine fields: Num Levels Choice, Total Pgs TF, Pgs To Write TF, Pgs Existing TF, Pgs Converted TF, Pgs To Convert TF, Pix TF, Icons TF, and Other Graphics TF, as shown in Figure 8.28. It's not necessary to connect them in the order listed.

3. Connect the Pages To Write TF to the Distributor2 component, as shown in Figure 8.29.

4. Connect the Pages Converted TF to the Distributor3 component, as shown in Figure 8.30.

5. Connect the inputs for the Pages Existing Arith component. Connect the Total Pgs TF component to the input connector called Left on the Pages Existing Arith component. Then,

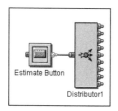

Figure 8.27
Connect the Estimate Button component to the Distributor1 component.

Figure 8.28
Connect the Distributor1 output connectors to the Trigger connectors on each of the nine fields.

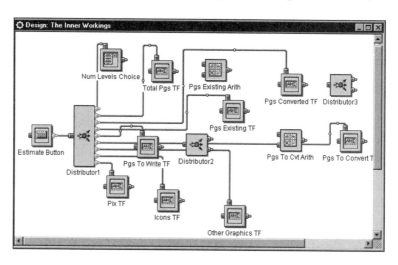

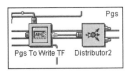

Figure 8.29
Connect the Pages To
Write TF and the
Distributor2 components.

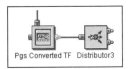

Figure 8.30
Connect the Pages
Converted TF and the
Distributor3 components.

Figure 8.31
Connect the inputs Total
Pgs TF and Pgs To Write
TF to the Pages Existing
Arith component.

Figure 8.32
Connect the inputs Pgs
Existing TF and Pgs
Converted TF to the Pages
To Cvt Arith component.

connect one of the output connectors of Distributor2 to the input connect called Right on the Pages Existing Arith component, as shown in Figure 8.31.

6. Connect the inputs for the Pgs To Cvt Arith component. Connect the Pgs Existing TF component to the input connector called Left on the Pgs To Cvt Arith component. Then, connect one of the output connectors of Distributor3 to the input connector called Right on the Pgs To Cvt Arith component, as shown in Figure 8.32.

7. Connect the output of the Pgs Existing Arith component to the Set Text input connector of the Pgs Existing TF, as shown in Figure 8.33.

8. Connect the output of the Pgs To Cvt Arith component to the Set Text input connector of the Pgs To Cvt TF, as shown in Figure 8.34.

9. Connect the inputs to the Expression Evaluator component. You must connect them to the correct input connectors. Use Table 8.3 to determine which components go to which input connectors.

   It might not be a lot of help, but Figure 8.35 shows the input connections for the Expression Evaluator.

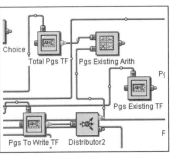

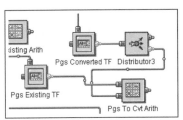

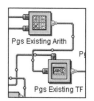

Figure 8.33
Send the output of the
Pgs Existing calculation
to the Pgs Existing TF
component.

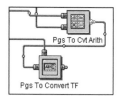

Figure 8.34
Send the output of the
Pgs To Cvt calculation to
the Pgs Existing TF
component.

Figure 8.35
The input connections
for the Expression
Evaluator are done.

Table 8.3 **Components and the input connector they connect to on the Expression Evaluator component.**

Component	Input Connector On The Expression Evaluator Component
Num Levels Choice	a
Distributor2 (Pgs To Write TF)	b
Distributor3 (Pgs Converted TF)	c
Pgs To Convert TF	d
Pix TF	e
Icons TF	f
Other Graphics TF	g

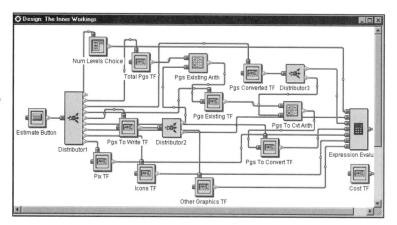

10. Connect the output of the Expression Evaluator to the input of the Cost TF component.

We're done building the design. Ready to start testing? Enter some sample numbers, and press the Estimate Cost button. Note that if you don't press Enter after entering some of the numbers, then you may need to press the Estimate Cost button more than once.

Just Say Generate

Now that the design is built, we can generate an application and run it without starting Java Studio or a browser. Start this phase by clearing the field values. The values in the calculated fields won't change unless they receive a number, so enter "0" in all the fields. Enter "0" in the Total Cost field as well, and press the Estimate Cost button a few times. Then, follow these steps:

1. Save your design.

2. From the Generate menu, choose Application. A Generate dialog box, as shown in Figure 8.36, will appear.

3. Click Next.

4. Java Studio offers to add a File menu, with the sole menu choice Exit, as shown in Figure 8.37. This is a good idea, because we didn't add a File menu and all applications need a way to exit. You can also choose to run the application after it's generated.

5. Click Next. On the next screen, click Finish.

If you chose to run the application automatically after it is generated, then you should see your design expressed as a real, live application, as shown in Figure 8.38.

Close Java Studio, and let's take a look at the contents of the BAT file, as shown in Listing 8.1.

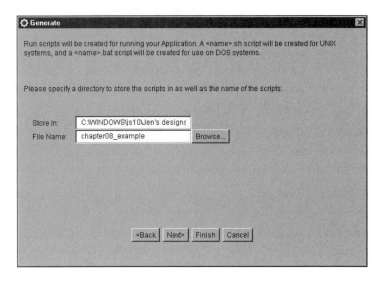

Figure 8.36
When you generate an application, Java Studio creates a BAT file for you to use to run the application.

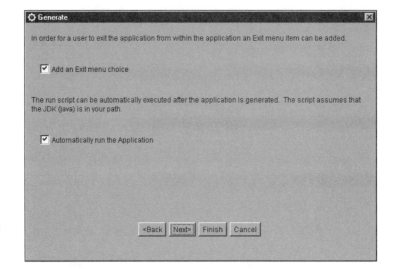

Figure 8.37
Java Studio adds a File menu to your application.

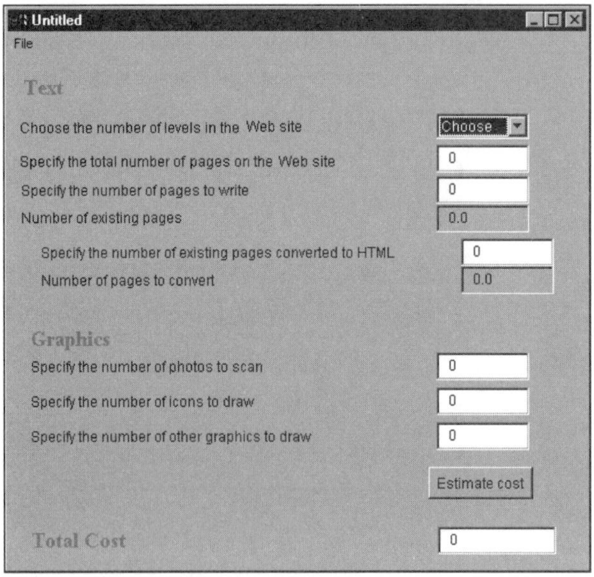

Figure 8.38
The finished application has a File menu and is ready to use.

Listing 8.1   The contents of the BAT file.

```
set JAVA_COMPILER=none
set DEPLOYDIR=C:\WINDOWS\js10\Jen's designs\classes
set CLASSPATH=%DEPLOYDIR%;%CLASSPATH%
set SERFILE=null
java -Dsun.js.vj.deploy.base="%DEPLOYDIR%" -
Dsun.js.vj.deploy.ser=%SERFILE% VJAd241d70ed8
```

The first four lines set up some environment variables, and the last line calls the Java interpreter to run the class file called VJAd241d70ed8.

Let's arrange it so that you can easily run this application. Start Windows Explorer, and find the BAT file that was generated by Java Studio. The name of the BAT file is the same as the name of your design. When you find it, right-click it, and send it to the desktop as a shortcut.

Display your desktop, right-click the BAT file icon, and choose Properties. Click the Shortcut tab, and review the contents of the Target field. For some reason, our Target field had two sets of "C:\" in it. If necessary, delete the first "C:\" and the extra quotes at the end of the Target field. In our example, we need a set of quotes around the Target because one of the directory names uses a space.

Click OK, and the icon for your shortcut turns into the DOS icon. Double-click the icon to run the application.

Out Of Environment Space
You might run into an error message when you run the application. If you get a message in the DOS window such as "Out of environment space" then you need to change the memory allocation for this application. Follow these steps:

1. To change the memory allocated for your application, right-click the shortcut, and choose Properties.

2. Click the Memory tab.

3. Open the Initial Environment drop-down field, and choose 512, as shown in Figure 8.39.

If 512 doesn't work, try stepping up to 768, then 1024, and so on until you find a memory allocation that works for you.

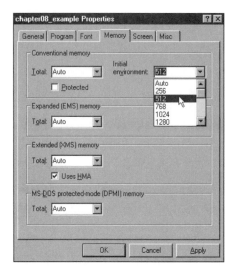

Figure 8.39
Change the memory allocation for your application by changing the settings on the Memory tab on your shortcut.

But Wait! Where Did You Get Those Numbers?

Yes, we understand that you want to be able to customize this application, and therefore you need to know what's going on under the hood in order to make it useful for you. In Chapter 9, we discuss the details about planning applications and exactly what you need to do to change our example to suit your purposes.

On to Chapter 9, then, shall we?

Chapter 9

Understanding Applications Built With Java Studio

We warned you in Chapter 8 that Java Studio isn't really suited for developing many applications. It lacks some built-in components necessary for larger programs. But we did build a useful estimation tool. So, let's take a look underneath the interface and see what drives our estimator.

First, a caveat—we know the application we built in Chapter 8 isn't a prime-time application. You have to press the Estimate Cost button several times, and you can't tab from field to field. It's also a fairly simplified view of what's involved in developing a services estimate for the cost in building a Web site. But it's a pretty nice tool to have for your internal use, and you can use this as a starting point for bigger and better applications. One of the nice abilities of Java Studio, of course, is that you can encapsulate a design into a Packaged Design, and then use the Packaged Design in other Java Studio Designs. For more information on Packaged Designs, see Chapters 12 and 13.

If you find yourself wanting to build other applications and are frustrated by Java Studio's lack of components, look for JavaBeans that you can import to make up for the missing components. For more information on importing JavaBeans, see Chapters 14 and 15. If you want to spend more time developing applications, then you should consider a full-fledged Java development environment. Generally, full development environments have features that, for example, allow a user to tab from field to field when entering data in a form. Take a look at Sun's Java Workshop, IBM's Visual Age for Java, Inprise's Jbuilder, or Microsoft's Visual J++.

For now, let's get back to the task on hand and take a closer look at our estimator application.

Planning The Application

The first question you should ask when you sit down to plan a Java Studio project should be, "Is this project an applet or an application?" Perhaps we're a bit prejudiced (okay, maybe a lot prejudiced), but it seems that most Java Studio projects are applets destined to run in a browser.

But there are times when a designer might want to build an application that is not accessible on the Web or run through a browser. One of the best reasons to create an application instead of an applet is that the application contains information that you don't want to make public. And although you can set up security procedures to prevent unauthorized access, the safest bet is to keep the application on your PC. Another reason to create a standalone application is that you might not want the overhead involved in running a browser to run your application.

We decided to keep the estimator project as a standalone application, so we chose to create the estimator as an application. Now, let's talk about how a Java application runs.

Java Compilers And Java Interpreters

As discussed in Chapter 1, Java Studio runs the Java compiler for you to generate an applet or an application. If you wanted to run the Java compiler yourself, you would go to the DOS shell and call the compiler with the **javac** command. If you view the contents of the JDK directory, you'll find a subdirectory called bin. In that subdirectory, you'll find the Java compiler, javac.exe.

You'll also find the Java interpreter, called java.exe. When the Java compiler compiles your design, it creates a file of bytecodes. This is the file that is theoretically platform-independent. It can run on any platform that has a Java Virtual Machine (JVM), which includes the Java interpreter.

Any developer worth his or her salt starts to worry about performance issues once they know users will be running an interpreter, and it's a valid concern. Java applications have not been known for their screaming performance, but Sun Microsystems is working on that. It's more of a problem with the JVMs than anything else, but it should improve as this technology matures. For more information on improving the performance of your Java Studio designs, see Chapters 20 and 21.

Errors When Running The Java Interpreter

To run the Java interpreter, your system needs to know where the Java interpreter lives. That's why we added it to your **PATH** statement in your autoexec.bat. Otherwise, you'll end up with an error when you try to run your Java application, as shown in Figure 9.1.

If your **PATH** statement has a lot in it (such as directories re-peated three times, like one of this book's coauthors' **PATH** statements), and depending on what else you have in your autoexec.bat, then you may receive an error about running out of environment space when you run your Java application, as shown in Figure 9.2. For example, if your autoexec.bat include several other statements that are setting environment variables, then your environment space is even more of a premium. We discussed how to fix this at the end of Chapter 8. You can right-click the BAT file or on the shortcut to the BAT file, and choose Proper-ties. Then, click the Memory tab, and change the amount of memory in the Initial Allocation field to 512. Click OK, and try running the BAT file again. If you're still running out of environ-ment space, step up the memory to the next level. If that still doesn't work, then you need to talk to a counselor about your memory addiction. (Actually, you shouldn't need more than 512K of memory to run this application.)

Now that we have the application-specific groundwork covered, let's delve into the details about the estimator project.

Figure 9.1
When your system doesn't know where the Java interpreter is stored, you receive an error message indicating that the Java interpreter is a bad command.

```
C:\WINDOWS\js10\Jen's designs>java -Dsun.js.vj.deploy.base="C:\WINDOWS\js10\Jen'
s designs\classes" -Dsun.js.vj.deploy.ser=null VJAd23765d902
Bad command or file name
```

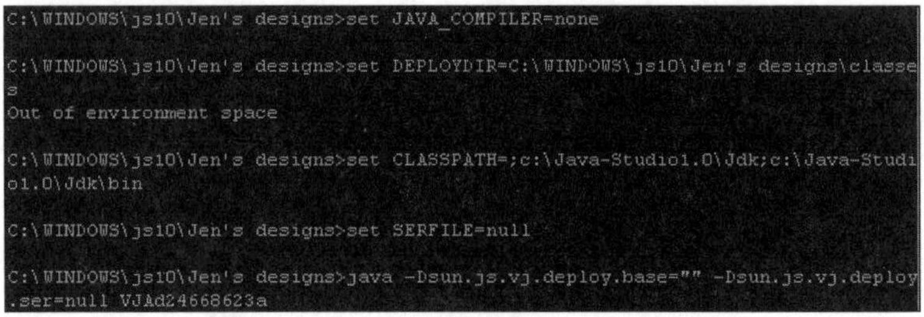

Figure 9.2
You might receive an
error about running out
of environment space
when you run your Java
application.

The Estimate Application

The methodology for the estimate application is based on the fact that a good portion of clients probably want to start a Web site as a vehicle for electronically distributing their existing hardcopy corporate collateral, white papers, documentation, and contact information. The estimater accommodates using multiple levels of hierarchy in the Web site, incorporating existing and new material into the Web site, and creating various kinds of graphics. In short, it handles estimating the development costs for a Web site that can be an attractive repository of information.

On the other hand, some businesses also use their Web sites as interactive mediums for communicating with their customers, conducting ecommerce, and building communities. If your client falls into this latter category, then you'll need a different estimation tool. You can modify this estimator by adding categories for developing chat boards, catalog shopping, and online applications.

The estimate methodology used in our application is based on two categories of information: the number of hours required to complete each task and the amount to charge per hour. For our example, we divide the work into the categories of text and graphics. We use an hourly rate of $50 for the text work, and $40 for the graphics work.

Table 9.1 illustrates the data we used for the formula.

The other factor is that we believe the number of levels of hierarchy in the Web site add another level of complexity to your tasks. We account for this by multiplying the hours required for the text tasks by 1.1 if there are two levels in the Web site, 1.2 if

About The Hourly Rate
You need to change the hourly rates in the estimator according to what the market bears in your area for Web development services. We've learned that rates for services are highly tied to geography. We chose numbers that have worked for us in previous bids for clients. You need to use the numbers that work for you and for your area.

there are three levels in the Web site, and 1.3 if there are four levels in the Web site.

With this data, you can understand why we used the formula

$$(a*(2*b + .25*c + 1*d))*50 + (.5*e + 3*f + 5*g)*40$$

where **a** represents the factor for the number of levels in the Web site.

Of course, your mileage may vary. Feel free to adjust, refine, and revamp this formula and the metrics embedded in it. Make sure the formula reflects your skills and is in accordance with your Web services' marketability.

Interface Design

When we built the labels for this application, did you notice the pattern we used when we created the labels? The labels that instruct users to choose or specify a parameter start with a verb. In contrast, the fields that are calculated have labels that start with a noun, such as "Number of existing pages." In this context, readers

Table 9.1   Data used to derive the estimation formula.

Task	Hours Per Page/ Graphic	Hourly Rate	Input Connector On The Expression Evaluator
Write new material for the Web site	2.0	$50	b
Clean up material already converted to HTML	0.25	$50	c
Convert existing hardcopy material to HTML	1.0	$50	d
Scan photographs as JPEGs; crop as necessary	0.5	$40	e
Draw an icon; typically used to represent the major sections of the Web site	3.0	$40	f
Draw other graphics of medium complexity for use on the Web site	5.0	$40	g

subconsciously understand that a phrase that starts with a verb is an instruction for them to take an action. This is our desired effect for the fields that need numbers entered by the reader.

The other interface design technique we used for the calculated fields was to display them as grayed out. We accomplished this by deselecting the Make Field Editable checkbox on the first tab of the customizer. The user is prevented from changing anything in the field, and gray fields visually cue users to not try to enter any data.

We also grouped the categories, so the text tasks are separated from the graphics tasks with a little more space. Likewise, the calculated results are also offset with a little extra space to add to the interface's readability.

Output

Ideally, we should format the output with a dollar sign, but we leave that as an exercise for you. Another task we could add to this design is to display the total hours involved in doing the work, because the client's next question is going to be "So, how long will the work take?"

If we can display the number of hours required to do the work, then we could also add a calendar to the page for you to flip through and specify a calendar date. Although Java Studio does not include a calendar component, one of the contributed JavaBeans included on this book's CD (and on the Web site) includes a calendar component. If you're interested, see Chapters 14 and 15 on importing JavaBeans.

What's Next?

Speaking of JavaBeans, in the next two chapters, we'll build JavaBeans. Besides being able to import JavaBeans to use while building applications, you can also use JavaBeans in other development environments. So, fire up your coffee grinder, and turn to the next chapter for more information on building JavaBeans.

Chapter 10

Building JavaBeans With Java Studio

Ahhhh, now we approach the heart of the matter. We suspect many of you picked up Java Studio because of its ability to create and import JavaBeans.

JavaBeans are chunks of software that you can use in visual development environments. In programmers' parlance, they are *reusable software components*. You can import JavaBeans into Java Studio to extend the functionality of Java Studio, as you'll see in Chapters 14 and 15. So, you can create a design in Java Studio, export it as a JavaBean, and then import it back into Java Studio. Or, more likely, you would create a Bean for exporting into Java Workshop or another visual development environment. Chapter 11 covers this in more detail.

Essentially, Beans are a means to an end. You use them as a part of your Java Studio design or as a part of a Java application you build in Java Workshop. You do not write HTML code that calls a Bean—you don't use Beans on your Web site (unless you're building a Web-based repository of JavaBeans, of course). To add functionality to your Web site, create an applet.

As a builder of JavaBeans, Java Studio is still a screwdriver in a garage of power tools. You can do it, and it's easy to do, but it's hard to build sophisticated Beans. If you are already a Bean programmer, then you may find Java Studio somewhat limiting, depending on the nature of the Beans you develop.

In this chapter, we will develop and test a design. After we are satisfied with its performance, we will modify it so we can generate the design as a Bean. After generating the Bean, we will start a new design, import our Bean, and examine how it holds up.

Develop And Test The Design

Remember the estimate application we built in Chapter 8? The final number was an estimate of the cost for developing a Web site. It would've been nice to format the final dollar amount a little more nicely, but Java Studio doesn't have any components to do that automatically. So, let's build a JavaBean that rounds a number to a whole number and adds a dollar sign. Then, we can import the JavaBean into Java Studio's component palette and use the new Bean as a component in our designs.

Let's step back for a moment and consider why we are generating a JavaBean. Both JavaBeans and Packaged Designs are methods to encapsulate a design for reuse. Why not generate the design as a Packaged Design?

As explained in Chapters 12 and 13, Packaged Designs are an easy way for you to take a design and encapsulate it for use in other Java Studio designs. It's easier and faster than importing a JavaBean. So, why would you generate a JavaBean? Generate a Bean if you want to use the Bean in other application-development environments that support JavaBeans, such as Sun's Java Workshop (which is on this book's companion CD-ROM) or Symantec's Visual Café. Java Workshop or Visual Café wouldn't know what to do with a Packaged Design, because it's unique to Java Studio.

If you know that you'll use your encapsulated design only within Java Studio, then it's worth considering generating it as a Packaged Design, instead of a JavaBean. We believe this design could be useful in other development environments, so we're going to develop the design as a JavaBean.

As we have done with other designs, we will develop the design and test it. Unlike other designs, we will only spend time arranging the items in the GUI window, and we won't add any labels.

Develop The Design

We start building a Bean like we start everything else in Java Studio—by opening a new design. If you don't already have Java

Tip

Warning: Danger Ahead

As you know, Java Studio crashes once in a while. Generating and importing JavaBeans seems to push the program's limits a little more than other development projects, so save your design frequently.

We also encountered some unrepeatable… uh…performance issues. We mean bugs. Or at least we think they're bugs—it's hard to follow up on them because they seem to happen erratically and unpredictably. We found ourselves wondering if the problem really happened or if we were just too tired to see straight. But enough odd things happened that we feel compelled to share them with you. As we encounter tasks that occasionally generated one of these bugs, we'll warn you about them.

Studio running, start it now. If you have another design open, save it. Then, open the File menu, and choose New. Follow these steps:

1. Add a Text Field component to your new design. In the Text Field Customizer, name the component Input TF, and add a trigger connector. Click OK.

   Before we go any further, let's save the design.

2. Open the File menu, and choose Save. You should save frequently as you work in this chapter.

3. On the Computation tab of the component palette, select the Math component, as shown in Figure 10.1.

4. Click in the Design window to the right of the Input TF component. In the Math Customizer, name the component Round Math, and choose round(X) in the Function drop-down menu, as shown in Figure 10.2. Click OK.

5. On the Data Flow tab of the component palette, select the Distributor component. Click in the Design window to the right of the Round Math component. In the Distributor Customizer, accept the default name Distributor1. Click OK.

6. Review your Design window. It should appear similar to Figure 10.3.

7. On the Computation tab of the component palette, select the Constant component, as shown in Figure 10.1.

8. Click in the Design window to the right of the Distributor1 component. In the Constant Customizer, name the component $ Constant. In the Value field, enter "$", as shown in Figure 10.4. It automatically comes with a trigger connector.

Figure 10.1
Select the Math component on the Computation tab.

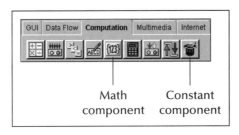

GUI | Data Flow | **Computation** | Multimedia | Internet

Math component   Constant component

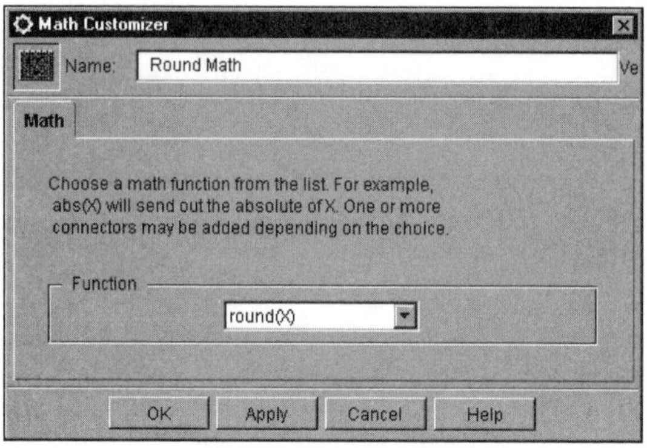

Figure 10.2
Choose the round(X)
function in the Math
Customizer.

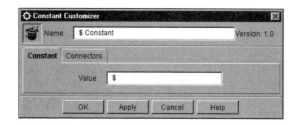

Figure 10.3
The Design window has
three components.

Figure 10.4
Add a Constant
component called $
Constant, and enter a
dollar sign in the Value
field.

9. On the GUI tab of the component palette, select the Text Field
component. Click in the Design window to the right of the $
Constant component. In the Text Field Customizer, name the
component Output TF, and add a trigger connector. Click OK.

10. Review your Design window. It should appear similar to
Figure 10.5.

11. On the GUI tab of the component palette, select the Button
component. Click in the Design window on the far left side.
In the Button Customizer, accept the default name Button1.

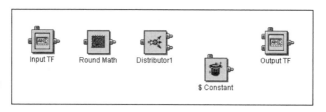

Figure 10.5
Your design now has five
components.

Now that all the components are in place, we can connect the components and test the design.

Connect The Components

The order in which you connect the components doesn't matter. So, use Table 10.1 as a checklist, and connect all your components. Then, verify your Design window against Figure 10.6.

Now, we can test the design. If you want, you can rearrange some items in the GUI window for the testing phase.

Test The Design

The objective of this design is to take a floating-point number, round it to a whole number, and add a dollar sign. So, type a number in the Input TF. Make sure it has at least one digit after the decimal. Now, click the button or press Enter. Your GUI window should show results similar to Figure 10.7.

Now that we have a design that works, we can make a few changes to turn it into a JavaBean.

Table 10.1   Connect the components.

Connect This Component	To This Component
Output connector on Button1	Trigger connector on Input TF
Output connector on Input TF	Input connector on Round Math
Output connector on Round Math	Input connector on Distributor1
Top output connector on Distributor1	Set Text connector (upper left) on Output TF
Bottom output connector on Distributor1	Trigger connector on $ Constant
Output connector on $ Constant	Prepend Text connector (lower left) on Output TF

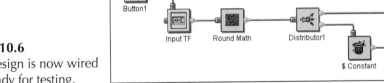

Figure 10.6
Your design is now wired and ready for testing.

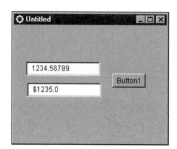

Figure 10.7
The design works.

Making It A Bean

Turning a Java Studio design into a Bean isn't quite as simple as going to the Generate menu and choosing JavaBean. You can do that, but you won't have a useful Bean, unless you're an experienced Bean programmer. If you are an experienced Bean programmer, you might be interested in the list of all the methods exposed by the process in Chapter 11. But for the rest of us, we're going to take a few simple steps to make this design Bean-friendly. The steps involved in turning this design into a Bean include adding External Connectors, hiding a text field, resizing the GUI window, and generating the Bean.

Add External Connectors

To add External Connectors, you select the External Connector component and wire it into your design. External Connector components become connectors on the Bean when you import it into Java Studio. Consider the connectors we want on this Bean. We want a trigger, so we can send a message through the component to display the results, and we want to be able to specify the string that the Bean operates on. Therefore, we need two External Connectors. Add External Connectors to the design using the following steps:

1. Right-click the Button1 component and choose Delete. The Button1 component was used as a placeholder during testing.

2. On the Data Flow tab on the component palette, select the External Connector component as shown in Figure 10.8.

3. Click in the Design window where the Button1 component used to be. In the External Connector Customizer, name the

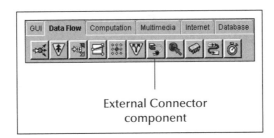

External Connector
component

Figure 10.8
Select the External
Connector component.

component Trigger EC, and accept the default selection of
Imports Messages, as shown in Figure 10.9. Click OK.

4. Select the External Connector component again on the
component palette. Click in the Design window to the left of
the Input TF component. In the External Connector
Customizer, name the component Import Number EC, and
accept the default selection of Imports Messages. Click OK.

5. Connect the output connector of the Trigger EC component
to the trigger connector on the Input TF component.

6. Connect the output connector of the Import Number EC
component to the Set Text input connector on the Input TF
component. Review your design. It should appear similar to
Figure 10.10.

Now, we have finished adding the External Connectors. Our next
step is to modify the appearance of one of the text fields.

Figure 10.9
Name the first External
Connector Trigger EC.

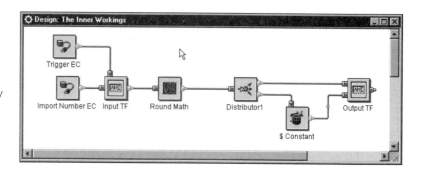

Figure 10.10
Your design should now have two External Connector components wired into the Input TF component.

Hide One Text Field

Think about the Bean we are creating. When you select this Bean from the component palette and place it in your Design window, what do you want to see in the GUI window? As it stands right now, two text fields appear. One reflects the number sent into the component, and the other reflects the number after it has been processed. We are going to hide the first text field, because it only displays the incoming number. Follow these steps:

1. Right-click the Input TF component, and choose Customize.

2. Click the Standard tab, and deselect the Enable and Show checkboxes, as shown in Figure 10.11. Click OK.

3. It may seem a little odd to have an invisible text field, but it's the right approach. Think of the Input TF as a container to hold the incoming number. You can still see the text field when it's selected, as shown in Figure 10.12.

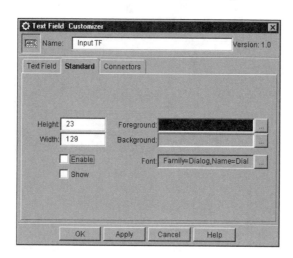

Figure 10.11
Disable and hide the Input TF component.

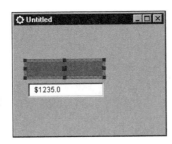

Figure 10.12
The Input TF component is invisible when it's not selected.

4. Position the Input TF component below the Output TF component. Then, move the Output TF component so it's in the upper-left corner of the GUI window, as shown in Figure 10.13.

With the text fields rearranged, we are ready to resize the GUI window.

Resize The GUI Window

We need to resize the GUI window to fit tightly around the Output TF component, because the size of the GUI window in the Bean design is the size of the visual components that appear in the GUI window when you import the Bean as a component. When we do this, the Input TF component is out of view on the GUI window. Resize the GUI window so it matches Figure 10.14.

The last thing we need to do is delete the contents of the Output TF component. Otherwise, the field starts with the values in the field when you save the design.

After clearing the Output TF component, save your design. Now, your design is ready to be expressed as a JavaBean.

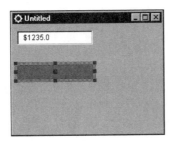

Figure 10.13
Move the text fields so Output TF is in the upper-left corner and Input TF is below.

Figure 10.14
Resize the GUI window so all you see is the Output TF component.

Generating A Bean

The last step in creating a JavaBean is to generate the design as a Bean, which Java Studio makes very easy. Follow these steps:

1. From the Generate menu, choose JavaBeans.

2. Java Studio generates a JAR file containing the Bean, so it asks you to specify the directory in which to start the JAR file and for the name of the JAR file, as shown in Figure 10.15. When you specify the name of the JAR file, don't include the .JAR extension. Java Studio adds an extension for you.

   After you specify the directory and file name, click Next.

   The file name you specify must be unique within the directory you specify. Otherwise, you receive an error message, as shown in Figure 10.16.

3. Java Studio asks you to specify the Java class name of the Bean. If you're not quite sure what a class name is, that's okay.

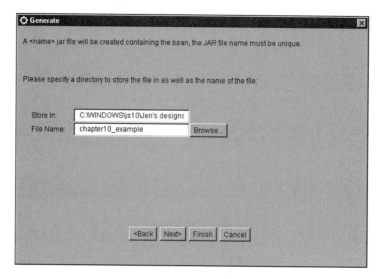

Figure 10.15
Specify the directory and the file name of the JAR file to be created by Java Studio.

Figure 10.16
Make sure the file name you specify is unique within the directory.

Chapter 11 describes class names, so you'll know what they are soon enough. Java Studio suggests a class name by appending the string "Bean" to the end of the file name you specified for the JAR file, as shown in Figure 10.17. Click Next.

4. Java Studio tells us that we have included External Connectors in our design and that we need to name the methods associated with each External Connector. (Again, Chapter 11 covers all the details, including a discussion about methods.) Java Studio suggests using the names of the External Connector components and appending the string "Method". Accept the suggested names, as shown in Figure 10.18, and click Next.

5. Java Studio now has the information it needs and is ready to generate a Bean. Click Finish.

6. Java Studio generates the code and creates the JAR file. When the Bean is complete, you receive a message, as shown in Figure 10.19.

If you take a look at the directory where you told Java Studio to store the Bean, you'll see a file called (in our case) chapter10_example.jar. Within that JAR file is a Bean called chapter10_exampleBean. We'll import that Bean to test our newly generated JavaBean.

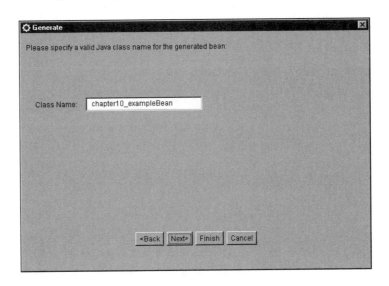

Figure 10.17
Specify the Java class name of the JavaBean.

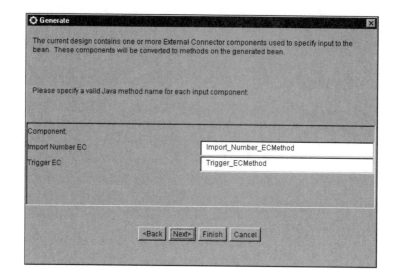

Figure 10.18
Specify the methods associated with the External Connector components.

Figure 10.19
The Bean has been generated.

Import The Bean And Test

Now that we have a JAR file, then we have some choices. We can import the Bean into Java Workshop or another visual Java development environment, we can import it into Java Studio, or we can import it into Sun's BeanBox. (For more information about the BeanBox, see Chapter 11.) For this chapter, we are going to import the Bean back into Java Studio. Follow these steps:

1. On the File menu, choose New.

2. Open the Import menu, and choose JavaBeans.

3. Java Studio asks you to name the directory of the JAR file containing the Bean, and the name of the JAR file, as shown in Figure 10.20. Click Next.

4. Java Studio examines the specified JAR file and lists all the Beans it found within the file. Then, Java Studio asks you to select which Beans to import into Java Studio. Select the Bean, and click Add, as shown in Figure 10.21. Click Next.

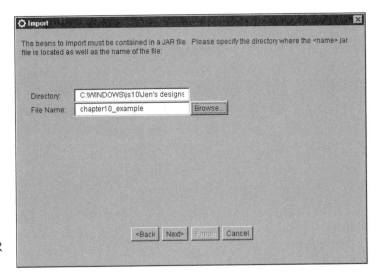

Figure 10.20
Specify the directory containing the JAR file and the name of the JAR file.

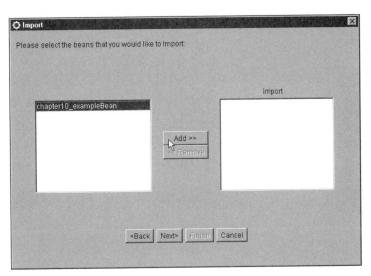

Figure 10.21
Select the Bean, and click Add.

5. Java Studio asks you to provide information that it will display about the Bean. In the first field, it asks for the display name of the Bean (which is the name that appears in a pop-up when you hold your cursor over the component), and Java Studio suggests the name of the Bean. In the second field, specify a short description that appears in the status bar when you hold your cursor over the component in the component palette. Leave the Bean name in the first field, and enter "Rounds a number and adds a $", as shown in Figure 10.22. Click Next.

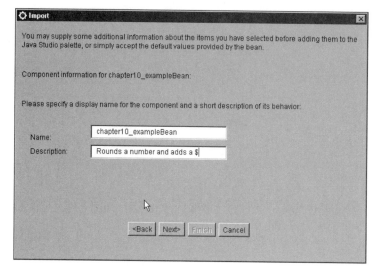

Figure 10.22
Supply the display
information for the Bean.

6. Java Studio lists the methods that can be exposed as connectors, and the methods are grouped into categories in a drop-down field. In the default category chapter10_exampleBean, four methods are listed. Select all four methods, then click Add, as shown in Figure 10.23. Click Next.

7. For each of the methods you choose to expose as connectors, Java Studio asks if you want to specify a description, and where on the component should the connector appear. Java Studio

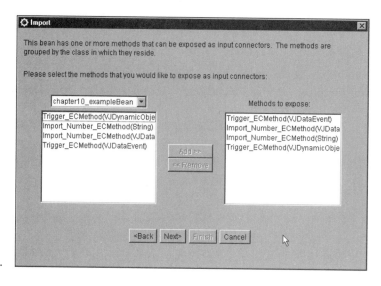

Figure 10.23
Select all four methods
with the default
category, then click Add.

puts trigger connectors on top of the component, so open the drop-down fields for both trigger methods, and choose North. Leave the default West location for both Import_NumberEC methods, as shown in Figure 10.24. Click Next.

8. Java Studio displays all the methods that can be exposed as output connectors. This component won't have any output connectors, so skip through the screen, as shown in Figure 10.25, and click Next.

Figure 10.24
Choose North for both trigger methods, and choose West for both Import_NumberEC methods.

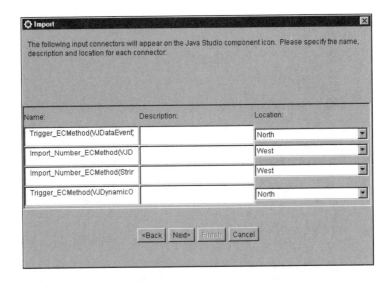

Figure 10.25
You can specify the methods to expose as output connectors here, but this component doesn't have any output connectors.

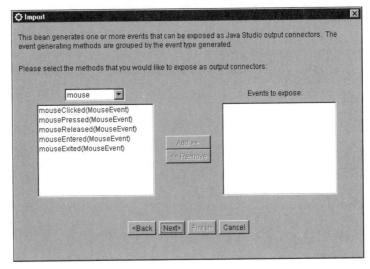

9. This component doesn't have any output connectors, so the next screen doesn't apply. If you chose to expose methods as output connectors, then you could add descriptions and choose their location on the screen shown in Figure 10.26. Click Next.

10. Java Studio offers an image to use as the icon on the component palette for this Bean. The default image is fine, but if you start importing more Beans, you need more images. Any image you acquire to use on the component palette should be 24-by-24 pixels. Store the images in the directory Java-Studio1.0\Js\intel-win32\bin, and you'll be able to choose the images from this screen. For now, accept the default image, as shown in Figure 10.27. Click Next.

11. Java Studio creates yet another JAR file that contains everything necessary to automatically import this Bean into Java Studio. You specify the directory in which to store the JAR file and the name of the JAR file. Java Studio, by default, uses your original JAR file name and prepends the string "VJ", for Visual Java. Use the default, as shown in Figure 10.28, and click Next.

12. Now, you can choose which tab on the component palette to use for the new component. By default, Java Studio suggests

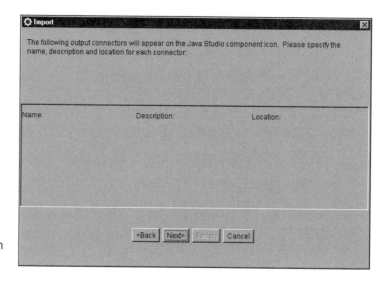

Figure 10.26
If you had output connectors, you would choose their location on the component.

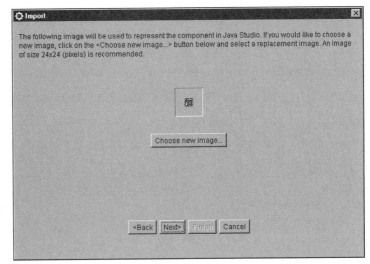

Figure 10.27
Choose an image for the icon representing the component on the component palette.

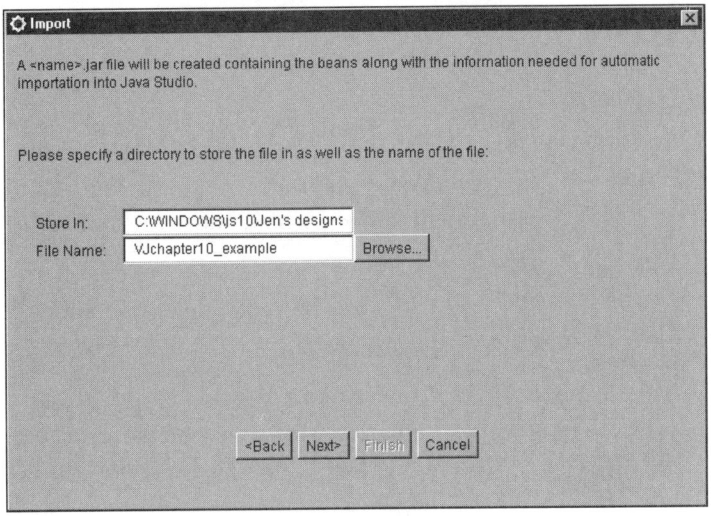

Figure 10.28
Specify the name and the directory of this JAR file, which contains the Bean ready for importing into Java Studio.

using the User tab, which is a new tab created for user-imported components. Leave the default, as shown in Figure 10.29, and click Finish.

Now, we're finished importing the Bean. If you check the directory where we've stored the files, you'll see two JAR files in addition to your original VJ design file. The first JAR file was generated when we generated the Bean. The second JAR file was generated when we imported the Bean.

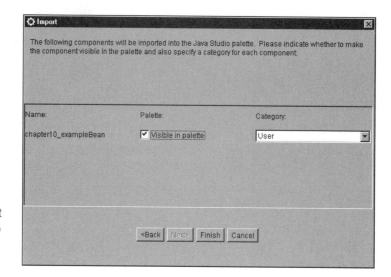

Figure 10.29
Choose the component palette tab on which to place the new component.

Warning, Part III

Once, after importing the newly generated Bean into Java Studio, all our previously imported Beans on the User tab disappeared. Java Studio replaced them with our new Bean as well as a bevy of blank Beans. It took us about 40 agonizing minutes to delete these 20 or so blank Beans.

Click the User tab on the component palette. See your new component? Let's take it out for a test drive.

Test The Component

This test will be very simple. We'll send a number to the component and see what it does to the number. Follow these steps:

1. On the User tab of the component palette, select the Chapter10_exampleBean component. Click in the Design window.

2. Java Studio displays a message, as shown in Figure 10.30. As discussed in Chapter 1, several Web browsers support JDK 1.1, including Netscape Navigator 4 beta 2 (and above) and Microsoft Internet Explorer 4 (and above). Click OK.

3. In the Chapter10_exampleBean Customizer, accept the defaults suggested by Java Studio, as shown in Figure 10.31. Click Close.

4. On the GUI tab of the component palette, select the Text Field component. Click in the Design window to the left of the Chapter10_exampleBean1 component. In the Text Field Customizer, click OK.

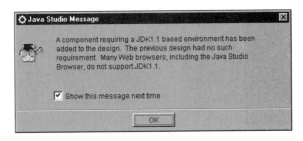

Figure 10.30
Java Studio generates
this message when you
add your Bean.

Figure 10.31
Accept the defaults in the
Chapter10_exampleBean
Customizer.

5. On the GUI tab of the component palette, select the Button component. Click in the Design window above the Chapter10_exampleBean1 component. In the Button Customizer, click OK.

6. Review your Design window. It should appear similar to Figure 10.32.

7. Connect the output connector of the Button1 component to one of the trigger connectors on top of the Chapter10_exampleBean1 component. You'll know which one to connect it to, because one of the trigger connectors causes the connection to turn red and fail to work, and the other one causes the connection to turn green and succeed. The trigger connector that succeeds is called Trigger_ECMethod(VJDynamicObject), as shown in Figure 10.33.

8. Connect the output connector of the Text Field1 component to one of the input connectors on the side of the Chapter10_exampleBean1 component. Again, one input connector will work and the other one won't work. The one that works is Import_Number_ECMethod(string), as shown in Figure 10.33.

Figure 10.32
Your Design window has three components.

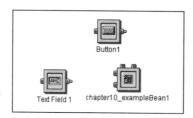

Figure 10.33
Each component (Button1 and Text Field1) connected to Chapter10_exampleBean1 connects to only one connector.

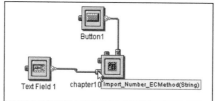

9. Pop over to the GUI window, and straighten it up a bit. Then, enter a number in the Text Field1 field, and press Button1. It works, as shown in Figure 10.34.

Continuing On

We're done. That wasn't too painful, was it? And now, you have developed a component that fills a gap in Java Studio's palette. Are you itching to learn more about JAR files, methods, classes, and other details of JavaBeans? Then, read on, because Chapter 11 covers exactly that.

Figure 10.34
The Bean, as an imported component, works as it should. Success!

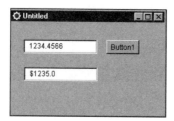

Chapter 11

Understanding JavaBeans Built With Java Studio

You can find a lot of good books on JavaBeans, but they usually start with the assumption that you're a Java programmer. This chapter is for you if you want to grind a few Beans without becoming a full-fledged coffee jockey, and it also includes a methods reference list if you really want all the caffeine.

We figure that you probably want to know enough about Beans to understand JAR files, methods, and classes. We'll take you there as well as explain the world of JavaBeans and the Bean we built in Chapter 10. Furthermore, we found an amazing lack of documentation on building JavaBeans in Java Studio, so we offer a reference at the end of this chapter for Bean programmers who want to know exactly which methods can be exposed on Java Studio Beans. Let's get started by exploring why you would want to create a Bean in the first place.

Why Build A Bean?

There are several reasons why you might want to build a Bean:

- You can extend Java Studio's functionality by importing the Bean.

- You can use the Bean in Java Workshop or another visual development environment.

- You can share your Bean with other developers.

Now, why create a Bean in Java Studio? Because there are Beans, and then there are Beans for Java Studio. As you will read in Chapters 14 and 15, not all JavaBeans are importable into Java Studio. Sun offers an extensive document that describes how to develop Beans for Java Studio. You can find it at **www.sun.com/studio/docs.html**. However, a Bean generated from Java Studio

159

will always be importable back into Java Studio. So if you want to create a Bean that you will use in Java Studio and other visual development environments, it's a good idea to use Java Studio. Or, you can download *JavaBeans for Java Studio: Architecture and API* or *JavaBeans for Java Studio: Cookbook* from **www.sun.com/studio/docs.html** and make sure your Bean complies. By the way, if you aren't sure if your Bean is compatible with Java Studio, just try importing it. Java Studio lets you know fairly quickly if a Bean's valid.

The rest of this chapter explores the basics of JavaBeans, offers a brief description of the JavaBean world, digs into the details about the JavaBean we built in Chapter 10, and lists all the methods in Java Studio Beans for Bean programmers.

The Lowdown On JavaBeans

Sun Microsystems, Inc. came out with the JavaBeans standard for public comment in September 1996. The JavaBeans 1.01 specification is available from **java.sun.com/beans/docs/spec.html**. Beans, in general, have had quite an impact on the Java industry. In this section, we'll discuss component technology, review some terms used for JavaBeans (*JAR files*, *methods*, and *classes*), describe how methods can be events or listeners, and talk about Sun's Bean Development Kit.

Component Technology Is A Wonderful Thing

JavaBeans are a pretty cool concept. As mentioned in Chapter 10, Beans are called *reusable software components*. We think a better description might be *Legos For Java*. In the old (pre-JavaBeans) days, once you built a useful piece of software, it took a fair amount of work to use that software in any other software. You had to customize the parameters and the connections to fit the new home of the software. JavaBeans have defined connections, just like The LEGO Group defined the space between the circles and the diameter of the circles on Legos. If you have a set of Legos at home, and you buy another set of Legos at Toys R Us, you know that your new Legos will fit into your existing Legos. No need to buy an adapter kit or anything else in order for all of your Legos to fit together.

JavaBeans can be used in any application development environment that understands JavaBeans, which is quite a few. It's that easy. Sun has defined the characteristics of JavaBeans, such as how connections work, and standardized the way Beans behave. No need to rewire the Bean to fit an application or change the Bean in any way.

When you build a Bean, you get to define your own Lego piece. Beans are stored in files called JAR files, as you'll see in the next section.

JAR Files, Classes, And Methods

JAR files are containers that hold a Bean and anything the Bean needs to run, such as audio files or graphics files. JAR files are called *JAR files* because they are *Java AR*chives. When you generate a Bean from Java Studio, you get a JAR file. When you import a Bean into Java Studio, you get another JAR file.

When you generated the Bean in Chapter 10, Java Studio instructed you to, "Enter a valid Java class name". So, what is a Java *class*? A Java class is a template or blueprint for a set of software objects. The template defines the variables and the behaviors for the software objects. Think of the components on the component palette in Java Studio. The Button component has certain defined characteristics and behaviors. When you select the component and click in a window, you are adding a specific instance of the Button component. By default, Java Studio names the instance Button1. In the Java world, this is called *instantiating* a class to create an *object*. In our example, the class is the Button component, and the object is Button1.

Java comes with a set of defined classes. Plus, you can declare your own class. But when you declare your own class, you are actually defining a *subclass* of one of the defined classes. Subclasses are classes that have a subset of the characteristics and behaviors of the parent class, and subclasses can add new characteristics and behaviors for members of the subclass. To specify a valid Java class name, specify a name that makes sense for the class, using letters of the alphabet and numbers. By convention, Java class names begin with a capital letter.

Classes that have some similarities are grouped into *packages*. Just so you can nod your head knowingly during the next Java discussion at work, all classes are in a package. Java has something called the *default package*, which is referred to as java.lang. One of the most common packages in Java is called the Abstract Windowing Toolkit, or the AWT. The package is referenced in code by java.awt. The package java.awt contains, among other classes, two classes known as java.awt.Frame and java.awt.Panel. When you generate a Bean from Java Studio, you are actually declaring a class that is a subclass of java.awt.Frame or java.awt.Panel. If your Bean contains a Menu component, then it is a subclass of java.awt.Frame. Otherwise, it is a subclass of java.awt.Panel. When a class is a subclass of a parent class, it is said to *extend* the parent class. So, your Bean extends either java.awt.Frame or java.awt.Panel.

A class defines methods, which can be used by all members of the class and any members of subclasses. Think of methods as the verbs of classes. Methods are also called the behaviors of a class. For those of you who know a smattering of programming, you can think of methods as functions (although object-oriented programmers might be offended at this analogy). When the creators of Java explained why the language doesn't have functions, they said that any function can be implemented by defining a class and creating methods for the class.

Methods, Events, And Listeners

Events are the way that objects communicate with each other. In Java Studio, components communicate with each other through messages. Sometimes, it's just a trigger message. Other times, it is actually data, such as a number or a string. All these activities are events.

Some methods handle events. These methods are called (amazingly enough) *event handlers*. When an event occurs, some objects want to be notified of the event. For example, any component wired to another component in Java Studio needs to know when a message is sent from the first component.

When an object wants to be notified of an event, it is called a *listener*. All event listeners have names that end in *Listener*. If you browse the names of methods available to be exposed by Java Studio at the end of this chapter, you'll notice some of the names include the word *Listener*, which indicates that they are listeners.

When an object wants to become a listener, it *registers* with the method that generates the event. When it is no longer interested in being notified of an event, it *unregisters*. When an object registers to be a listener, it uses a method that starts with the word *add*, and it includes the word *Listener* in parenthesis. When an object unregisters, it uses a method that starts with the word *remove*, and it includes the word *Listener* in parenthesis.

Now that you have had a five-minute lesson in JavaBean terminology, you are better equipped to understand how to generate and use JavaBeans in Java Studio. If you want to delve deeper into JavaBeans, you will need to use Sun's Bean Development Kit, which we'll discuss in the next section.

Bean Development Kit

To help you develop JavaBeans, Sun offers a software tool called the Bean Development Kit (BDK). The BDK is not a full-fledged development tool—it's just some free software that you can use to test the behavior of your Beans. Sun offers it so that every Bean developer has the same arena in which to test Beans. Sun calls it a "standard reference base."

The BDK is available on this book's companion CD-ROM. Or, to download the BDK, go to **java.sun.com/beans/software/ bdk_download.htm**. The BDK contains a variety of items, but the one to install and use right now is the BeanBox. After you have the BeanBox installed, you can import your Bean and play with it. This can also be useful if you are interested in importing a Bean into Java Studio, but you want to see what it does before you import it.

Now that you know the basics of JavaBeans, let's take a look at the other technologies developing with the world of JavaBeans. This will give you some context for Beans.

About The JavaBeans Standard

JavaBeans, as a standard, is very active and moving forward all the time. To better keep up on the world of JavaBeans, see the online resources listed in Appendix B. But this section gives you a quick review of several issues associated with JavaBeans, including InfoBus 1.1, the JavaBeans Activation Framework, Enterprise JavaBeans, and bridging other technologies, such as ActiveX, with JavaBeans.

InfoBus

InfoBus is a new specification that Sun is defining as a "standard extension" of Java. *Standard extension* is Sun's term. Basically, it means that the specification isn't included in the core definition of JavaBeans, but Sun wants it to become widely adopted. So, it's not quite part of the standard, but it's close.

InfoBus was a technology originally developed by Lotus and adopted by Sun. It is an application programming interface (API) that allows InfoBus-aware Beans (and other Java technologies) to communicate with each other in more powerful ways than previously available. InfoBus is certified as 100% Pure Java.

Because it is a standard extension of Java, it can be included by vendors implementing Java platforms, but it's not required. InfoBus requires JDK 1.1 or higher. If you are building Beans in Java Studio 1, and you intend to use these Beans in an application development environment with other Beans that happen to use InfoBus, then you probably won't be able to use the full capabilities of the InfoBus technology. The Beans generated in Java Studio 1 are not InfoBus-aware.

JavaBeans Activation Framework

JavaBeans Activation Framework (JAF) is a tool from Sun for Beans developers. It allows Beans to determine a data's type (whether it is a number and, if so, what kind of number; whether it is a string; and so on) and to determine the operations that can be performed on the data. Essentially, it is a set of classes available in a JAR file called activation.jar, and it is implemented as a standard extension to Java. JavaBeans Activation Framework requires JDK 1.1 and currently isn't implemented in Java Studio 1.

Enterprise JavaBeans

Enterprise JavaBeans is a proposed application programming interface for Java that makes it easier for developers to build larger applications with JavaBeans. The final draft of the specification was released by Sun in March 1998, and as this book goes to press, it has not been implemented in JDK 1.1, nor does it appear to be forthcoming in JDK 1.2. When it is implemented, developers will be able to build, for example, applications that are transaction oriented, such as inventory control systems. They will also be able to build JavaBeans server applications. For now, JavaBeans are still meant for smaller projects, but this proposed API gives you an idea of where JavaBeans and Java Studio are headed.

Bridging Other Technologies With JavaBeans

As you may know, ActiveX is a set of object-oriented technologies from Microsoft, and some people believe that ActiveX competes with Java and JavaBeans. ActiveX software that runs in a browser window is similar to Java applets. ActiveX environments, at least for now, are limited to Windows 95/98, Windows NT, and Macintosh platforms. ActiveX technology is not specific to a software language. For example, you can write ActiveX controls using C++ or Microsoft's Visual Basic.

Sun offers a way for JavaBeans and ActiveX components to talk to each other through a bridge. The bridge, called the *JavaBeans Bridge for ActiveX*, is a part of the BDK when you download the BDK for Windows (Sun says they will evaluate customer demand for bridges on other platforms if ActiveX libraries are developed for other platforms.) The bridge allows you to use JavaBeans within ActiveX containers. For example, you could use JavaBeans within an Internet Explorer application with the bridge. So, if someone objects to the idea of using JavaBeans because they are incompatible with ActiveX technologies, you can point them to Sun's JavaBeans Bridge for ActiveX.

Whew! That was a quick review of some interesting developments for Beans. Now, we can get back to the work at hand and discuss the details of the Bean we built in Chapter 10.

About Our Bean

We built a Bean to use as a component on the component palette in Java Studio. The purpose of the Bean is to take a number, round it to a whole number, and slap a dollar sign at the beginning. Let's take a look at the final state of the Design window, as shown in Figure 11.1.

Other than the External Connector components, it looks like a fairly standard design. On the other hand, the GUI window looks a little different. As you'll see in the next section, we took some unusual steps with the GUI window.

Interface Design

The GUI window went through some interesting changes during the development of this design. When we finished creating the functionality of the design and were testing it, the GUI window appeared as shown in Figure 11.2. Then, we went through several steps to hide the Input TF component, and we resized the GUI window so the Input TF component was no longer visible. Why?

Figure 11.1
The final state of the Design window for the Chapter 10 Bean.

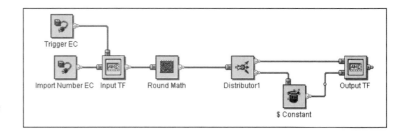

Figure 11.2
The GUI window, as it appeared before hiding a Text Field component.

We hid the Input TF component because we only wanted one text field to appear when the Bean was placed in a design. Other components use a similar approach by displaying only the results of the operation performed by the component. Our Bean has a similar function as the components on the Computation tab, and the components on the Computation tab have a similar design in terms of their appearance in the GUI window. For example, the Arithmetic component only displays the result of the operation, not the inputs. We wanted to set up our Bean the same way.

To hide the Input TF component, we opened the customizer for the component. Then, we clicked the Standard tab, and deselected the Enable and Show checkboxes. By deselecting the Enable checkbox, it removed the possibility that any user could change the contents of the Text Field. By deselecting the Show checkbox, it meant the Text Field would not appear in the GUI window. It appears as a dark gray box when you select it, but it is invisible when it is deselected.

The next unusual thing we did was resize the GUI window so that the Input TF component was not showing in the GUI window, even if it was not invisible. We did this because, when you generate a Bean, the size of the GUI window is the size of the Bean when you place it in the Design window. Anything showing in the GUI window appears in the GUI window when you import the Bean. So, we resized the window to make it fairly small, and the Output TF component was centered in the GUI window. Figure 11.3 displays the GUI window after we moved the Text Field components and resized the GUI window.

Remember how we said the only unusual item about the Design window was the External Connector components? Let's take a look at those components.

External Connectors

Figure 11.3
Resize the GUI window as small as possible.

By adding the External Connector components, you explicitly identified connectors for your Bean. You could generate a Bean from a design that lacked External Connectors. The problem is that you are faced with a dizzying array of methods to expose.

Tip

Resizing The GUI Window

To achieve the best results when you resize the GUI window, move the Output TF component to the upper-left corner of the GUI window. When you resize the window, you reduce the amount of space on the right side of the window and on the bottom of the window, but not on the top or on the left. So, move the components you need to appear to the upper-left corner, and you can resize the window appropriately.

Without the background or experience of a JavaBean programmer, it's hard to know which methods to expose to get the results you want. Take a peek at the reference list in the next section, "Bean Programmers' Reference Of Methods." That's the list you can choose from when you don't include External Connector components. You can still choose from the list when you include External Connector components, but by including External Connector components, you get another category of methods called External Connectors. Think of this category as your shortcut to methods to choose.

When you include External Connector components, then you are offered two methods to expose for each External Connector component. For example, in our Bean, we added two External Connectors called Trigger_EC and Import_Number_EC. The methods we could expose included the following:

- Trigger_ECMethod(VJDataEvent)

- Trigger_ECMethod(VJDynamicObject)

- Import_Number_ECMethod(VJDataEvent)

- Import_Number_ECMethod(String)

The methods with the parameter VJDataEvent are not valid connections. So, you could avoid some confusion by not exposing the methods that use the parameter VJDataEvent. The rest of the methods that you can choose to expose are listed in the next section.

Bean Programmers' Reference Of Methods

This section contains a list of methods available to expose as input connectors or output connectors. When you generate a Bean from Java Studio, you don't have any control on the methods used in the Bean. However, when you import a Bean into Java Studio, it creates another JAR file containing the Bean, and you can control which methods to expose as input connectors and which methods to expose as output connectors. This section lists those methods by category.

For information on developing JavaBeans for Java Studio using other tools, see *JavaBeans for Java Studio: Architecture and API* or *JavaBeans for Java Studio: Cookbook* at **www.sun.com/studio/docs.html**.

Input Methods

If you include External Connector components in your design, the first category of methods is always External Connectors. Then, the following method categories are available for input connectors:

- VJDesignPanel
- Container
- Components
- Object

The rest of this section lists the methods grouped by category.

VJDesignPanel

- removeListenerForVJPaint
- addListenerForVJPaint(VJPaintListener)
- setTiledImage(boolean)

Container

- removeAll
- removeContainerListener(Container)
- printComponents(Graphics)
- addContainerListener(ContainerListener)
- setLayout(LayoutManager)
- paintComponents(Graphics)
- remove(int)
- remove(Component)

Components

- addMouseMotionListener(MouseMotionListener)
- addFocusListener(FocusListener)

- printer(Graphics)
- setLocale(Locale)
- removeNotify
- setName(String)
- remove(MenuComponent)
- removeMouseMotionListener(MouseMotionListener)
- removeComponentListener(ComponentListener)
- hide
- repaint(long)
- removeFocusListener(FocusListener)
- resize(Dimension)
- repaint
- show
- addMouseListener(MouseListener)
- printAll(Graphics)
- removeMouseListener(MouseListener)
- deliverEvent(Event)
- list(PrintWriter)
- list
- nextFocus
- enable
- setBackground(Color)
- addNotify
- show(boolean)
- disable
- setBounds(Rectangle)
- list(PrintStream)
- setVisible(boolean)
- setFont(Font)

- addComponentListener(ComponentListener)
- setForeground(Color)
- setEnabled(boolean)
- addKeyListener(KeyListener)
- requestFocus
- layout
- update(Graphics)
- validate
- paint(Graphics)
- setSize(Dimension)
- removeKeyListener(KeyListener)
- paintAll(Graphics)
- invalidate
- doLayout
- add(PopupMenu)
- setLocation(Point)
- setCursor(Cursor)
- enable(boolean)
- transferFocus
- dispatchEvent(AWTEvent)

Object

- notify
- notifyAll
- wait
- wait(long)

Output Methods

The following categories of methods are available for output connectors:

- Mouse
- Key
- Component
- Container
- Focus
- mouseMotion

The rest of this section lists the methods grouped by category.

Mouse

- mouseClicked(MouseEvent)
- mousePressed(MouseEvent)
- mouseReleased(MouseEvent)
- mouseEntered(MouseEvent)
- mouseExited(MouseEvent)

Key

- keyTyped(KeyEvent)
- keyPressed(KeyEvent)
- keyReleased(KeyEvent)

Component

- componentResized(ComponentEvent)
- componentMoved(ComponentEvent)
- componentShown(ComponentEvent)
- componentHidden(ComponentEvent)

Container

- componentAdded(ContainerEvent)
- componentRemoved(ContainerEvent)

Focus

- focusGained(FocusEvent)
- focusLost(FocusEvent)

mouseMotion

- mouseDragged(MouseEvent)
- mouseMoved(MouseEvent)

In The Next Section

So far, we have covered how to build applets, applications, and JavaBeans using Java Studio. The only item left in the Generate menu is Packaged Designs. Although we've briefly discussed Packaged Designs here and there, we haven't covered them in detail. Chapter 12 contains the details regarding how to create Packaged Designs. Then, in Chapter 13, we'll talk about the Packaged Design created in Chapter 12.

Chapter 12

Building Java Studio Components

Think of building Java Studio components, called Packaged Designs, as a home improvement chore. It's something that can be pretty useful, and it can be satisfying to build, but you're probably not going to do this work on anyone else's house.

A Packaged Design is a Java Studio design that has been generated as a Packaged Design and, typically, automatically imported back into Java Studio as a component on the component palette. As you read through this chapter, you'll notice a lot of similarities to the principles we discussed in Chapters 10 and 11 on building JavaBeans. But, building Packaged Designs is easier and quicker.

When you generate a Packaged Design, you generate a JAR file. However, Packaged Designs are only for use in Java Studio. Even though a JAR file is generated when you generate a Packaged Design, the JAR file isn't valid to use in other JavaBean tools. For example, when we tried loading a JAR file from a Packaged Design into the BeanBox, we received the message displayed in Figure 12.1.

After we discuss Packaged Designs here and in the following chapter, we'll have covered all four items in the Generate menu—applets in Chapters 6 and 7, applications in Chapters 8 and 9, JavaBeans in Chapters 10 and 11, and Packaged Designs in Chapters 12 and 13.

So, have you been longing for a component that is missing from Java Studio's component palette? We found ourselves wishing, a

Figure 12.1
The BeanBox doesn't like Packaged Designs' JAR files.

```
Jar file d:\book\chapter12_example.jar didn't have any beans!
```

175

number of times, for a simple programming structure called a **For** loop. For those of you unfamiliar with the term, we wanted to be able to use a structure that would generate X number of pulses or trigger messages. We also wanted to be able to specify the number that X represents. Well, pull up a chair and pour some coffee. We're going to build a design that counts X times, which we'll be able to use as a modified **For** loop.

Building A Java Studio Component

This design is not *exactly* a **For** loop. It's more like a counting machine, because it generates numbers counting from one to our specified number X. Because Java Studio uses any message as a trigger message, we can use the generated numbers as trigger messages.

Here are the steps we'll go through to build this design:

1. Build the section where we add 1 to the current number.
2. Build the section where we collect the input number (X, in our previous discussion) and compare the current number to the input number.
3. Build the front and back ends of the design, which are the Count button that starts the design and the Output components.
4. Make the connections between the components.
5. Clean up the GUI window.
6. Test the design.
7. Add External Connector components.
8. Generate the Packaged Design.

If you haven't already done so, save your current design, and start a new design in Java Studio.

Build The Add 1 Section

This section uses four components: Constant, Merger, Arithmetic, and Distributor. Figure 12.2 shows the components used in this section.

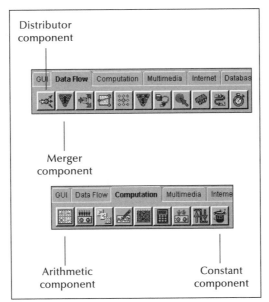

Figure 12.2
This section uses Merger and Distributor components on the Data Flow tab, and Arithmetic and Constant components on the Computation tab.

Let's start with the Arithmetic component.

1. On the Computation tab of the component palette, select the Arithmetic component. Click in the middle of the Design window.

2. Name the component Add 1 Arith. Click the Set The Right Value To A Constant checkbox, and enter the number "1" in the field, as shown in Figure 12.3. Click OK.

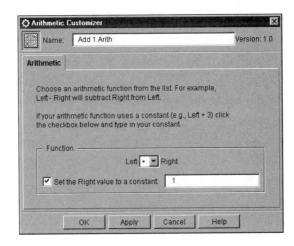

Figure 12.3
Add an Arithmetic component called Add 1 Arith.

3. From the File menu, choose Save to save your design.

4. On the Data Flow tab, select the Merger component. Click in the Design window to the left of the Add 1 Arith component. Let the name of the component remain Merger 1. Click OK.

5. On the Computation tab, select the Constant component. Click in the Design window to the left of the Merger 1 component. Name the component 0 Constant, and leave the default value 0 in the Value field. Click OK.

6. On the Data Flow tab, select the Distributor component. Click in the Design window to the right of the Add 1 Arith component. Leave the name of the component as Distributor1, and add two more connectors, as shown in Figure 12.4. Click OK.

We are now done with the Add 1 section, and your Design window should appear similar to Figure 12.5. While we're thinking of it, save your design.

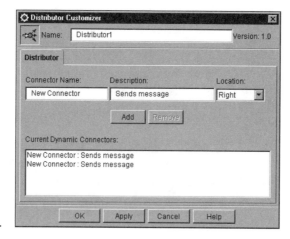

Figure 12.4
Add two more connectors to the Distributor1 component.

Figure 12.5
The Design window now has the Add 1 section, which adds 1 to the current number and distributes the resulting number.

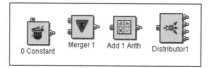

Build The Input Collection And Compare Section

This section uses four components: Text Field, Constant, Relational, and If. Figure 12.6 shows the components used in this section.

1. On the GUI tab, select the Text Field component. Click in the Design window above the Merger1 component. Name the component Input TF, and add a connector to trigger the component. Click OK.

2. On the Computation tab, select the Constant component. Click in the Design window to the right of the Input TF component. Name the component Input Constant, and add the connector labeled Add A Connector That Sets The Value Of The Constant. Click OK.

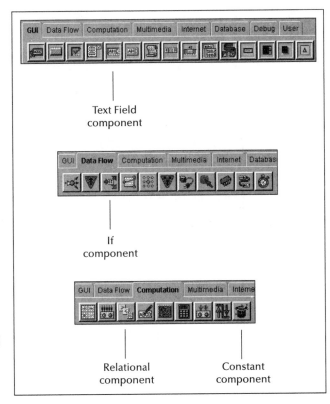

Figure 12.6
This section uses a Text Field component on the GUI tab, an If component on the Data Flow tab, and Relational and Constant components on the Computation tab.

3. On the Computation tab, select the Relational component. Click in the Design window to the right of the Input Constant component. Name the component LessThan Rel, and select the function Is Less Than from the drop-down list, as shown in Figure 12.7. Click OK.

4. On the Data Flow tab, select the If component. Click in the Design window on the far right side. Accept the default name of the If 1 component. Click OK.

We have now completed this section, and your Design window should look similar to Figure 12.8.

Build The Bookends: Count Button And Output

In this section, we use three components. We use a Button component, a Distributor component, and a List component, as shown in Figure 12.9.

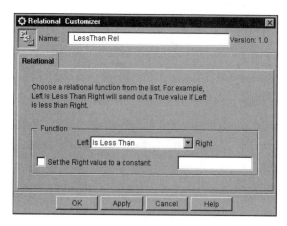

Figure 12.7
Add a Relational component that evaluates whether the left input is less than the right input.

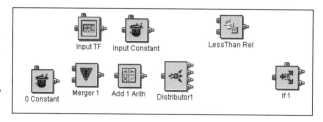

Figure 12.8
The Design window now has eight components.

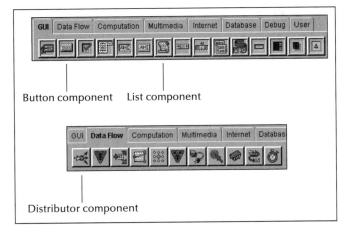

Figure 12.9
This section uses Button and List components on the GUI tab, and a Distributor component on the Data Flow tab.

1. On the GUI tab, select the Button component. Click in the Design window on the far left side. Name the component Count Button, and specify the button caption as Count. Click OK.

2. On the Data Flow tab, select the Distributor component. Click in the Design window to the right of the Count Button component. Leave the default name of the component as Distributor2, and add one more connector for a total of three output connectors. Click OK.

3. On the GUI tab, select the List component. Click in the Design window on the far right side. Name the component Output List, and add a connector that clears the list. Click OK.

Now, we have added all the functional components for this design. Go ahead and save it, then we'll wire the components together.

Make The Connections

We'll make the connections in chunks. First, we will present a table that lists the connections, and then we'll show you the results in a figure so you can verify your work:

- Table 12.1 lists the connections for the first section, and Figure 12.10 displays the connections made using Table 12.1.

- Table 12.2 lists the next set of connections, and Figure 12.11 displays the connections made using Table 12.2.

Table 12.1   Connections for the first section.

Make A Connection From	To
Output connector of the Count Button component	Input connector of the Distributor2 component
Top output connector of the Distributor2 component	Bottom input connector (named Clear) of the Output List component
Middle output connector of the Distributor2 component	Trigger connector (top) of the Input TF component
Bottom output connector of the Distributor2 component	Trigger connector (top) of the 0 Constant component
Output connector of the Input TF component	Input connector of the Input Constant component
Output connector of the 0 Constant component	Bottom input connector of the Merger1 component

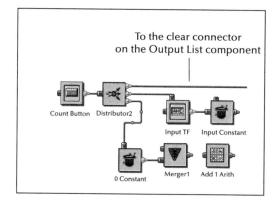

Figure 12.10
The first set of connections is done.

- Table 12.3 lists the final set of connections, and Figure 12.12 displays the completed view of the connectors.

Our remaining tasks, before generating the Packaged Design, are to clean up the GUI window, test the design, and add an External Connector component.

Clean Up The GUI Window

Take a look at the GUI window. Add a text label, and name it Input Label. Specify the label caption as "Specify the number to count to". Click OK.

Table 12.2   Connections for the second section.

Make A Connection From	To
Output connector of the Merger1 component	Input connector of the Add 1 Arith component
Output connector of the Add 1 Arith component	Input connector of the Distributor 1 component
Output connector of the Input Constant component	Bottom input connector of the LessThan Rel component
Top output connector of the Distributor1 component	Trigger connector (top) of the Input Constant component
Second output connector of the Distributor1 component	Top input connector of the LessThan Rel component
Third output connector of the Distributor1 component	Input connector of the If component
Bottom output connector of the Distributor1 component	Top input connector of the Output List component

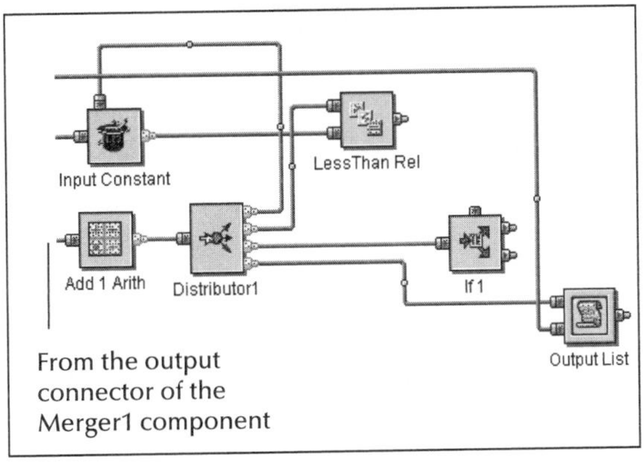

Figure 12.11
The second set of connections is done.

Now, take a few minutes to rearrange the items in the GUI window so they appear similar to Figure 12.13. Next, we're ready to start testing.

Test The Design

Enter a number in the first field, and click the Count button. The design starts counting at one. As it generates a number, it sends the number to the Output List component.

After you're satisfied that the design works as you expected, then we can move on to adding an External Connector.

Table 12.3 Connections for the third section.

Make A Connection From	To
Output connector of the LessThan Rel component	True/False connector (top) of the If component
Top output connector (True) of the If component	Top input connector of the Merger 1 component

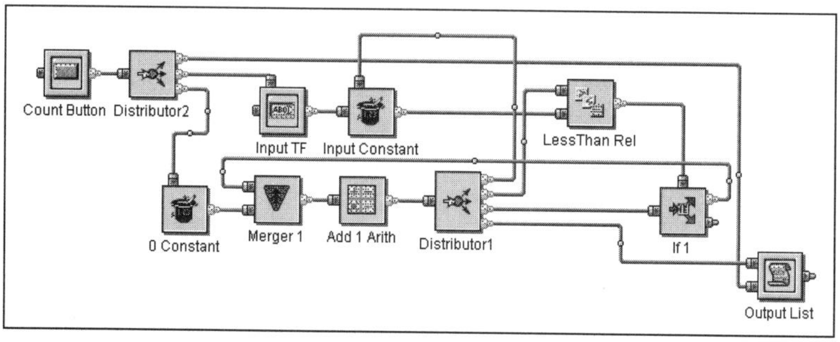

Figure 12.12
All the current connections are complete.

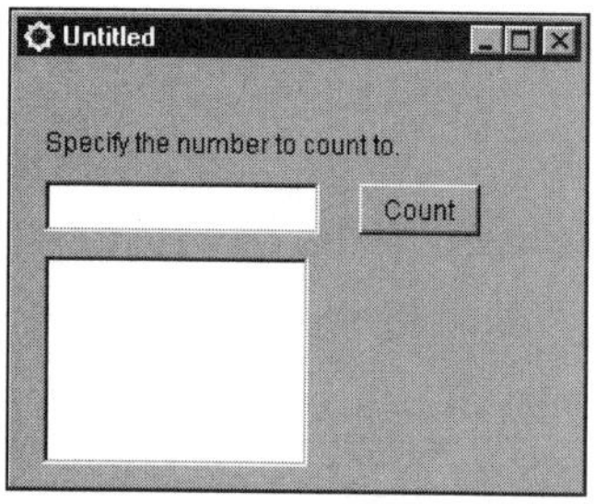

Figure 12.13
Clean up the GUI window.

Add An External Connector

We used the Output List component only for testing. Now, we can remove it and replace it with an External Connector.

1. Right-click the Output List component in the Design window, and choose Delete.

2. Right-click the Distributor2 component, and choose Customize. Remove the extra connector, and click OK.

3. By removing a connector, you probably lost a connection from the Distributor2 component. Reconnect any connections that are necessary. You should have one connection that goes to the trigger connector of the Input TF component, and

one connection that goes to the trigger connector of the 0 Constant component.

4. On the Data Flow tab, select the External Connector component. Click in the Design window on the right side, where the Output List component used to be. Name the component Output EC, and select Exports Messages, as shown in Figure 12.14. Click OK.

5. Connect the bottom output connector of the Distributor1 component to the input connector on the Output EC component.

6. Switch to the GUI window. Now that you've deleted the List component, you might need to do a little rearranging, and you will need to reduce the size of the GUI window.

With the testing completed and the design slightly modified with an External Connector, we're ready to generate a Packaged Design.

Generating A Packaged Design

Before we generate a Packaged Design from our design, save the design. After all, we don't want to take any chances. Then, follow these steps:

1. On the Generate menu, choose Packaged Design.

2. Specify a location and a file name for the JAR file. By default, it uses the name of your design as the name for the JAR file. Do not specify a file extension, because Java Studio automatically appends the .JAR extension to your file name. Click Next.

Figure 12.14
Add an External Connector that exports messages.

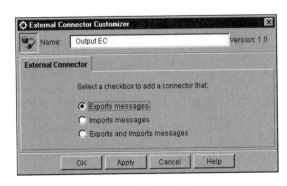

3. Specify a name for the component and a description. The description appears below the component palette when you hold your cursor over the new component. You can use Figure 12.15 as an example of what to specify for your own design. Click Next.

4. If you like, you can choose another image for your component. We're going to just accept the default image. Click Next.

5. You can choose to automatically import the component, which we will do. We can also choose the tab on the component palette. Open the drop-down field, and choose Data Flow. Click Next.

6. Because we included an External Connector component, we can choose where the connector appears on the component. Leave it on the East side. Click Next.

7. Click Finish.

Java Studio chews through the design and then automatically imports the Packaged Design as a component on the tab of the component palette.

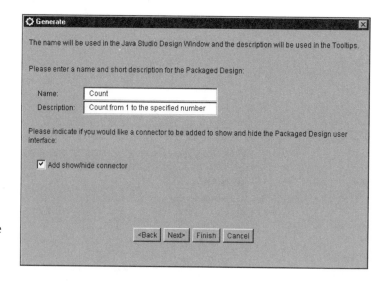

Figure 12.15
Specify the name of the component and a description.

Continuing On

That's it! Your design is now sitting on the Data Flow tab, happily ready to generate all the numbers you need. In Chapter 13, we really get up to our elbows in this project by digging into some of the details of generating Packaged Designs.

Chapter 13

Understanding Java Studio Components

After going through the trials of generating a JavaBean, generating a Packaged Design was easy, don't you think? With this capability, you can revamp the entire component palette, or at least, you can add those components you've been looking for.

Probably the most confounding aspect of generating a Packaged Design is that you get a JAR file containing the Packaged Design. When you review your files, there is no obvious difference between JAR files containing JavaBeans and JAR files containing Packaged Designs. This isn't a problem if you are using the JAR files to add components to Java Studio, but it *is* a problem if you need real live JavaBeans.

It's interesting to observe what happens when you import the JAR file of a Packaged Design into Java Studio. You can import the JAR file as a Packaged Design, or you can import the JAR file as a JavaBean. Java Studio recognizes a Bean inside the JAR file, and it imports the Bean as a component on the component palette seamlessly, even though the JAR file was generated as a Packaged Design.

On the other hand, if you try loading a JAR file containing a Packaged Design into Sun's BeanBox, you receive a message that the JAR file doesn't contain any Beans. So, depending on your goal, you might need to keep track of which JAR files contain Beans and which JAR files contain Packaged Designs. Or, you could just try importing or loading the file to see what happens.

In this chapter, we'll first work through the details of the component we built in Chapter 12. Then, we'll take a look at using Packaged Designs in general.

Understanding The Count Design

The Count design we built in Chapter 12 was meant to fill a hole in Java Studio's component palette. Lacking any component that would generate a given number of messages, we created the Count design. We can use this as a **For** loop or as a general-purpose counting machine. Let's take some time to understand the Count design. First, let's revisit the final state of the design, as shown in Figure 13.1.

The heart of the design is the Arithmetic component that adds one to the current number and the Relational component that evaluates whether the current number is less than the input number. In the upcoming sections, we'll review the Arithmetic component, then the Relational component, and finally the If component, which ties the Arithmetic and Relational components together.

About The Arithmetic Component

We customized the Arithmetic component so that it will always add one to the current number. We could, of course, change it so that the user could specify the increment value, but that is left as an exercise for you if you need that feature.

The Arithmetic component needs, as input, the number to add one to. Of course, to start, we need to send it the number zero so that the first loop results in the number one. After the first loop, the Arithmetic component needs the current number.

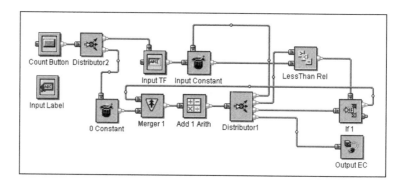

Figure 13.1
The final state of the Count design.

Mistrials And Misdemeanors

In working on this design, we tried several approaches. For a while, we used a Sequence Generator component to generate a series of numbers. Our thought was that we could capture a generated number, evaluate whether it was the target number, and if not, send a signal to the Sequence Generator to generate the next number. Unfortunately, this approach seemed to mostly result in infinite loops rather than logical conclusions.

After we switched to using the Arithmetic component, it seemed that we needed to use Adapter components before the If component and before the Relational component to keep the design going. Otherwise, the signal going through the design stopped at those two components. But later, during testing, we removed the Adapter components and the design worked just fine. Who knew?!

You can experiment with other approaches for this design, but we recommend you review Chapters 22 and 23 to learn how to use the Debug component before doing so.

In order to send the Arithmetic component a zero on the first loop, we used a Constant component that we set to zero. A Constant component won't send out its number unless triggered, so we added a trigger connector that is connected to the Count button. To allow the Arithmetic component to get input from either the constant or the current number, we used a Merger component. Fortunately, the Merger component sends a message when a message is received at either input connector—we don't have to trigger it to send out the message. Figure 13.2 illustrates this section of the design.

After the Arithmetic component sends a number to its output connector, the output number needs to be sent to a lot of components. The output number performs the following tasks:

Figure 13.2
The Arithmetic component receives input from either a Constant component or the current number.

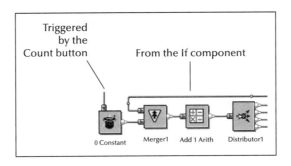

Triggered
by the
Count button

From the If component

0 Constant   Merger1   Add 1 Arith   Distributor1

- Triggers the Input Constant component.

- Sends the current number to the Relational component for evaluation.

- Sends the number to the If component, so the number can be routed back as the current number if the Relational component sends a true message to the If component.

- Sends the number to the Output EC component.

Notice that two of the connectors of the Distributor component are sent to the Relational component area, as we'll discuss in the next section.

About The Relational Component

The Relational component evaluates the current number and determines if it is less than the input number. The input number, of course, is the number entered by the user. The Relational component sends a true or false message, depending on the results of the evaluation. The true or false message is sent to the If component, which we'll discuss in the next section.

The Relational component receives the input number from a Constant component. We collected the input number with a Text Field component and triggered the Text Field component with the Count button in order to send the number to the Constant component.

We used a Constant component because, essentially, we needed to store the input number. We triggered the Constant component to send its stored number when the Arithmetic component finishes adding one to the current number. By sending the signal from the Arithmetic component, we can control when the signal reaches the Relational component. We want the Relational component to evaluate the newly generated current number, which is available only after the Arithmetic component finishes its operation.

The Relational component waits until it has both input numbers before performing its evaluation. When it receives both numbers, a true or false message is sent to the If component. Figure 13.3 illustrates this area of the design.

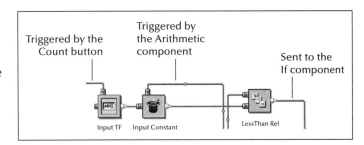

Figure 13.3
The Relational component receives the input number and the current number, which comes from the Arithmetic component.

About The If Component

The If component is the fork in the road of this design. If the If component receives a true message, it sends the current number back to the Merger component, which sends the number to the Arithmetic component (Figure 13.4). If the If component receives a false message, the message is not sent anywhere. The design stops, and because we've been sending the current number to the Output EC along the way, it has received the right number of signals.

That's about everything there is to know about the Count design, besides the fact that it works. Now that we understand this particular design, let's step back and take a look at Packaged Designs in general.

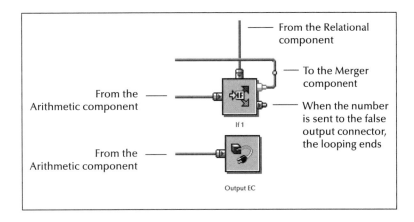

Figure 13.4
The If component receives the current number and a true or false message from the Relational component.

Understanding Packaged Designs

There are several issues we need to cover about Packaged Designs. They include:

- Building an interim design

- Preparing the GUI window

- Using External Connectors

- Bugs and bafflers

- Images for components

- Removing components

Building An Interim Design

In our Count design, we started by sending the output to a List component instead of to an External Connector component. Why? Because we needed to build an interim design before adding the External Connector components. This is a good practice to adopt when you're working on a design that ultimately will have External Connectors. You may remember that we did this when building a JavaBean.

The purpose of an interim design is to get the main functionality of the design working, providing immediate feedback so you know if you're on the right track. After you have all the details worked out, then you can add the External Connectors. Otherwise, if we developed the design using External Connectors from the beginning, then we'd need to generate the design as a Packaged Design and use it in a new design in order to test the design. Pretty cumbersome, when it's much easier to just create an interim design.

Of course, when you remove the component unique to the interim design and add External Connectors, you'll still need to test it. But so far, we've found that when we build an interim design, the designs have worked as expected.

Preparing The GUI Window

This is a refrain that, by now, you probably have memorized. Before finishing the design, the GUI window needs to be the right size and the fields need to be cleared. Otherwise, the GUI window shows up full size when you add the component generated from your design to a new design, and the fields appear with numbers already in them. This is a consistent behavior, whether you are generating an applet, application, JavaBean, or Packaged Design.

Using External Connectors

As you noticed, adding External Connectors creates slightly different paths depending on whether you are generating a JavaBean or a Packaged Design. When we added External Connectors and generated a JavaBean, Java Studio added two connectors on the new component for each External Connector in the design. When we generated a Packaged Design, only one connector was added to the component for each External Connector in the design.

One aspect of External Connectors takes a little thinking. In order for your generated component to have an *output* connector, the External Connector component needs an *input* connector. Figure 13.5 illustrates External Connectors with input and output connectors, and the resulting connectors on the generated components.

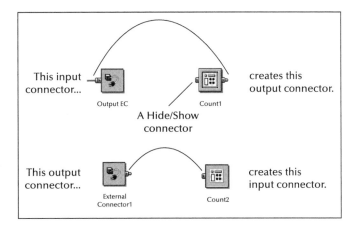

Figure 13.5
The External Connector component takes some thought, because it's a little confusing.

Bugs And Bafflers

We know you won't be shocked when we say that we encountered some odd behaviors in Java Studio when working on Packaged Designs. Fortunately, generating Packaged Designs seems less buggy than generating JavaBeans. We haven't always been able to re-create the strange occurrences, but we describe them here, so you can beware.

As you know, when generating a Packaged Design, you can choose to automatically import the component onto the component palette. When we did this, it renamed another component we had previously imported as a Bean to the same name we chose for the Packaged Design component.

We already know that JAR files are created when generating both JavaBeans and Packaged Designs. We found that a design, when generated as a Bean and then imported as a component, generated the JDK 1.1 warning message (shown in Figure 13.6) when adding the component to a design. The same design, when generated as a Packaged Design and automatically imported, did not generate the warning when the new component was added to the design.

When you delete a component from the component palette, you need to close Java Studio and restart if you are going to import a component that has the same name as the one you deleted. Otherwise, you will receive a warning message, as shown in Figure 13.7.

Images For Components

If you intend to add more than one or two components to Java Studio's palette, it's a good idea to find some other icon images to

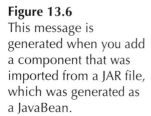

Figure 13.6
This message is generated when you add a component that was imported from a JAR file, which was generated as a JavaBean.

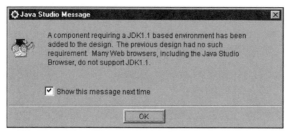

Figure 13.7
You receive this message when you try to import a component that you previously deleted.

use. Java Studio is a visual tool, so those icons on the palette are a big clue to you as the user. Java Studio only offers one image for all imported JavaBeans and Packaged Designs, although it appears to use the images differently. Figure 13.8 displays the same image used as an imported JavaBean and an imported Packaged Design. As you know, images for icons preferably need to be 24-by-24 pixels in size.

Removing Components

As you create more Packaged Designs and import them as components, you might find that you need to delete a component from the palette. Deleting components from the palette is relatively simple.

Figure 13.8
The first component was imported as a JavaBean. The second was imported as a Packaged Design.

Open the Customize menu, and choose Palette. Java Studio displays the contents of the palette, as shown in Figure 13.9. To delete a component, find it in the Customize Palette window. Select it, and then click the scissors icon in the Customize Palette window.

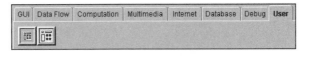

Figure 13.9
Use the Customize Palette window to delete a component from the component palette.

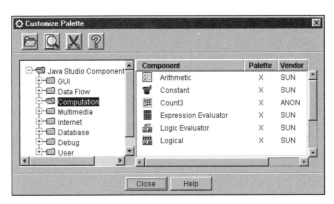

If you want to make a change to a component that you generated from a Packaged Design, you need to delete the component from the palette. Then, make the changes in your Java Studio design, and generate it as a Packaged Design again. This is little frustrating, especially when you just need to make a minor change to the component, but for now, it's the only way to modify a component.

More Excitement Ahead

You are hereby certified capable of creating Packaged Designs with the best of 'em. Fortunately, you may be able to find a Bean importable into Java Studio that saves you the trouble of creating a Packaged Design. Chapters 14 and 15 discuss how to find JavaBeans to import into JavaStudio and how to use them as Java Studio components.

Chapter 14

Extending The Power Of Java Studio By Importing JavaBeans

You've already seen that you can add features to Java Studio's palette by generating your own designs as JavaBeans or Packaged Designs and importing them to the palette as components. In this chapter, you'll skip the creating phase and go directly to importing Beans from other sources.

Open technology is a powerful concept. By publishing the specifications for a technology, any developer can write code conforming to the standards. The result, in the case of JavaBeans, is that a variety of JavaBeans exist that you can import into JavaStudio to extend its functionality. However, this issue raises some questions. Such as, how can you find JavaBeans to use? Are they free? Can all JavaBeans be imported into Java Studio? These questions and more are answered in this chapter and in Chapter 15.

In this chapter, we'll import some JavaBeans as components, and then improve one of our existing designs with the newfound power of these Beans. In Chapter 15, we'll discuss how to find JavaBeans. For additional JavaBean resources, see Appendix B.

Now, let's go import someone else's Beans.

Gather Some Beans

Where do you go when you want to find some JavaBeans? Chapter 15 answers this question in some detail, so, for now, we're going to use some Beans that ship with Java Studio. We'll also import a Bean available on this book's companion CD-ROM.

If you bought Java Studio on CD, then look in the CD's contrib directory. Contrib contains 21 JAR files, and the JAR files contain 25 Beans. We are going to import two JAR files. For a

▶Tip

Free Beans For Everyone

We believe that as Java Studio gathers steam and builds a larger user base, then more JavaBeans will become available. Until Java Studio, creating a Bean took more expertise and tools than a casual Web developer had in pocket. With the advent of Java Studio, that barrier is removed.

complete list of the JAR files and Beans in the contrib directory, see Chapter 15.

If you downloaded Java Studio from the Sun Web site, you can find the JAR files at **www.sun.com/studio/contrib**. Or, if you want to search Sun's site for the Beans, search for *contributed components* (that's what Sun calls them).

Sun warns Java Studio users that contributed components are not as thoroughly tested as the components included on the component palette. Therefore, Sun provides no technical support for the contributed components. Some of the components don't even have a Help file. But, we found that several of the components are useful and no more buggy than Java Studio. (Hey, quit snickering!)

There are other places to find Beans, but not as many as you might think. (We discuss this in Chapter 15.) Also, some Beans might be free, but it's more likely that you'll have to shell out some bucks. Sometimes, Beans only cost $25 or $30. But, for serious, big Beans, you can find yourself looking at upwards of $200 or so.

On this book's companion CD-ROM, we included some other Beans for you to try. The developers of these Beans kindly allowed us to include the demo version of the Beans that are sold commercially. Some of the other Beans are freeware, offered by the developers for the pleasure of sharing Beans. All the Beans included on this book's CD-ROM are compatible with Java Studio. But when you search for Beans on the Web, you might run into some JAR files that aren't so compatible.

No, Not That One—You Need A Compatible JavaBean

Among the Beans living in JAR files around the Web, some are compatible with Java Studio and some are not. How will you know? Well, it's hard to tell without importing the JAR file. But you won't lose much by trying to import it, so you might as well put the JAR file to the test. When you import a JAR file, Java Studio immediately tries to load all the necessary classes. If any are missing, it gives you a message that it cannot import the JAR file, as shown in Figure 14.1.

Figure 14.1
Java Studio warns you up
front if a Bean doesn't
work in Java Studio.

Here are two rules of thumb that can help you find compatible
Beans for Java Studio:

- Beans developed for JDK 1.1 work more often than Beans
  developed only for JDK 1.02.

- Beans using the letters VJ in their names are usually developed
  for Visual Java environments, which means that they will
  probably work in Java Studio.

Remember, these are rules of thumb—you'll find Beans developed
for JDK 1.1 and Beans containing VJ in their names that don't
import into Java Studio.

By now, you know what to look for, so let's import our Beans.

Importing The Bean

In this section, we'll import three JAR files:

- Synchronizer.jar

- VJLines.jar

- VJMultiLineLabel.jar

The first two JAR files are in the contrib directory on Sun's Java
Studio CD. The third Bean is on this book's CD-ROM.

If you don't already have Java Studio running, start it now. Follow
these steps:

1. Copy Synchronizer.jar, VJLines.jar, and VJMultiLineLabel.jar
   from their source directories to your hard disk. A good location for them is in a subdirectory of the JDK directory. The
   JDK directory might be a subdirectory of the Java Studio
   directory, usually Java-Studio1.0. For example, copy the files
   to c:\Java-Studio1.0\Jdk\lib\JARs.

▶Tip

Faster File Selection

Did you notice that we selected this JAR file a little faster than in previous endeavors? Earlier, we laboriously typed the full directory name in the Directory field (after all, the documentation tells us to do so). Quite by accident, we discovered this shortcut. By using the Browse button to select the file, and skipping specifying the directory, the proper directory name is filled in the Directory field for you.

2. In Java Studio, open the Import menu, and choose JavaBeans.

3. In the Import window, click Browse, and navigate to the directory containing the JAR files. Select the first JAR file, and click Open, as shown in Figure 14.2.

4. In the Import window, your selected file and its directory should now appear in the Directory and File Name fields. Click Next.

5. The Bean inside the JAR file is displayed in the left window. Select the Bean, click Add, and then click Next.

6. You can choose which tab on the component palette to use as the home for the Bean. Accept the default setting, which means the Beans are imported to the User tab. Click Finish.

Repeat Steps 1 through 6 for the remaining two JAR files. When you import VJLines.jar, you will find three Beans in the JAR file, as shown in Figure 14.3. Your User tab should appear similar to Figure 14.4.

Now that we have imported the three Beans, we can take a previous design and improve it using our newly imported Beans (don't worry if you didn't save past projects—we've supplied a copy of the design on this book's CD-ROM).

Improving A Design

In Chapter 4, we put the finishing touches on an order form. Figure 14.5 shows the final version of the design's GUI window.

Figure 14.2
Click Browse, and then navigate to the directory containing the JAR files.

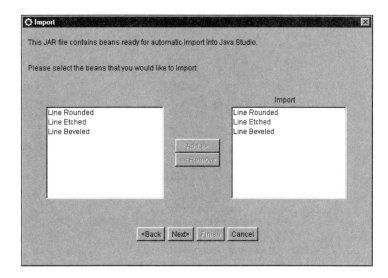

Figure 14.3
When you import VJLines.jar, select all three Beans for importing.

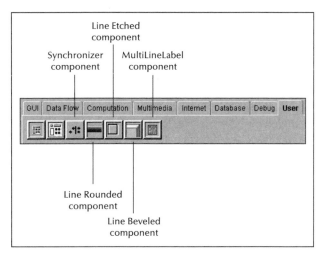

Figure 14.4
Your User tab should have five new Beans on it.

With our new components on the User tab, we can easily improve this design. First, we'll improve its functionality, and then we'll improve its appearance.

Improving Functionality

If you don't have Java Studio running, start it now. Then follow these steps:

1. From the File menu, choose Open. Display the contents of this book's CD-ROM, and select the file chapter04_example.vj.

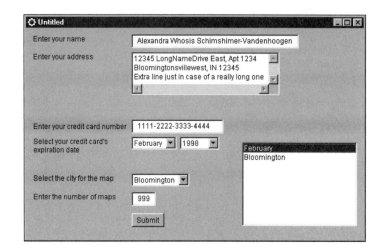

Figure 14.5
The order form from Chapter 4.

 Tip

Disconnecting Connections

If you haven't discon-nected any components in a while, here's a quick refresher. To disconnect a connection, right-click the connection, and choose Disconnect. Or, go to the end of the connection (where it enters an input connector), click and hold the input connector, and pull away from the input connector.

2. From the File menu, choose Save As. Save chapter04_example.vj with a new file name, such as order_form_new. Remember, Java Studio adds the .VJ file extension for you.

3. Switch to the Design window. One of the problems with this design is that as soon as a user selects an item from a drop-down menu, such as Credit Card Expiration Month, the item is immediately sent through the Merger component to the List component. However, the rest of the data is not sent to the List component until the user presses the Submit button. The Synchronizer component can help fix that. Select the Merger1 and List1 components and move them further to the right on the Design window.

4. Disconnect all the input connectors for the Merger1 compo-nent, and disconnect the bottom input connector (the Clear connector) on the List component, as shown in Figure 14.6.

Figure 14.6
The Design window, after you've finished the disconnections.

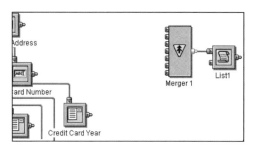

5. On the User tab of the component palette, select the Synchronizer component, and then click the Design window to the left of the Merger component.

6. In the Synchronizer Customizer, add five more connectors to the two default connectors, as shown in Figure 14.7. You need a total of seven input connectors. Click OK.

7. Use Table 14.1 to make the connections from the other components to the Synchronizer.

Figure 14.7
Add five more connectors for a total of seven connectors.

Table 14.1   Connections to the Synchronizer1 component.

Connect This Component	To This Input Connector On The Synchronizer1 Component
Customer Name	1st Input Connector
Customer Address	2nd Input Connector
Credit Card Number	3rd Input Connector
Credit Card Month	4th Input Connector
Credit Card Year	5th Input Connector
Cities	6th Input Connector
Number of Maps	7th Input Connector

8. Connect the output connectors of the Synchronizer1 component to input connectors of the Merger1 component, as shown in Figure 14.8.

9. Right-click the Distributor1 component, and choose Customize. Or, select the Distributor1 component, go to the Customizer menu, and choose Selected Component. Display the last connector in the list, select it, and click Remove, as shown in Figure 14.9.

10. Now, we need to add a new button to clear the list. On the GUI tab, select the Button component. Click the Design window. Name the component "Clear Button", and specify the button caption as "Clear".

11. Connect the output connector of the Clear Button component to the bottom input connector on the List1 component.

By adding the Synchronize component, all the input messages are collected before being sent to the Merger component. Now that the form's output is easier to process, let's improve the design's appearance.

Figure 14.8
Connect the output connectors of the Synchronizer1 component to the input connectors of the Merger1 component.

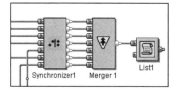

Figure 14.9
Remove the last output connector on the Distributor1 component.

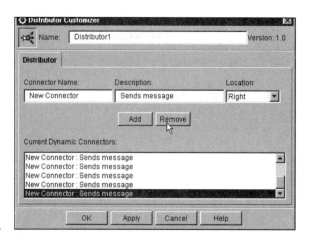

Improving Aesthetics

In this section, we'll change one of the labels to make it easier to maintain, and we'll add some lines to visually differentiate areas of the form. Let's start by deleting some of the existing labels.

1. In the GUI window, look for the two labels that, together, state "Select your credit card's expiration date". Select one of the labels, open the Edit menu, and choose Delete. Select the other label, open the Edit menu, and choose Delete.

2. On the User tab, select the MultiLineLabel component. Click the GUI window to the left of the Credit Card Expiration Month component. Name the component "Credit Card Exp Date Label". Now, click the Edit button at the end of the Text field. Enter the text "Enter your credit card's expiration date." as shown in Figure 4.10. Click OK.

3. Click the Edit button at the end of the Font field. In the Family list, scroll to find the font Dialog. Select it, as shown in Figure 4.11. Click OK, then click Close to close the MultiLineLabel Customizer.

Figure 14.10
Edit the Text field in the MultiLineLabel component.

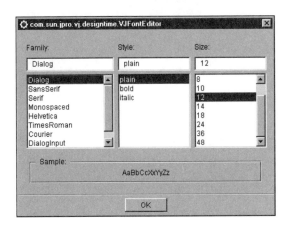

Figure 14.11
Select the Dialog font.

4. Look at the GUI window, and review the results. Align the new label to the left with the other labels, then align it to the top of the Credit Card Month and Credit Card Year components.

5. Align the tops of the Submit and Clear buttons near the bottom of the GUI window.

   Notice how the form in the GUI window has four areas: name and address, credit card information, map information, and buttons. Let's add lines to more clearly differentiate between these areas.

6. On the User tab, select the Line Etched component. Click the area below the Address Text Area. In the Line Etched Customizer, change the thickness to 2. Click the Standard tab, and change the width to 100. Click OK. Then, review the thickness of the line in the GUI window. Select the line, and stretch it so it is almost the width of the form, as shown in Figure 4.12.

7. Because items aligned to the left always use the leftmost item as the alignment post, make sure the line is *not* the leftmost item. Then, select the line and some of the labels. Open the Layout menu, and choose Align Left.

8. After you are satisfied that the line is a pleasing width, add another Line Etched component between the credit card information and the map information.

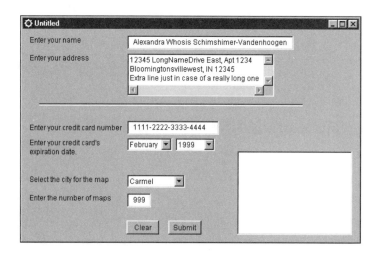

Figure 14.12
Add a Line Etched component.

In our current design, we have a List component that prevents us from making this line the same width as the previous line. However, for future designs, if you need lines the same width, you can use one of two techniques:

- Use the Layout|Equalize Width command.

- View the customizer for the first line, and determine the number used to specify the width. (In our design, it's 459.) Then, use the same number to specify the width on the other line components.

9. Add another Line Etched component between the map information and the buttons. Your finished design should appear similar to the design shown in Figure 4.13.

Mission Accomplished

Take some time to play with your design. The Submit and Clear buttons work like a champ, and the design is easy to use and understand, which is our primary goal. In Chapter 15, we'll dive deeper into the issues of importing JavaBeans from other sources and scavenging for Beans to use in Java Studio.

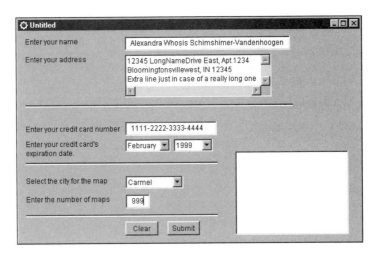

Figure 14.13
The finished design looks lovely, just lovely.

Chapter 15

Understanding How To Import JavaBeans

Perhaps this chapter is misnamed. It's not hard to understand how to import JavaBeans—at least the basics of the process are straightforward. The trick is knowing where to find Beans, how to choose them, and how to use them once you've got 'em.

In Chapter 11, we spent some time discussing JavaBeans. But in this chapter, we'll talk about how you can make the most of your time and productively use JavaBeans from other sources.

Where Do You Find JavaBeans?

When we began working on this chapter, we set out to identify the best JavaBean repositories. After some research, more research, and then some serious digging, we regret to report that, although a few sites offer some collections of JavaBeans, publicly available JavaBeans are not nearly as ubiquitous as we had hoped. So, with that forewarning, where does that leave you? Actually, you have a good start with the Beans already on your plate.

Surprise! You Have More Beans

Okay, maybe you're not really surprised, because you imported some of these Beans in Chapter 14. But, let's take a few minutes to discuss the bonus Beans provided by Java Studio. As you read in the last chapter, the Java Studio CD-ROM's contrib directory stores JAR files containing Beans. Or, if you downloaded Java Studio from the Web, the bonus Beans are available at **www.sun.com/studio/contrib**.

The Beans in the contrib directory are shipped by Sun with Java Studio. They are a collection of Beans created by Sun and other Bean developers that conform to Java Studio's specifications.

Because these Beans were written explicitly for Java Studio, the process of importing them is slightly different than for other Beans. For more details on this, see "Importing JavaBeans And Deleting Components" later in this chapter.

Table 15.1 lists the Beans stored in the contrib directory. Except where noted, the name of the component (after the Bean is imported) is the same as the name of the Bean.

With these contributed components, you have your choice of another 25 Beans to add to Java Studio's component palette. But because we are so dedicated to providing you with the most resources possible to make your working life easier, we found more Beans for you, which are presented in the following section.

Other Sources For Beans

Essentially, there are four categories of Bean resources:

- Commercial development companies who develop JavaBeans, such as Jscape or the KL Group.

- Professional developers who are either independent or working with just one or two other associates, such as Wildcrest Associates (developers of the MultiLineLabel Bean we use in Chapter 14), Scotty's MiniBeans, and JohnnyBeans.

- Casual hobbyists—people who develop Beans for fun at home.

- Independent Web site companies that collect JavaBeans for the mutual benefit of the Bean community, such as the Java Applet Rating Service at **www.jars.com**.

The categorizations are helpful, because it helps you know where to look for Beans and what to expect when you find them. The commercial development companies are more likely to have full-featured, rich Beans for a premium price. For example, Jscape offers several Beans in a package called Jscape Form for $120. Their Jscape Widgets package is $800. Professional developers are more likely to offer useful, smaller Beans with accordingly smaller prices. Wildcrest Associates offers their MultiLineLabel Bean for $29 for an individual license.

Table 15.1   Beans you already have.

JAR File Name	Bean Name	Description	Vendor	In The Design Window
ArgentCoffeTable.jar	ArgentCoffeeTable	Displays data in a table. You specify the number of rows, number of columns, and other attributes.	Argent Software	ArgentCoffeeTable1
dbaccessCoco.jar	Coco-DBAccess	A more sophisticated version of the Database component.	Thought, Inc.	Coco-DBAccess 1
	TableOutputCoco	Table output for the Coco-DBAccess component; receives the results of the database query performed by Coco-DBAccess.	Thought, Inc.	TableOutputCoco 1
	ValidationTextCoco	Validates input for the Coco-DBAccess component.	Thought, Inc.	ValidationTextCoco 1
EventAdapter.jar	EventAdapter	Provides information about an event. For example, if you send it a mouse event, then it outputs the x location of the mouse, the y location, the number of clicks, and a true/false indicating whether the mouse click indicated a pop-up trigger.	Sun Microsystems	Event Adaptor1
FormGateway.jar	FormGateway	Collects data and sends it to a CGI script for processing; outputs the results of the CGI script.	JohnnyBeans	FormGateway1

(continued)

Table 15.1 Beans you already have (continued).

JAR File Name	Bean Name	Description	Vendor	In The Design Window
HashTable.jar	HashTable	Implements a *Hash Table* in a Bean. A Hash Table is a data structure similar to a table, except each item in the table has a unique value, called a *key*, associated with it. Values are stored, retrieved, and deleted using keys.	JohnnyBeans	HashTable1
IBS.jar	IBS	Instant Basic allows you to enter a Basic program, which is interpreted by the Bean. It determines the number of input or output connectors needed by the program.	Halcyon Software	IBS1
Konstants.jar	Konstants	Generates one of four constants: newline, tab, pi, or E.	JohnnyBeans	Konstants1
NetTransport.jar	NetTransport	Sends messages over a network; enables separate designs to communicate with each other. Does not work in applets (see Chapter 18 for more information).	JohnnyBeans	NetTransport1
ServerSocket.jar	ServerSocket	No documentation exists for this component.	JohnnyBeans	ServerSocket1

(continued)

Table 15.1   Beans you already have *(continued)*.

JAR File Name	Bean Name	Description	Vendor	In The Design Window
Socket.jar	Socket	No documentation exists for this component.	JohnnyBeans	
Synchronizer.jar	Synchronizer	Similar to the Adapter component, except the Synchronizer waits until a value has been received by all input connectors before sending out the values.	Sun Microsystems	
TableToText.jar	TableToText	Takes table input and formats it as text.	Scotty's Minibeans	
VJCalendar.jar	Calendar	Displays a calendar, month view.	Jscape	
VJChartT	VJChart (name of component is Chart)	Draws a chart using input data. Charts can be line, bar, stacking bar, pie, or scatter charts.	KL Group	
VJDateTextField	DateTextField (name of component is Date TextField)	Very similar to a Text Field component, except it provides the slashes used in dates, such as 9/18/98, and it provides some error checking so you can specify the minimum and maximum dates.	Jscape	
VJImageCanvas	VJImageCanvas (name of component is Image Canvas)	Allows you to add an image to your design.	Jscape	

(continued)

Table 15.1 **Beans you already have** *(continued).*

JAR File Name	Bean Name	Description	Vendor	In The Design Window
VJImageListBox	imageListBox	No documentation exists for this component, and we received a Java Studio error when importing it.	Jscape	imageListBox1
VJLines	Line Rounded	Draws a three-dimensional rounded line.	Scotty's Minibeans	Line Rounded1
	Line Etched	Draws a line that looks like it has been carved into the background of the design.	Scotty's Minibeans	Line Etched1
	Line Beveled	Draws lines that enables you to frame an image and make it appear beveled.	Scotty's Minibeans	Line Beveled1
VJLiveTableT	Table	Displays table data in a variety of formats, and outputs either the entire table or the user-selected portion of the table.	KL Group	Table1
VJProgressBar	Progress Bar	Displays a numerical value indicating percent completed.	Jscape	Progress Bar1
VJRadioBox	VJRadioBox	Displays radio buttons, which are choices that are mutually exclusive. Useful when you want to present a finite set of options to your users and choosing more than one option is not valid.	Sun Microsystems	VJRadioBox1

As mentioned earlier, a good place to look for Beans is
www.jars.com. We believe this collection is more complete that
any others we found. Note that some of the Beans posted there
are freeware, some are shareware, and some are commercial Beans.
Please respect the rules for using shareware and commercial
Beans. Each source for a Bean will explain what they need from
you. For example, you may be able to use a demo Bean for evaluation. If it fulfills your need, you will be asked to pay for it. If not,
you will be asked to destroy the JAR file.

You can also explore the Bean Development Kit (BDK), offered as
a free utility by Sun Microsystems. The BeanBox, part of the
BDK, comes with 15 Beans you can use for experimentation.

For a comprehensive list of resources for JavaBeans, see Appendix
B. In the appendix, we list every resource we found for Beans,
along with any comments we have about the resource.

Now that you are equipped with Beans, we can proceed with a
discussion about importing and deleting them.

Importing JavaBeans And Deleting Components

You can import JavaBeans, lots of Beans, into Java Studio. The
maximum number of components you can have in Java Studio is
unclear to us. But keep this in mind—the more components on
the component palette, the slower Java Studio runs. Java Studio is
somewhat of a CPU hog already, so this point is relevant. This
section describes how to import JavaBeans; it also describes how
to delete components from the component palette.

Importing JavaBeans

There are two kinds of Beans to import: regular Beans and Beans
written for Java Studio (or other visual Java environments). The
main difference is that when you import a Bean written for Java
Studio, you are not given a list of methods to choose as input
connectors or output connectors. By not being forced to ponder a

Figure 15.1
Enlarge the palette to display more than 23 Beans on a tab.

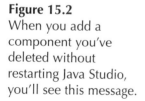

▶Tip

Enlarge Your Palette

If you find that you import more than 23 Beans to the User tab of the component palette, the 24th and successive Beans are hidden from view. To fix this problem, simply enlarge the palette by clicking and dragging the bottom edge of the palette, as shown in Figure 15.1.

considerable list of methods, the process of importing the Bean is fairly quick. When you import a regular Bean, you are presented with a list of methods (as discussed in Chapter 11).

The Beans described at the beginning of this chapter don't allow you to select methods to expose. They come with the connectors already defined. However, when you import a non-Java Studio Bean, how do you know which methods to expose? Sometimes, it's easy to tell. If the Bean is similar to the Text Field or Text Area components where text is displayed, then it's probably a good idea to expose a method called **setString** or **setText**. It's an educated guess that methods with those names generate an input connector that allows you to set the text to display.

If the methods you choose to expose don't seem to work as expected, then you can always delete the component, restart Java Studio, import the Bean again, and try to expose different methods. You need to restart Java Studio before importing a second time, because Java Studio forces you to. Otherwise, you'll receive the message shown in Figure 15.2.

Before you import any Bean, you should consider taking one more step and moving the JAR file to your hard disk. After you import the Bean to Java Studio, as long as it remains on the palette, Java Studio looks for the JAR file when it starts.

If Java Studio can't find the JAR file, the palette gives you an error message, then the components with the missing JAR files

Figure 15.2
When you add a component you've deleted without restarting Java Studio, you'll see this message.

appear on the palette as blank icons. Fortunately, when the JAR files are back where Java Studio expects them to be, the icons for the components reappear. This is why we told you, in Chapter 14, to take the time to move the JAR files to your hard disk, before importing them.

Deleting Components

To delete a component from the palette, open the Customize menu, and choose Palette. Find the component you want to delete, select it, and click the scissors button on top of the Customize Palette window.

Deleting a component from the palette does not actually delete the Bean on your hard drive. This is good, because you don't want your Beans deleted just because you're removing them from Java Studio's component palette. It means that if you change your mind, you can import the Bean again, because the JAR file is still sitting on your hard drive.

When deleting components, here are two tips that can make your life easier:

- Before you start deleting components, save your current design. If you have been working for more than a couple hours, close Java Studio, and restart it. If you have been working for more than half a day, restart Windows. We found that Java Studio seemed to crash more often when deleting components then during other operations, and closing and restarting tended to minimize the problems.

- If you are deleting more than a couple of components, look at the warning message you receive when you delete a component. Consider deselecting the checkbox that indicates whether you want to see this message every time you delete a component. The advantage of deselecting it is that the deletion process goes much faster and seems to crash less often. The disadvantage is that there is no obvious way to see the warning again.

Beans, Ready For Grinding

After reading this chapter, you should be pretty well equipped to go out and scrounge for Beans. While you're looking, don't forget that Appendix B provides you with a list of locations for Beans. In Chapters 16 and 17, we'll forge on to bigger designs with Java Studio and connect a Java Studio design to a database.

Chapter 16

Connecting To Databases With Java Studio

By now, you should have a handle on the basics of placing and customizing components, so you're ready to build an applet that does some "real work"— reading and writing records to and from a simple text database file.

A wise person (my wife, to be exact) has noted that much of the challenge of modern life is about *stuff management*— the endless keeping track of what you've got, where it is, how to use it, and (all too often) where to get it fixed.

With that concept in mind, we're going to tackle the essentials of building database connections by creating an applet to handle a common stuff management problem—the warranty information for all your computer and office equipment. (If you're trying this at home, you can record all your appliances and audio-visual gear instead—or for that matter, your daughter's Beanie Babies collection.)

When we're finished, your database applet (we'll call it the Warranty Tracker) will let you record, find, and report basic warranty information about your gear. Along the way, you'll pick up a few techniques on using Java Studio to develop database-enabled applets and applications.

Your Objective: The Warranty Tracker

By the time you've worked your way through to the end of this chapter, the GUI for your Warranty Tracker applet should look something like the applet shown in Figure 16.1. Your completed

221

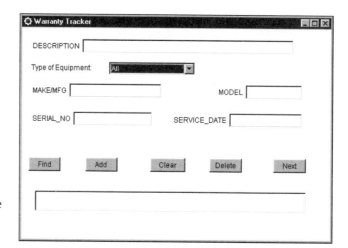

Figure 16.1
Sample interface for the completed Warranty Tracker applet.

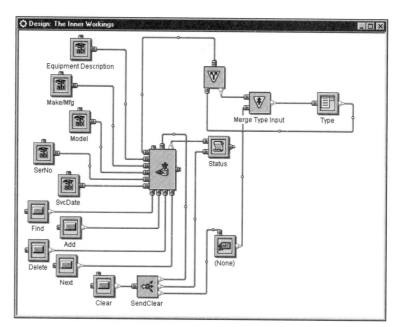

Figure 16.2
Sample Design window view of the Warranty Tracker applet.

design should look similar to the Design window shown in Figure 16.2.

You'll be using the Java Studio components listed in Table 16.1 to build this applet. If you would like any additional information on the care and feeding of a particular component, please see Appendix A.

Table 16.1   Components used for the Warranty Tracker applet.

Component Button	Name	Description
	Button component	Lets you add functionality to applets and give clear indications of their use.
	Choice component	Displays or sets the value of a specific field in the database. In the Warranty Tracker, the Choice component will be used to select or identify the class of equipment that a record belongs to, such as Printer or Copier. When we create the Choice component, we'll have you name it the Type component. For clarity's sake, that's also how we refer to it elsewhere in the text.
	Distributor component	Allows you to *multicast* a particular value to the input connectors of multiple components, so several components can receive the value at the same time.
	Label component	Has two purposes in the Warranty Tracker: to describe (within the interface) the purpose or use of another component and to pass a fixed value (the label's own caption) to another component for functional use.
	List component	Displays the current status of the applet and the results of the most recent Find, Add, and Delete operations.
	Merger component	Allows you to send messages from multiple sources to a single input connector for displaying the results.

(continued)

Table 16.1   Components used for the Warranty Tracker applet *(continued)*.

Component Button	Name	Description
	SimpleDBAccess component	Creates the connection between the applet and a *flat* (nonrelational) database file. In our case, that's the WARRANTY.SDF file—a comma-delimited collection of information about typical office equipment.
	Splitter component	Lets you connect separate input and output connectors to a single bidirectional port on the SimpleDBAccess component. Specifically, you use the Splitter to connect a Choice component to a specific field so that it can display or set the value of that field.
	ValidationTextField component	Allows you to enter new records into the database file and to display existing records from the database file in response to a query.

Getting Set Up

To get started, you'll need to copy over the sample file we've provided on this book's companion CD-ROM:

1. Copy the file WARRANTY.SDF from the Chapter 16 folder on this book's CD-ROM into Java Studio's home directory on your system.

2. Move any other SDF files stored in Java Studio's home directory into another folder or location. (The SimpleDBAccess component works most reliably during design when it's located by itself in the Java Studio directory.)

You'll use this *simple data file* (hence the .SDF extension) as the data source for your applet. It's just a comma-delimited text file, so you can open it in any editor if you want to take a look. (The text format details of this file are provided in the next chapter.)

NOTE

Keep in mind that we're using the SimpleDBAccess component for our connection to a flat text database file—the operative word being simple. Our Warranty Tracker has great potential as a helpful utility, but its real purpose is to initiate you into the exciting world of Java database development.

The Plan Of Attack

We're going to build the Warranty Tracker in three stages:

1. First, we'll set up all the interface elements—the fields, labels, and buttons that control the Warranty Tracker's functions. While you don't *have* to start this way, we've found that it helps to know where you're going before you start building the underlying structure.

2. Next, we'll add the "plumbing"—all the functional connectors that make the various components work together.

3. Finally, we'll plug in the database itself, via the SimpleDBAccess component.

A little testing, a little cleanup, and you'll be ready to create order and beauty out of your warranty records.

Building The Warranty Tracker GUI

Okay, let's get started. First, let's create a new design in Java Studio and then add the GUI elements.

Configuring The GUI

One of the most useful aspects of Java Studio is its real-time representation of the GUI for your applet or application. Because it's so easy to set up the GUI's size and appearance, we'll go ahead and do that first, so we're building the finished product from the get-go. Follow these steps to configure the GUI:

1. You've been working on other projects up to now, but let's start this one with a clean slate. On the File menu, choose New.

2. Click the GUI window to select it, and choose GUI Window from the Customize menu, as shown in Figure 16.3.

3. Reset the default dimensions, the title, and just for fun, the background color of the GUI window:

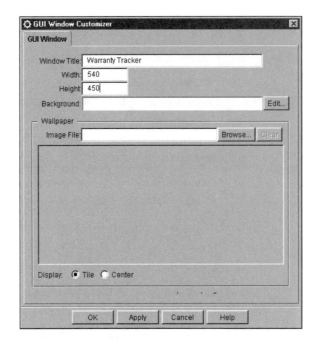

Figure 16.3
Customizing the GUI window.

- Set the window name to Warranty Tracker.

- Set the window size to 540 (width) by 450 (height).

- Select Ivory or some other suitable color for the background (just remember, you'll be looking at it for a while, so don't pick anything too obnoxious).

4. Click Apply to view your results, and click OK when you're happy with the settings.

5. Minimize the GUI window so you don't get distracted and start fiddling with the various elements (well, that's what *we* do).

6. Resize the Design window to give yourself plenty of working room.

Setting The Text Fields

Now, we'll add the visible parts of the Warranty Tracker interface. We'll start by adding the text fields you'll need. Follow these steps:

About Tab Order

You're about to make a form with fields that most users will want to Tab through (pressing the Tab key to move from field to field). Because you want users to Tab from field to field in a reasonable order—usually top left to bottom right—we'll tip you off up front that Java Studio sets the tab order to the reverse of the order in which you add the fields to the design. (If you've ever done any inventory control, you'll recognize this as an LIFO—last in, first out—process.) Therefore, we're going to have you add the ValidationTextFields in reverse order, so they'll have a logical tab order when the Warranty Tracker applet is used.

1. Select the Database tab on the toolbar, click the ValidationTextField component, and place the component on the bottom-left side of the Design window.

    (You can put the component anywhere you want, of course, but since we've done this already, you can benefit from our fiddling-time.)

2. In the customizer, rename the component "SvcDate". Leave the Editable checkbox checked as shown in Figure 16.4.

3. Click Apply to modify the first component.

4. Repeat the process described in Steps 1 through 3 to create the following fields. Make sure you use the following field names (they have to match exactly with the names of the corresponding columns in the sample WARRANTY.SDF database file):

    *   Make/Mfg
    *   Model

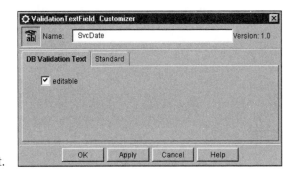

Figure 16.4
Modify the customizer for the ValidationText-Field fields of your Warranty Tracker applet.

Tip

Hey, My Labels

If you happen to peek at the GUI window, you'll see all your ValidationText-Field fields labeled N/A. Don't worry, nothing's wrong—ValidationText-Fields take their labels from the name of the database field to which they're attached. We haven't attached the database component yet, so they don't know who they are. That will straighten out when you add the Simple-DBAccess component.

Tip

Design Shortcuts

Don't forget, you can press and hold the Ctrl key when clicking in the Design window, and Java Studio will place another instance of the previous component onto the design. Also, when you're adding multiples of the same type of component, use the customizer's Apply button rather than the OK button. This leaves the customizer dialog box open for the next component, and saves you the system time of closing and opening the dialog box.

- SerNo

- Description

If they don't match exactly, the database won't connect properly, and you'll get a long and alarming list of Java errors.

5. When you're adding the Description component, click the Standard tab on the customizer, and change the width to 200, so you'll have plenty of field room to be descriptive.

6. Because this is kind of an advanced applet and we're trying to avoid having to deal with connector-spaghetti at the end of the process, take a few minutes now to arrange your components in the Design window—something along the lines of the layout shown in Figure 16.5.

7. To prevent any surprises, save your work in the Java Studio directory, under the name "WARRANTYTRACK". (Remember, Java Studio adds the .VJ extension automatically.)

Add Buttons For Function And Profit

Next, we'll add the four buttons that we need to represent and launch our functions. Follow these steps, using Figure 16.6 as an example:

1. On the tool palette, select the GUI tab, then click the Button component. Place the first of four Button components along the bottom of the Design window.

2. In the Button tab of the customizer, name this button "Find", and change the caption to "Find". You don't need to make any other changes, so click Apply.

3. Ctrl+click in the Design window to place three more buttons. Name and caption them as "Add", "Clear", and "Delete". Be sure to leave plenty of room between the four buttons.

That will do it for the fields and buttons (only two more elements to go!).

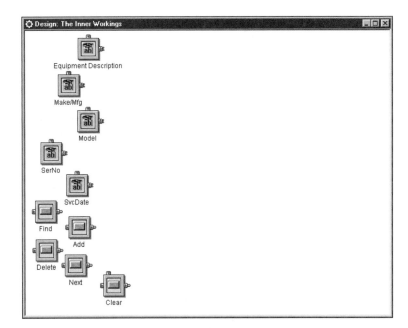

Figure 16.5
Sample layout of GUI elements in the Design window.

Figure 16.6
Sample customizer settings for Warranty Tracker buttons.

Set Equipment Categories In A Selection Pull-Down

Our applet assumes that your equipment can be assigned to specific *categories*, so we need to provide a means to select them—but we don't want this to just be another text field, or we'll have to deal with typos and other user creativities. Instead, let's add a pull-down select list and predefine some values for the categories of stuff you're going to track. Follow these steps, using Figure 16.7 as an example:

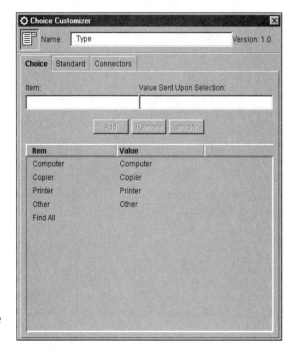

Figure 16.7
Define your equipment categories in the Choice Customizer.

1. On the GUI tab of the tool palette, select the Choice compo-nent, and place it somewhere in the upper right of the Design window.

2. In the Choice Customizer, set the name to "Type". (We'll refer to this as the Type component from now on, by the way.)

3. Define the categories of equipment you want the Warranty Tracker to store for you. (Our sample file contains records for computer and office equipment, but when you do your own, you might define other categories for your selections.)

    a. First, select the default Item for this component, which is labeled Choice.

    b. Change the value in the Item and Value Sent Upon Selection fields to "Other".

    c. Click Modify to record your changes.

4. Add the following categories to your selection list by entering each one in the Item fields and clicking Add. (By default, Java Studio automatically fills in the Value Sent field with the same value.) You can enter them in any order, but make

►Tip

Needed: A Null Choice

Our experience, such as it is, tells us that a selection list has one particular quirk. Because (by definition) there's always something selected in the list, the component always has a defined value. Not a bad thing, really, except when you want to, say, do a Find for all records. Then, you realize that the currently selected value, whatever it is, is going to be applied to your search and limit your search results. What you need is a selection that has no value, so you can apply it before doing a search, and it won't limit the results. Lucky for you, we saw this one coming (well, okay, we figured it out while testing the applet), and we'll show you how to add this null choice to the Type component.

sure you enter these selection terms accurately, because they need to match the data that's in the sample WARRANTY.SDF database file:

- Computer
- Copier
- Printer
- Find All

When you add the Find All selection to the Type component (the last item in the preceding list), set the Value Sent field for this selection to null by deleting the content of the field, leaving it blank as shown in Figure 16.8. If you have other categories that you know you want to add, however, feel free to customize the list.

5. On the Connectors tab, check the Selects A String value option. (This will allow the database to select the corresponding type when we find a particular record.)

6. Click OK to save your settings, and close the customizer.

   Our user will need to know what this selection list is used for, so let's add a descriptive label.

7. Click the GUI tab on the toolbar, select the Label component, and then place the component in the bottom-right corner of the design, out of the way of our future labyrinth of connections.

8. In the label's customizer, change the Label caption to read "Type of Equipment:" and click OK. See Figure 16.9 as an example.

Make Room For Applet Status

Finally, there's one more interface element to add—a *status* component. The status component will enable us—and the

Figure 16.8
Configuration of the null value Type component selection.

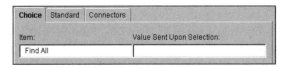

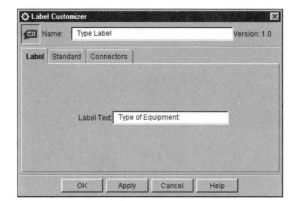

Figure 16.9
Customizer settings
for the descriptive
Type label.

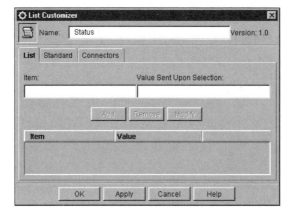

Figure 16.10
Customizer settings for
the Status list
component.

applet's future users—to see what's going on. Follow these steps,
using Figure 16.10 as an example:

1. On the GUI tab of the tools palette, select the List component, and add it to your design. (We put ours off to the
   middle right of our design, because that's where it eventually
   connects to the SimpleDBAccess component.)

2. In the customizer, name the component "Status".

3. Select the Connectors tab, add a connector that clears the
   list, and click OK. This will keep us from leaving old and
   confusing messages lying around in the display.

That will do it for your functional interface components. Save
your work, and then it's time for a little visual reinforcement.
Let's clean up the GUI a bit, so we can see some tangible progress.

Open your Warranty Tracker GUI window, and see what kind of mayhem you've got going there. In our experience, components often seem to slap themselves into arbitrary places—but that's what the Layout|Align function is for, right?

Take a few minutes now to bring some semblance of order to your GUI, but don't worry about fine-tuning it yet. As a guide, you may want your GUI to resemble the "after" example in Figure 16.11. If you need a refresher on "making it look nice," see Chapter 4.

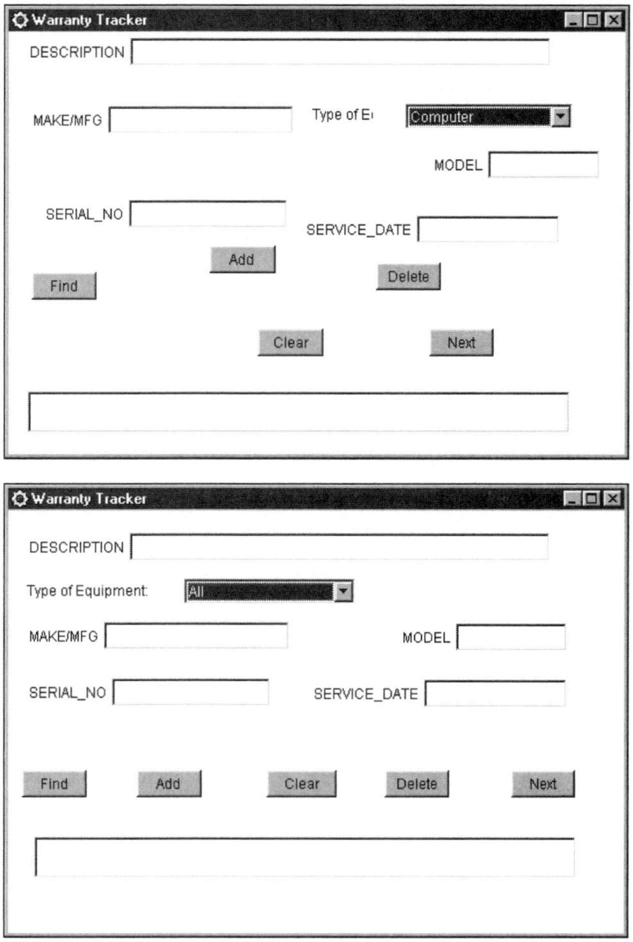

Figure 16.11
Before and after examples of a rough design for the interface of the Warranty Tracker applet.

Adding The Functional Structure

We now have the visible stuff on board and a kind of a mental road map of where we're going with this applet's design and function. Let's add the functional components that will make the Warranty Tracker work.

Built-In Functions: Find, Insert, And Delete

We have four buttons, so you might surmise that we'll have four functions to build—but this is not the case. As it turns out, three of these are already done for you: The SimpleDBAccess component comes equipped with **Find**, **Insert**, and **Delete** functions, so all you have to do is insert the buttons and attach them to the right connectors. (In fact, the Clear button also has a corresponding SimpleDBAccess function, but we're going to complicate that one a little bit, so we'll deal with it next.)

Here's a brief description of how the **Find**, **Insert**, and **Delete** functions work.

The Find Function

The SimpleDBAccess component's Find connector triggers the component to collect criteria from any input fields to which it's connected, search the database for any records matching that criteria, and make them available for output. By definition, that means that it searches for any criteria currently displayed as data within the applet's fields. So, when you're actually using the applet, you'll have to clear the fields before you can select the type of equipment you want to find. (And yes, you spotted it— you'll have to document this behavior in the interface with prompting text, because we're not building a help structure for this applet. We can predict you'll have users who will ignore, forget, or misunderstand your crystal-clear instructions. You certainly have *our* sympathies…)

Tip

Updates The Hard Way

The SimpleDBAccess component has no ***Update*** *or* ***Modify*** *function, so if you ever need to change a record, you'll have to retrieve it by using the* ***Find*** *func- tion, make your changes, and insert the newly defined record into the database. Then, you'll have to remember to go back and delete the original version. (Remem- ber, the component's full name is SimpleDBAccess; if you want something more robust, you'll need to buy or obtain a different component or JavaBean.) We'll leave it up to you to decide if or how to notify your users.*

The Insert Function

The Insert connector works the same way, adding the data cur- rently displayed in the fields to the database file. This also applies if you're displaying an existing record and trigger the **Insert** function—the SimpleDBAccess component doesn't have any mechanism for checking for uniqueness. So, it will merrily repli- cate that record in the database.

Before we wrap up the design, we'll add some text prompts to the interface to remind the user to click the Clear button before adding a new entry.

The Delete Function

The Delete connector follows suit, tracking down the record currently identified in the field display and deleting it. (By default, the user gets a confirmation dialog box first—a nice touch.)

Because these functions are built-in, and we've already put the buttons in place, we don't need to do anything more with them right now. We'll drag in all the necessary connections in the next section.

Setting Up The Clear Function

The Clear button has a slightly expanded function in the War- ranty Tracker—we want it to not only clear the fields in the GUI but also reset the Status display and clear the current selection from our Type component. So, what we need to do is distribute the Clear message to multiple connectors—using, as you probably guessed, a Distributor component.

Spread The Wealth: The SendClear Distributor

Your modified Distributor component will simultaneously clear out all the fields and displays to which it's connected. To build it, follow these steps, using Figure 16.12 as an example:

1. Click the Data Flow tab on the toolbar, and select the Dis- tributor component. Place it at bottom center of your design.

2. In the customizer, change the component's name to "SendClear".

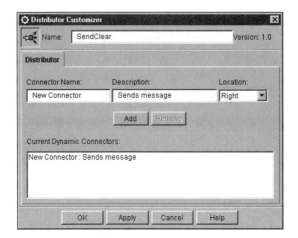

Figure 16.12
Customizer settings for the SendClear component.

3. Add another output connector to the component. Enter "ClearChoice" as the name of the new connector, leave the description and location as-is, and click Add.

4. Click OK to make the changes to the component. (We'll draw the connections in a few moments.)

All Or Null—Or Both?

We know from setting up the Type component earlier that we have to be able to set the current value of its selection list to null, so we can do an open search on all records. To take care of this, we're going to add an invisible label and trigger it with the Clear button to send its caption—which just happens to be Find All— to the Type component, as shown in Figure 16.13. (Nifty, eh?)

To create this Find All caption, follow these steps, using Figure 16.14 as an example:

1. Click the GUI tab on the toolbar, and select the Label component. Place it on the bottom right of your design (about 5 o'clock, for those of you old enough to remember analog clocks).

2. In the customizer, name the component "ClearType", and enter "Find All" as the label text. When this label name hits the Type component, it will select the null value we need.

3. Select the Connectors tab in the customizer, and check the Triggers The Component option.

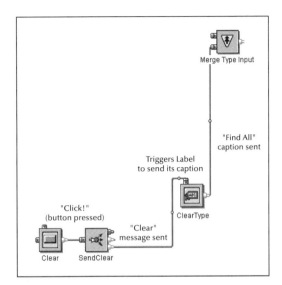

Figure 16.13
Triggering a null
selection.

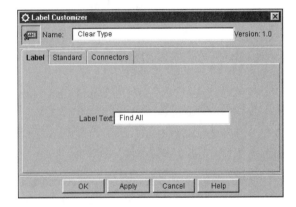

Figure 16.14
Customizer settings for
the Find All Label
component.

4. Click OK to implement your changes, and close the customizer.

Making Room: The Merge Type Component

So far, so good. Now, we have to make room for the Find All label
caption to connect to the selection list.

A quick glance at the Type component reveals only one input on
the left side of the component—the input that you added when
you created the component. This is the Selects A String input,
which is exactly what we need. When a string of text is sent to
this input, the component selects the matching item from the list
and pushes its value out the door of its output connector.

However, the SimpleDBAccess component needs access to the selection list, too, so it can get and set selection values. We'll solve that problem by inserting a Merge component in front of the Type component. That way, we can send it a selection string from either source, and the Type component will handle it. To set this up, follow these steps, using Figure 16.15 as an example:

1. On the Data Flow tab on the toolbar, select the Merge component, and drop it onto the design just to the left of the Type component.

2. In the customizer, change the name of the component to "Merge Type Input".

Wiring The Clear Function

Now that we've got all the pieces in place, let's draw the connections to complete the **Clear** function. Follow these steps, using Figure 16.16 as an example:

1. Connect the Clear button output to the SendClear (Distributor component) input.

2. Connect one of the SendClear outputs to the Trigger input of the ClearType label.

3. Connect the output of ClearType to one of the inputs of the Merge Type component.

4. Connect a second output of the SendClear distributor to the Clear input of the Status component. (We'll connect the

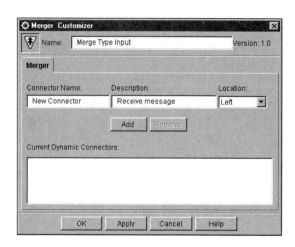

Figure 16.15
Customizer settings for the Merge Type component.

Tip

Example: One Find Day...

Suppose you need to find all the equipment records for computers. You'll want to select Computers in the Type list, and then click the Find button, right? (Right!) That's exactly what we want you to be able to do, so we need to make sure that the Type component can pass its selection (in this case, Computers) to the database to drive the query.

third SendClear output to the SimpleDBAccess component in just a minute.)

Closing The Loop: Connecting The Type Component

Since we're in the neighborhood, let's finish building the infrastructure for the Type select list. What we need is a way to connect the Type component to the SimpleDBAccess component, so that we can either:

- Send the current list selection to the database during a **Find**, **Insert**, or **Delete** function, or

- Display the selection that's sent *from* the database as part of a set of **Find** function results.

Fortunately, that's just what the Splitter component was built for. To create this connection to the SimpleDBAccess component, follow these steps, using Figure 16.17 as an example:

1. On the Data Flow tab on the toolbar, select the Splitter component, and drop one onto your design, just to the left of your Merge Type Input component.

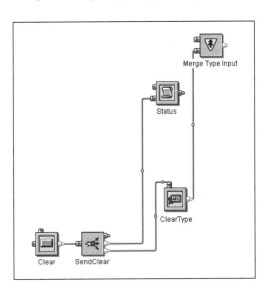

Figure 16.16
Example of the Clear button's connections.

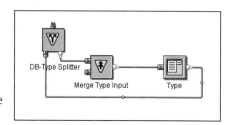

Figure 16.17
Connections for the Type component.

2. In the customizer, name the component "DB-Type Splitter". (We've omitted the name from our illustrations, so that you can see all the connections more clearly. You don't have to, though.)

3. Connect the output on the bottom right of the Splitter to the available input of the Merge Type component.

4. Connect the output of the Merge Type component to the Select string input on the Type component.

5. Connect the output of the Type component to the single-direction input (bottom left) of the Splitter component.

Now, you can see how our little selection loop works:

- If you select a value from the list, the Type component sends it to the Splitter. The Splitter forwards the selection to the database through its bidirectional connector. (It *will*, that is, when we connect the database a little later in this chapter.)

- If you generate a selection value from the database—normally as a result of a Find—SimpleDBAccess sends it to the Merge Type input. Merge Type immediately pushes the value through its output connector to the Type list input, prompting the Type to select the matching value from its list of possibilities.

- If you click the Clear button, the SendClear distributor triggers the ClearType label. The label passes its caption (Find All) to Merge Type. Merge Type passes it along to the Type list, prompting the Type component to select the matching null value from its list of possibilities.

That pretty much does it for the infrastructure. In the next section, we'll drop in the database and wire the last of the connections.

▶Tip

Reality Check

Quite frankly, we found the SimpleDBAccess component to be a bit more finicky than we expected. It was fairly easy to disrupt the connection to the database file or to have trouble linking to a source file that was stored elsewhere on the system. After you make the connection, it works fine, but don't be surprised if you have to move your source files into the Java Studio directory, or tinker with the end-of-record marker, or other such fiddlings-around. When you're ready to develop more than just practice applets, you'll probably want to use a more robust database connection component. Then again, maybe it was just our systems, and you'll have no trouble.

Connecting The Database

The star of our Warranty Tracker applet is the SimpleDBAccess component, which you'll use to connect all your ValidationTextFields with the WARRANTY.SDF source file that you copied from this book's companion CD-ROM at the start of this chapter.

Adding And Configuring The SimpleDBAccess Component

Caveats notwithstanding, the process of inserting the SimpleDBAccess component and linking it to the database is fairly straightforward:

1. Click the Data Base tab on the toolbar, and select the SimpleDBAccess component.

2. Drop the component in the blank spot at the center of your design. The default configuration for the component (shown in Figure 16.18) includes all the functional connections you'll need—Find, Add, Delete, Next, Clear, and Status—but has no data connections yet.

3. In the customizer, enter the following specifications for this database connection, using Figure 16.19 as an example:

    a. Leave the user name and password at the defaults. These values are normally used for connecting to remote, secure SQL databases that require access authorization. We're just linking to a simple text file, so we're not worried about these settings.

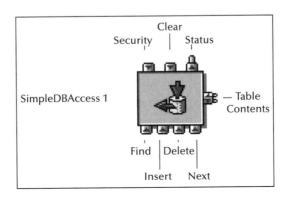

Figure 16.18
Default connectors for the SimpleDBAccess component.

Figure 16.19
Customizer settings for the SimpleDBAccess component.

b. Modify the default URL shown to append the full path to the location where you stored WARRANTY.SDF. If you followed our recommendation and copied it to the root Java Studio directory (shown as *JavaStudio* in the following code, but your settings may differ), then you should modify the URL as follows, changing

```
jdbc:SimpleText
```

to read, if you're on a Windows system:

```
jdbc:SimpleText:c:\JavaStudio\js\intel-win32\bin
```

or (if you're on a Solaris system):

```
jdbc:SimpleText:c:\JavaStudio\js\Solaris\bin
```

Note the colon that precedes your full path statement—don't leave that out or the connection will fail.

c. For this exercise, leave the default driver in place. When you switch to a more robust connector (typically using JDBC or other format), you'll specify the appropriate JDBC (or other) driver.

4. When your cursor exits the URL field, Java Studio lists all the simple text databases (as defined by the .SDF extension) found at that location in the Tables list field. If you entered your URL correctly, the Warranty database file will be among those listed. (The Phonebook database file shipped with Java Studio may be available also, if you're in the application root directory.)

   In addition to listing each SDF file in the URL location, Java Studio reads the column names from each file's header. When you select a specific database, Java Studio lists its column names (say *that* three times, quickly!) and automatically selects them for linking.

5. Click the Connect button, and Java Studio modifies the SimpleDBAccess component, adding a bidirectional connector specific to each column in the database file. When you connect to the WARRANTY.SDF source file, for example, Java Studio will add connectors for SvcDate, SerNo, Model, Make/Mfg, Description, and Type, as shown in Figure 16.20.

Before we link these inviting connectors, let's take one more look at the final design, as shown in Figure 16.21. For a look at the fully connected SimpleDBAccess component, see Figure 16.22.

Figure 16.20
Expanded
SimpleDBAccess
component with
WARRANTY.SDF
connectors added.

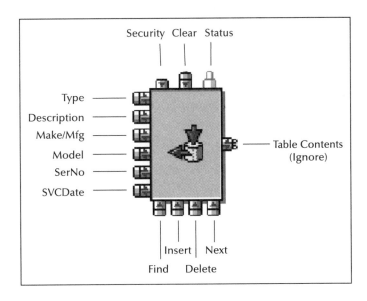

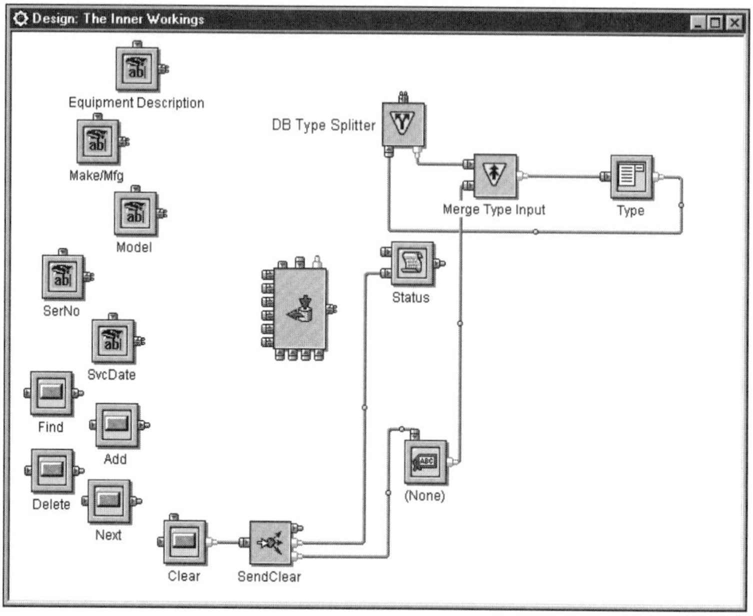

Figure 16.21
Completed (but
unwired) design of the
Warranty Tracker.

►Tip

Get Prompted

*Your results can get a little
confusing if you
misconnect any of the
Validation TextFields to the
wrong ports on the
database—the fields will
still work, but you could
end up with model
information showing up
where you expect the
service date. So, when
dealing with a gnarly set
of connections, like a
SimpleDBAccess compo-
nent, use the connector
prompts. Before you lock
in a connection, let your
cursor hover over the
connector, and you'll see
a balloon label that
identifies the connector.*

Wiring It All Up

Finally, we get to the fun part—connecting the dots! (Is it our
imagination, or is there a certain back-to-playtime trend going on
here?) Let's link all the fields and buttons with the
SimpleDBAccess component, so we can fire up the applet and try
it out.

Just for the sake of being orderly, we'll start at the top of the
SimpleDBAccess component and work our way around clockwise
(the order of your connectors may vary from ours, depending on
the order in which you added them). Follow these steps, using
Figure 16.22 as an example:

1. Drag a connection from the last available output connector of
   the SendClear distributor component (ours is below the
   database component, at roughly 6 o'clock) to the input on
   the very top of SimpleDBAccess.

2. The next database connector to the right is the Status output.
   Connect it to the available input on the left of the Status list
   component.

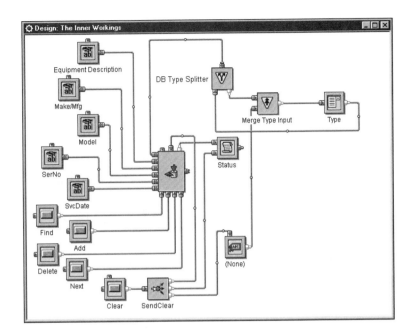

Figure 16.22
Final connector
arrangement for the
Warranty Tracker.

3. Skip the bidirectional connector on the right side of the database component. We are outputting our results directly to their respective fields, so we didn't need a Table container and we won't be using this output.

4. Connect the output of the Next button to the Next input on the bottom right of the database connector.

5. Connect the output of the Delete button to the Delete input on the bottom of the database connector, next in line clockwise from the Next input.

6. Continuing clockwise around the database connector, connect the output of the Add button to the Insert input.

7. Finish up the buttons by connecting the output of the Find button to the Find input at the bottom-left corner of the database component.

8. Connect the outputs of the ValidationTextFields to the inputs of the SimpleDBAccess component in the same fashion, continuing in a clockwise direction through the fields SvcDate, SerNo, Model, Make/Mfg, and Description.

9. Last but not least, connect the bidirectional Type output to the bidirectional input of the DB-Type Splitter.

Congratulations—you've wired up your first database connection!

Take a quick look at the GUI window, and you'll see that the N/A labels that used to adorn your ValidationTextFields have been replaced with the actual field names they represent. (Figure 16.23 shows an example of the final GUI window.) This is okay for our purposes here, but it's something to keep in mind for future development.

Testing The Warranty Tracker

Now, you're ready to put the Warranty Tracker through its paces. Although they're probably self-evident, we'll do a quick review of the applet's functions, just so there won't be any surprises.

Finding Records

To use the **Find** function, follow these steps:

1. Click the Clear button to empty all the fields.

2. Enter your search criteria in the appropriate field. To find all the equipment of a specific type, select the type from the pull-down list.

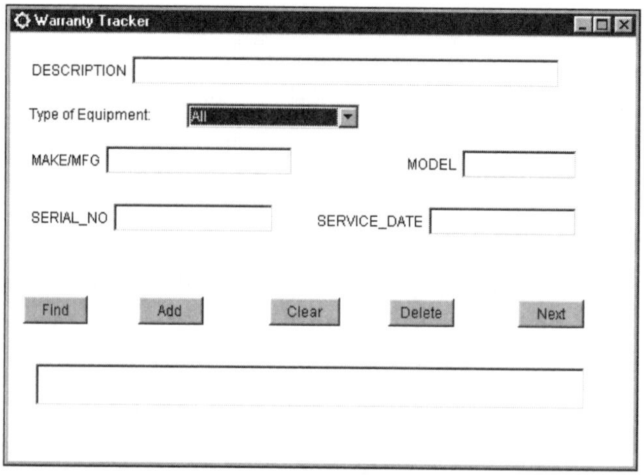

Figure 16.23
Final GUI design of the completed Warranty Tracker.

Tip

Column Names Matter

As you can see, displaying the actual column names is a mixed blessing. It effortlessly identifies the field in the GUI, but the usability of the terms used for column headers may leave something to be desired. If you have any plans to use the Simple-DBAccess component for useful work, be sure to name (or rename, it's only a text file, after all) the columns in your SDF file in an interface-appropriate manner.

For example, select Computers on the pull-down list, and the database will return three records (unless you've edited the source file, of course).

3. Click the Find button, and Java Studio will search the WARRANTY.SDF file for any matching records.

   The Status field displays a message telling you how many records were found, if any.

4. Click the Next button to cycle through the found set. There's no **Back** function available with SimpleDBAccess, but the **Next** function loops continuously through the found set—so if you click Next after viewing the last found record, Java Studio displays the first record again.

Adding Records

To use the **Add** function, follow these steps:

1. Click the Clear button to empty all the fields.

2. Enter the information for your new equipment record in all the fields. SimpleDBAccess doesn't offer any error checking or validation (your *field* components support it, but the database component doesn't), so there's no required fields or error messages to contend with.

   To get reasonable responses, be careful to enter reasonable data—GIGO (garbage in, garbage out) still holds true, even more so in this day and age.

3. Select the appropriate Type for this equipment record.

4. Click the Add button.

   Java Studio displays a message telling you that one record was inserted (unless there are errors of some sort).

Duplicating Records

To duplicate an existing record, follow these steps:

1. Perform a Find that retrieves the record you want to duplicate as part of its found set.

2. Cycle through the results as needed until that record is displayed in the Warranty Tracker.

3. Click the Add button. There is no data-checking or uniqueness required, so Java Studio adds the record as-is to the database and displays the appropriate message in the Status field.

Modifying Records

To modify an existing record, follow these steps:

1. Perform a Find that retrieves the record you want to modify as part of its found set.

2. Cycle through the results as needed until the record is displayed in the Warranty Tracker.

3. Modify the record as needed, and click the Add button. Java Studio adds the new record to the database and displays the appropriate message in the Status field.

4. Repeat the Find, and cycle through the results until the original record is displayed. Click the Delete button, and Java Studio deletes the original record, leaving the updated record in the database.

Deleting Records

To delete a record, follow these steps:

1. Perform a Find that retrieves the record you want to delete as part of its found set.

2. Cycle through the results as needed until the doomed record is displayed in the Warranty Tracker.

3. Click the Delete button, and Java Studio deletes the record from the database file and displays the appropriate message in the Status field.

When you're sufficiently reinforced and impressed with yourself for your new programming skills (and rightly so, we might add), you need to make one more design and clean-up pass at the GUI. Contrary to some results we've seen, your job's not done until the interface is ready for the uninitiated user.

▶Tip

Notepad Users Beware

Java Studio's online help casually mentions that you can create your own simple database text files using Notepad, which is true, but after some experimentation, we found it necessary to use Ctrl+Backspace to insert each end-of-record marker. Just so you know.

Cleaning Up The Interface

Basically, you have two tasks before you:

- Make the interface appealing and neat by lining up the fields and buttons and presenting the functions in a logical way. If you need help remembering how to move things around with some semblance of control, refer to Chapter 4.

- Add whatever hints, prompts, or tips you feel are necessary. (If you're feeling adventurous, you could try to launch an External component containing help information.)

Figure 16.23 showed an example of what the final GUI might look like.

Track Those Warranties!

Okay, you're done—stick a fork in it and call it "My First Java Database Applet"! While we readily concede that the Warranty Tracker is not exactly a mission-critical application, we hope that you can find some worthwhile uses for it. Feel free to modify the structure and choices, or replace the source file with your own, if you want to put it to other uses.

You could even try it out on your grade-school youngster, if you have one lounging around. If you tell the little nipper that he or she is "helping you test a Java applet", they might not notice that you've got them doing data entry drudge work!

Continuing On

In the meantime, now that we've fast-tracked through the database connection process, we're going to explain some of the whys of what we did in the next chapter, and offer some general perspectives on designing and developing database connections. We hope you'll join us!

Chapter 17

Understanding How To Connect To Databases With Java Studio

When you combine the portability of a Java applet or application, the ease of use of Java Studio, and the power of a relational database, a lot of interesting and productive things can happen.

Afull exploration of the art and science of using Java Studio to create database interfaces probably deserves its own book, which means we're somewhat limited for space here. In this chapter, we'll focus on the high points. Besides, any serious database connectivity requires the use of third-party add-ons—each of which has its own vagaries and surprises, and requires detail outside the scope of this book.

Snapshot: The Database Development Process

It seems likely that you might be using Java Studio for your first steps into the world of Java development. (If so, then extra points for Sun's marketing and product positioning efforts.) We also surmise that you might be moving up from static HTML into the world of database-driven pages and interaction. This means that you are trying to assimilate the terms, technologies, and syntax of Java programming at the same time that you have to figure out how to get actual work done and cross items off your To Do list. (We know, we've been there.)

That being the case, we wanted to give you a quick outline of the things we've learned along the way about the development process. We hope you'll find this helpful as you're building your Java Studio database applications—not to mention your own

Tip

A Little Editorial License

For brevity's sake, we're bending the terminology for a few minutes. In the upcoming sections, we refer to all Java-based database connection constructs as database applications, regardless of whether they take the form of Java applets or standalone Java applications. We're not recommending one form over the other or ignoring the many wonderful benefits of applets. In this chapter, we're just looking at things from the database perspective.

skills. We'll share this experience in the form of three simple guidelines, briefly described in the following sections. (And stop that groaning—this won't hurt a bit!)

Guideline 1: Know Where You're Going

Figure out what you want your database application to do—that is, identify what problem you're solving or what benefit you're offering. Don't just think, "Oh, I need an address book." Think through the idea, all the way down to the implications and uses. Think of what your users want and need out of this application. If you're planning a Web-based application, consider how it fits into the rest of your site.

After you know what you want the application to do, figure out what you'll have in your hands when the application is done doing whatever it's supposed to do. Sketch a rough design of the look and feel of the outcome—whether it's a database-generated page or table, a form, or any other object. Chances are, you'll either spot some function or display that you hadn't thought about, or you'll be able to suppress some of your surplus creativity and toss out an item or two that you don't really need.

Guideline 2: Plan For The Long Haul

Now that you've thought through what you want your application to do, think about the next generation. Try to foresee what future uses your application might be called on to support, and make sure that you build the necessary hooks and foundations into your current design. Think of this as the *what about* question, as in "What about needing to sort the data?" or "What about being able to replicate records?"

For example, an address book lets your users register to get email reminders about your upgrades, but what about linking it to your orders? That way, users won't have to reenter their address information. Or, how about automatically adding each registrant to the email list for the users' group in their area? Or...well, you get the picture.

▶Tip

Guideline 3: Travel Light, And Take The Shortest Route

"Nice-to-haves" are probably your worst enemies—they can clog
up your design and chew up your time and budget faster than you
can say "mission statement." Resist the temptation to wander off
on some cool or nifty feature in favor of taking the straightest
possible path to the least complicated solution that delivers the
desired results. (We're especially susceptible to this one ourselves.
You should have seen the original plans for Chapter 16's sample
application!)

This is another reason to know where you're going. Obviously, if
you don't, you can't tell whether you're wandering off-task,
trailblazing a great new application, or just plain lost.

There, that wasn't so bad, was it? Now, we'll cover some specifics
about databases and Java Studio by looking at the "behind the
scenes" details of some of the steps you took in Chapter 16.

Developing The Warranty Tracker

Now that you've been through the basic Java Studio database
development process with us, we want to share some of the hard
knocks we came across. We'll point out a couple of pitfalls, for
example, involving the sequence in which you perform certain
steps. We'll look at the Structured Query Language (SQL) under-
pinnings of the functions that come with the SimpleDBAccess, so
you can jump to SQL-based advanced components more comfort-
ably. Finally, we'll explain our use of the null value in more detail
and explore some techniques of effective looping.

Modifying The GUI Window Up Front

If you worked through the earlier examples in this book, you may
have developed several applets and applications without bothering
to formally rename and reconfigure the GUI window. We did so in
this instance out of personal preference, but there's also a practical

advantage—the revised GUI window name shows up as such in the Windows taskbar, making it easier to spot when you want it.

Adding The SimpleDBAccess Component Last

In addition to the comments earlier in this chapter about the benefits of a consistent design process (not to mention our own personal preferences), there was a practical reason why we developed the interface first, then the plumbing, and then added the database component last. We wanted to avoid lockups and crashes. We found that Java Studio seemed to have occasional problems when we started with the database and worked our way out to the interface, so we just reversed the sequence. Again, your mileage may vary.

The Meanings Behind The Functions

When your design triggers the Find, Insert, Delete, or Next connectors of the SimpleDBAccess component, what it's really doing is triggering the component to issue a *database query statement*. (All such statements are called *query* statements, even if they're giving an instruction—such as "insert" or "delete"—rather than asking a question. It's a programmer thing.)

For example, the SimpleDBAccess component interprets the Insert trigger to mean "Issue a query statement that inserts the current data from all available fields into the datasource as a new record." (In our case, the datasource is the text file WARRANTY.SDF.) The fact that the statement automatically includes *all* fields is simply a design decision by the folks at Thought, Inc., who created the SimpleDBAccess component.

Likewise, the fact that SimpleDBAccess doesn't have an Update connector is a design decision—the result being that, if you want to update a record in your application that uses SimpleDBAccess, you have to do the Find-Revise-Add-Delete Original dance. (There's nothing wrong with these decisions, by the way. Thought, Inc., gave away the component for free, so surely they have the most say on what goes into or gets left out of it.)

We mention this simply to make you aware that when you decide to venture forth and do more advanced database application programming in Java Studio, you'll be using other database connection components. You'll need to evaluate those components carefully for their functions and flexibility. There are no set standards and very little magic to the concocting of components—just decisions, usually made for business, competitive, technical, or marketing reasons.

Of course, if you use a component with more flexibility and freedom, you'll need to know more about structuring and expressing queries. SQL has several competing standards and comes in various flavors (like Unix), but there are plenty of references and classes out there to help.

The Importance Of Being Null

When we decided that we wanted our Warranty Tracker to have a pull-down list of equipment types (rather than a field where any old values could be entered), we opened up a couple of issues that made it more complicated than the other fields. For example, there were a couple of places where you were nulling around with empty values that might have seemed a bit arbitrary, possibly even confusing.

So, in keeping with the "do first, talk later" format of this book, here's our thinking on this null business.

Explaining The Find All Selection

When you customized the Choice component (the one called Type that stores the various categories of equipment), you added a selection named Find All that had no value. This was our workaround for one of the default characteristics of a pull-down select list: Left to its own devices, a select list, by default, always has a value selected. This gives you unexpected results any time you want to do an open Find on all available records, because the default list value jumps in and limits the results.

To address this quirk, you added the "Find All =" selection. We could have called the selection "Null" to make things clearer for you (the developer), but then we would have confused the users. There shouldn't be any actual records in the database with a type of Find All, of course.

If you were using a different database access component (instead of SimpleDBAccess), you might have had more control over the Find function, such that you could list specific fields to include in the search. If so, you wouldn't have to worry about the default selection unless you were including it in the query on purpose.

Including The Find All Label

After we had the "Find All =" selection established, we needed to find a way to tell the Type component to select it. More to the point, we needed to have it selected when we clicked the Clear button to empty all the other fields in preparation for a Find action. The easiest and fastest way to send a specific (unchanging) text string in Java Studio is to put it in a label and then use a connector from the Clear button to nudge the label to send it.

Put together, that's why you created the Find All label. (We made it nonshown, of course, because nobody needs to see it but us.)

Looping Through Splitter And Merge Components

In addition to the null value issues raised by our Type list, our design made it slightly more complicated to get the "type of equipment" value in and out of the database. So, we built a loop around the Type component, using the Splitter and Merge components.

Figure 17.1 shows the before and after views of connecting the Type component to the SimpleDBAccess component. Figure 17.2 shows before and after views of the merged inputs.

Juggling Input And Output: Splitting A Bidirectional Connector

When you link a SimpleDBAccess component with a simple database text file, the component adds a bidirectional connector for each field of the database to which it is linked. These bidirectional connectors make it possible for the component to:

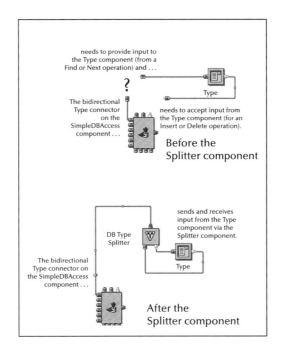

needs to provide input to
the Type component (from a
Find or Next operation) and . . .

?

Type

The bidirectional
Type connector
on the
SimpleDBAccess
component . . .

needs to accept input from
the Type component (for an
Insert or Delete operation).

**Before the
Splitter component**

sends and receives
input from the Type
component via the
Splitter component.

DB Type
Splitter

Type

The bidirectional
Type connector on
the SimpleDBAccess
component . . .

**After the
Splitter component**

Figure 17.1
Splitting the Type
connector of the
SimpleDBAccess
component.

- Send the values it gets from the database in response to a Find or Next operation.

- Take in the values that are entered in the fields to which they are connected, so the component can insert or delete them into or from the database.

This is no problem when the SimpleDBAccess component is connected directly to a ValidationTextField, because those field components also have bidirectional connectors. You just click 'em together, and they do all the work.

It gets a little more tricky, however, when you want to use a selection list (in Java Studio terms, the Choice component) to display and set the value for a field, because the selection list has separate, single-direction input and output connectors. You have to split the connection to the SimpleDBAccess component into separate input and output *channels*. Not surprisingly, that's why we placed the Splitter component there:

- The bidirectional connector on top of the component accepts the matching bidirectional connection from the SimpleDBAccess component.

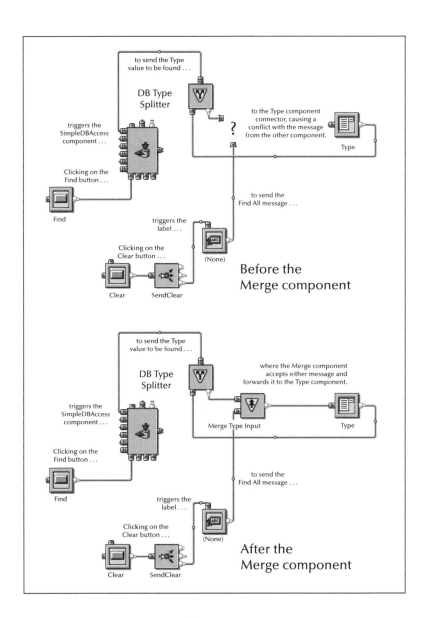

Figure 17.2
Using the Merge component to allow multiple inputs.

- The Splitter's output connector allows values coming *from* the database to get through to the Type component so that it will select and display them. (If we didn't need the Merge component for other reasons, as you'll see in a moment, we'd just plug the Splitter's output directly into the Type component.)

For example, when you perform a Find All for a specific manufacturer (such as Sony), the database sends the type value for the first matching record (such as Television) through the Splitter into the "select string" input of the Type selection list component, which promptly selects and displays the value Television.

- The Type component's output connector—which sends the currently selected value from the list, when asked to do so— connects back around to the Splitter's input-only connection so that the "type selected" value can be reported back to the SimpleDBAccess component.

  For example, when the SimpleDBAccess component processes a Find, Insert, or Delete action, it asks all the fields to report their current values (so it can find, insert, or delete them from the datasource). The Type component sends its current selection through its output, back through the Splitter, and back to the SimpleDBAccess component.

Setting The Selected String: Merging Two Inputs

Next, we had to allow both the Find All label and the database to send their respective values to the Type component. In other words, the Type component had to accept a "select this string" value in two circumstances:

- When the user presses the Clear button, triggering the Find All label to send itself.

- When the database component performs a Find query and wants to send the value of the Type field for the (first) found record to the Type component, so that it would select and display it along with the other fields.

Because we knew we didn't have to worry about handling both inputs at once (the interface won't process a Find and a Clear at the same time), we set a Merge component in front of the Type component's "select string" input. Then, we connected one input port to the Find All label and left the other ready for input from the database connector. (The fact that the database connector input goes back through the Splitter component just adds a little extra excitement.)

That's pretty much the sum of our lessons learned from developing a basic database application in Java Studio. (There were a few others, but this is a family publication.) Before we close, however, we want to share with you a few techniques for creating your own simple text database file, so that you can continue to use the SimpleDBAccess component for your own basic projects.

We realize that this is merely a starting point for you, of course; if you're going to try to do real work with Java-driven database connectivity, you'll move past the SimpleDBAccess component and into the realm of custom components and third-party JavaBeans. Even though each component or Bean will be unique, we hope the groundwork you've laid here will help make this effort easier.

Creating Your Own Simple Text Database

If you want to strike out on your own, use a text editor to create a file with an .SDF extension that follows this format:

```
.SDFTYPE,NAME1,NAME2,EMAIL, (and so forth)
"111","John","Brown","jb@company.com"
"222","Sally","James","sj@company.com"
"333","Toby","Tyler","tty@company.com"
```

The content has to follow these rules:

- The first line contains the field names. All caps are required, but you don't need quotes around them. Spaces are not allowed, so use underscores to string multiple words together.

- The first entry of the first line has to be in the form ".FIELDNAME". It must start with a period, then the letters "SDFTYPE". In the actual records, this first field can contain any kind of data, and it doesn't have to be a numeric ID.

- Each line has to end with a hard return—a regular word wrap is not sufficient.

What's Next?

Now that you know how to do "real work" with database connections, your Java Studio developments have more value and meaning—and consequently more risk. The next chapter follows along by taking on the serious concerns of applet/application security. Chapter 18 will show you what you can do in Java Studio to make sure that your work behaves in the best interests of your users.

Chapter 18

Building A Secure Design

Do you have virus-checker software on your computer? Most people do. But do you have virus-checker software that checks all Java applets you encounter while browsing the Web? Most people don't. The reason is simple—Java applets are pretty darn safe, as you'll find out in this chapter.

The name of this chapter is a bit of a misnomer, because it's very difficult *not* to build a secure design when you're working with Java. In Chapter 19, we'll discuss the reasons for this. In this chapter, we'll explore how to build a design that triggers the safety net built into Java, and how to get around it—safely, of course.

Note that we use a component in this chapter that requires the 1.1 version of the JDK. This means that you will need a rather up-to-date browser to perform the steps in this chapter. Your best bet is to use Netscape Navigator 4, Internet Explorer 4, or later versions of these browsers to complete the steps in this chapter. The applet viewer included with Java Studio does not understand components using the JDK1.1.

In the first part of this chapter, we'll build two simple designs that exchange messages with each other and generate them as applets. After testing the applets, we'll approach this project from a slightly different angle.

Building Two Designs

In this section, we'll build the first design, called Chap18_Send, and then we'll build the second design, called Chap18_Receive. After both designs are built, we'll generate each design as an applet and then test the applets.

The first design, Chap18_Send, consists of a text field and a button. The user enters text in the text field and then presses the button. The text message is sent to the second design, Chap18_Receive. Chap18_Receive listens for messages from Chap18_Send. When Chap18_Receive receives a message from Chap18_Send, Chap18_Receive displays the text message.

If you don't already have it running, start Java Studio. If Java Studio is already running and you have a design open, save the design. Then, open the File menu, and choose New.

Building The First Design

To build these two designs, we need a component that is not shipped on the Java Studio component palette. Therefore, we'll first import the needed component. Then, we'll build the first design.

Import The Component

If you bought Java Studio on CD-ROM, then look on the CD for the directory called contrib and find the NetTransport.jar file. If you downloaded Java Studio from the Sun Web site, the contributed components, including NetTransport.jar, are available at **www.sun.com/studio/contrib**.

Remember, Sun provides no technical support for contributed components. We use the NetTransport component in this chapter, and in our experience, it hasn't caused any problems.

After you locate the NetTransport.jar, then you are ready to add it to the component palette by following these steps:

1. Copy the NetTransport.jar file to a subdirectory of your JDK directory, which is a subdirectory of your Java-Studio1.0 directory.

2. In Java Studio, open the Import menu, and choose JavaBeans.

3. In the Import window, click the Browse button, and navigate to the NetTransport.jar file. Select the file, and click Open, as shown in Figure 18.2. Click Next.

The Nature Of Contributed Components

Okay, we believe the NetTransport component hasn't caused us any problems. But in the interest of full disclosure, we had some problems early in the research phase for this chapter, while experimenting with components that exercise the security rules of Java. The NetTransport component was among the files we imported. At one point during our experimentation, we ended up being totally unable to save any designs. Even if we started a new design and placed just one standard component in it, we received an error message when trying to save the design, as shown in Figure 18.1. Reinstalling Java Studio seemed to solve the problem. We don't know if a particular component caused this problem or not. Just keep this in mind in case you find yourself in the same situation.

Figure 18.1
One of the components we imported seemed to cause problems saving designs.

Figure 18.2
Import the NetTrans-port.jar file as a JavaBean.

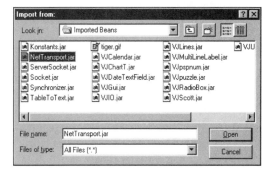

Figure 18.3
The NetTransport component is now in the User tab in the component palette.

4. The NetTransport component appears in the left list. Select NetTransport, and click Add to move the component to the right list. Click Next.

5. You can leave the default, so the NetTransport component appears on the User tab in the palette, as shown in Figure 18.3. Click Finish.

We now have the necessary component on the palette, so we can continue with our task of building the Chap18_Send design.

Build Chap18_Send

The Chap18_Send design is very simple. It includes Text Field, Button, Distributor, and NetTransport components. To build the design, follow these steps:

1. Add a Button component to your blank design. Name the Button component "Send Message Button". For the Button caption, enter "Send Message". Click OK.

2. Click in the GUI window. Select the Button component, and resize it so the entire button caption appears.

3. Add a Text Field component to your design. Name the component Message TF, and add two connectors. Add one connector to trigger the component, and add a second connector to clear the text. Click OK.

4. In the Design window, add a Distributor component from the Data Flow tab to the right of the Send Message Button. Leave the default name for the Distributor, and click OK.

5. On the palette, click the User tab. Select the NetTransport component, shown in Figure 18.3. Click in the Design window to add the component. You will receive a message from Java Studio warning you that a component requiring the JDK 1.1 has been added to the design. Click OK.

6. In the customizer for the NetTransport component, leave the default name as NetTransport1. In the Remote Host field, enter "localhost"; in the Remote Port field, enter "6001"; and in the Local Listening Port field, enter "7001", as shown in Figure 18.4. Click OK.

7. Use Table 18.1 to connect the components. Note that the NetTransport component seems to have the connectors reversed. The connector on the left side is called Outgoing, and the connector on the right side is called Incoming. We'll discuss this in Chapter 19.

8. With all the components connected, take a few minutes to neatly arrange the components in the Design window and in the GUI window. Resize the GUI window so it is only large enough for the Text Field and Button components.

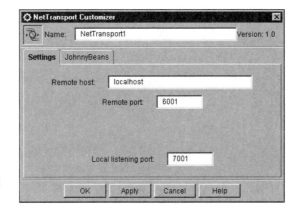

Figure 18.4
Set the Remote Port to 6001, and set the Local Listening Port to 7001.

Table 18.1   Connect the components.

Connect This Connector	To This Connector
Button Pressed output connector of the Send Message Button component	Input connector of the Distributor1 component
Top Output connector of the Distributor1 component	Trigger connector of the Message TF component
Bottom Output connector of the Distributor1 component	Clear Text connector (bottom left) of the Message TF component
Send Text output connector of the Message TF component	Outgoing connector (left side) of the NetTransport1 component

9. Open the Customize menu, and choose GUI Window. In the Window Title field, enter "Send Message". Click OK. Your GUI window should appear similar to Figure 18.5.

10. Save the design as Chap18_Send.

Chap18_Send is now complete. Let's build Chap18_Receive.

Building The Second Design

The second design, Chap18_Receive, listens for messages sent by Chap18_Send and displays them in a Text Field component. The

Figure 18.5
The final appearance of the GUI window of the first design.

design includes Text Field and NetTransport components. To build the design, follow these steps:

1. On the File menu, choose New.

2. Add a Text Field component to the right side of the Design window. Name the component "Message TF". Click OK.

3. On the palette, click the User tab. Select the NetTransport component, as shown earlier in Figure 18.3. Click in the Design window to the left of the Text Field component. You will receive a message from Java Studio warning you that a component requiring the JDK 1.1 has been added to the design. Click OK.

4. In the customizer for the NetTransport component, leave the default name as NetTransport1. In the Remote Host field, enter "localhost"; in the Remote Port field, enter "7001"; and in the Local Listening Port field, enter "6001", as shown in Figure 18.6. Click OK.

5. Connect the Incoming connector, on the right side of the NetTransport component, to the Set Text input connector of the Message TF component.

6. With all the components connected, take a few minutes to neatly arrange the components in the Design window and in the GUI window (okay, with only two components, it won't take long, but it's worth a few seconds of your time). Resize the GUI window so it is only large enough for the Text Field component.

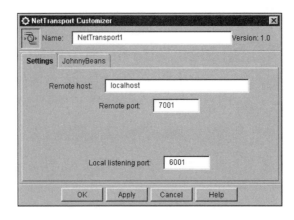

Figure 18.6
Set the Remote Port to 7001, and set the Local Listening Port to 6001.

Figure 18.7
The final appearance of the GUI window of the second design.

7. From the Customize menu, choose GUI Window. In the Window Title field, enter "Receive Message". Click OK. Your GUI window should appear similar to Figure 18.7.

8. Save the design as Chap18_Receive.

Chap18_Receive is now complete. Let's generate both designs as applets.

Preparing For Testing

In this section, we'll open Chap18_Send and generate it as an applet. Then, we'll open Chap18_Receive and generate it as an applet. Using the HTML code generated by Java Studio during the applet generation process, we'll create an HTML file that calls both applets.

Generating The Applets

After you generate one applet, you duplicate the steps to generate the second applet. To generate the applets, follow these steps:

1. At this point, you should already have Chap18_Receive open, so let's generate this design first. On the Generate menu, choose Applet.

2. In the Generate window, specify the name of the HTML file that is generated. By default, Java Studio suggests the same name as the design. Use the default, and click Next.

3. In the next window, you can choose the browser to use to view the applet. Change the default from the Java Applet Viewer to None. We're not quite ready to view the applet yet. Click Next.

4. In the next window, you can choose whether the applet displays in the browser window or whether the applet generates its own window. Choose In The Browser Window. Click Next.

5. Click Finish. When you see the Generated Applet message, click OK.

6. From the File menu, choose Open. Navigate to the directory containing Chap18_Send. Select the file Chap18_Send, and click Open.

7. From the Generate menu, choose Applet.

8. In the Generate window, specify the name of the HTML file that is generated. By default, Java Studio suggests the same name as the design. Use the default, and click Next.

9. In the next window, you can choose the browser to use to view the applet. Change the default from the Java Studio Browser to None. Click Next.

10. In the next window, you can choose whether the applet displays in the browser window or whether the applet generates its own window. Choose In The Browser Window. Click Next.

11. Click Finish. When you see the Generated Applet message, click OK.

You have generated both designs as applets. Now, we are going to create an HTML file that includes **<APPLET>** tags to call both applets.

Creating The HTML File

To create the HTML file, you need a simple text editor, such as Notepad or WordPad. If you are unfamiliar with these utilities, which are a part of the Windows systems, click your Start button, select Programs, select Accessories, and look for either the Notepad or WordPad shortcut. You can choose either application or use another text editor of your choice.

To create the HTML file for testing, follow these steps:

1. Open the text editor of your choice.

2. Open the Chap18_Send.html file. (Be sure to choose the html file and not the vj file.) It should be in the same directory as your design. The file should appear similar to Listing 18.1, except the name of the file specified on the **CODE** parameter is probably different, as well as the width and height.

▶Tip

Can't See It All?

If the lines are too long for you to see, look for a word wrap feature in your text editor. This wraps the lines around so you can see all of the text.

Listing 18.1   A typical Chap18_Send.html.

```
<APPLET
  NAME="chap18_send"
  CODE="VJad35210cbda"
  CODEBASE="classes"
```

```
  ARCHIVE="chap18_send.zip"
  WIDTH="336"
  HEIGHT="104"
>
</APPLET>
```

3. We need to add some HTML code to make this a valid file. Limber up your fingers, and add the highlighted HTML code shown in Listing 18.2.

Listing 18.2   Add some HTML code to make Chap18_Send.html a valid HTML file.

```
<HTML>
<HEAD>
<TITLE>Testing two applets</TITLE>
</HEAD>
<BODY>
<APPLET
  NAME="chap18_send"
  CODE="VJad35210cbda"
  CODEBASE="classes"
  ARCHIVE="chap18_send.zip"
  WIDTH="336"
  HEIGHT="104"
>
</APPLET>


</BODY>
</HTML>
```

4. Save your file. Make sure, if you are asked, that you save it as a text file.

5. In your text editor, open the file Chap18_Receive.html. It will appear similar to Listing 18.1, except it will have a unique file name specified on the **CODE** parameter.

6. Copy the contents of the Chap18_Receive.html file.

7. Open Chap18_Send.html. Place your cursor on the blank line after the **</APPLET>** tag and just before the **</BODY>** tag, and paste so the contents of the Chap18_Receive.html file are pasted into Chap18_Send.html. Your file should now appear similar to Listing 18.3.

**Listing 18.3   The Chap18_Send.html file now has the code
for both applets.**

```
<HTML>
<HEAD>
<TITLE>Testing two applets</TITLE>
</HEAD>
<BODY>

<APPLET
  NAME="chap18_send"
  CODE="VJad35210cbda"
  CODEBASE="classes"
  ARCHIVE="chap18_send.zip"
  WIDTH="336"
  HEIGHT="104"
>
</APPLET>

<APPLET
  NAME="chap18_receive"
  CODE="VJad3520e9270"
  CODEBASE="classes"
  ARCHIVE="chap18_receive.zip"
  WIDTH="208"
  HEIGHT="77"
>
</APPLET>

</BODY>
</HTML>
```

8. Save the file (Chapter18_Send), and close the text editor.

The HTML file is now constructed, and it calls both applets. It's time for testing.

Testing The Applets

As noted early in this chapter, you need a browser that understands the JDK 1.1, which means you need Netscape Navigator 4, Internet Explorer 4, or a higher version of either browser. To test your applets, follow these steps:

1. If it's not already running, start the browser of your choice.

2. On the File menu, choose Open. Navigate to the directory containing Chap18_Send.html. Select the file, and open it.

3. Notice what happens as the file loads. You'll see the Starting Java message at the bottom of the window, and then messages as each applet loads. After the applets load, place your cursor on one of the gray boxes representing an applet. You'll see a message, as shown in Figure 18.8.

What's wrong? The problem is that we generated the designs as applets, and Java applets have special security restrictions. We'll discuss this in detail in Chapter 19. For now, our task at hand is to solve the problem, which won't be too hard because the solution to this problem appears in the next section. So, close your browser and we'll move on.

Try That Again: Two Applications

An obvious way to get around the security restrictions imposed on Java applets is to use Java applications instead of applets. Although this isn't very helpful if you're trying to publish the design on the Web, it will at least prove that the problem with the designs is that they are applets, not that the designs contain errors. This process will demonstrate that our designs actually work when the security restrictions are lifted.

To use this approach, follow these steps:

1. If Java Studio is not already running, start it.

2. On the File menu, choose Open. Open Chap18_Send.vj.

3. On the Generate menu, choose Application.

4. In the Generate window, leave the default directory and file name. Click Next.

5. In the next Generate window, leave Add An Exit Menu Choice selected and deselect the choice to automatically run the application, as shown in Figure 18.9. Click Next.

6. Click Finish.

Figure 18.8
The applets can't talk to each other.

Applet chap18_send   can't start: exception: java.lang.NullPointerException

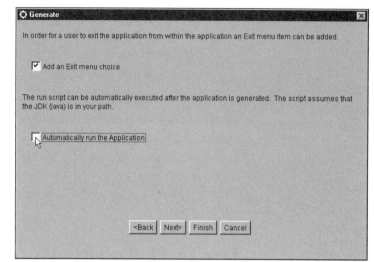

Figure 18.9
Do not automatically run the application after it generates.

7. After you receive the Application Generated message from Java Studio, click OK.

8. Repeat Steps 1 through 7 for Chap18_Receive.vj.

Now you have two applications. Let's test the applications.

9. Using the Explorer or My Computer, find the directory where you have stored the designs, the generated applications and applets, and the BAT files, which were created when you generated applications from your designs.

10. In the directory, look for Chap18_Receive.bat. Double-click the file to run it. A DOS window should appear. Look in the DOS window for any error messages. There are two common error messages that need to be resolved before you can progress. If you don't see any error messages, go to Step 11. Otherwise, read the sidebars (on the next page) addressing the error messages that you might receive.

Figure 18.10
Running the Chap18_Receive application.

11. After you successfully start the Chap18_Receive application, a window eventually appears, similar to the one shown in Figure 18.10.

12. Look at the window displaying the contents of the directory that contains all your designs and generated files. Look for Chap18_Send.bat. Double-click the file, and watch the DOS

Out Of Environment Space

If you are out of environment space, check the contents of your autoexec.bat file in your C:\ (or other root) directory. You have too many characters specified for environment variables. This includes statements like **set path=**, **set classpath=**, and **set temp=**. Reduce the number of items after the equal sign for each statement. For example, you can put a **REM** statement in front of your **set classpath** statement, so it's not used at all for now. You can also delete anything from your **set path** statement except your Windows directory and the location of the Java interpreter, which is probably C:\Java-Studio1.0\Jdk\bin. Save your autoexec.bat, close all programs, and reboot. Then, try running the Chap18_Receive application again.

Bad Command Or File Name

If you receive a bad command or file name error after the command that starts with **java**, it's likely the Java interpreter is not in your path. Edit the autoexec.bat in your C:\ (or other root) directory, and check for a statement beginning with **set path=**. It should include a directory, such as C:\Java-Studio1.0\Jdk\bin, so the complete statement might look like this: **set path=c:windows; c:\Java-Studio1.0\Jdk\bin**. Save the file, close all programs, and reboot. Then, try running the Chap18_Receive application again.

If you still receive the bad command or file name error message, it's possible your Java interpreter is in a different directory. Click the Start button, and choose Find|Files Or Folders. Search for the file java.exe. When you find it, note the directory, and specify it on the path statement in your autoexec.bat file.

window that opens. If you successfully made it this far, you shouldn't receive any more error messages, but check, just in case. After the application loads, a GUI window appears that looks similar to Figure 18.11.

13. Test the application by typing a word or phrase in the text field in the Send Message application. When you are finished typing, click the Send Message button. Watch it appear in the Receive Message application. The two, independent applications are communicating with each other.

Figure 18.11
Running the Chap18_Send application.

Congratulations! You have built two Java applications. One sends messages, and the other receives and displays the messages.

Padlocks On Your Coffee

The world of Java security is complex. Chapter 19 presents a 20-minute tour of Java security, and you'll learn why the Chap18_Send and Chap19_Receive designs generated as applets didn't work.

Chapter 19

Understanding Secure Designs

"We like security; we like the pope to be infallible in matters of faith, and grave doctors to be so in moral questions so that we can feel reassured." Blaise Pascal hit the nail on the head when he wrote this in 1670. We like security. In Java, secure software is the name of the game.

In this chapter, you'll get an informed executive-level tour of Java security. After reading the first section, you won't necessarily be ready to write your own digital signatures for Java applets, but you'll know the main components of Java security, why it is important, and the future of Java security. In the second section, you'll find a review of the design we built in Chapter 18. You'll see why the applets didn't work, and you'll learn about other issues associated with developing secure designs.

Security And Java

This section is your tour of security issues in the world of Java. We'll discuss the following topics:

- Why security is an issue
- Microsoft's ActiveX security
- JavaBeans security
- Why Java is safe
- The future of Java security

Let's start by facing the biggest question first, Why does anyone care whether Java is secure or not?

Java Security

Remember when the general public began to use online resources? People understood that they could find software online, and they could download the software to use on their own computers. But everyone was warned—make sure you have good virus protection. Make sure you only download from sites that you know are reputable. Make sure you say grace before clicking the Save button. Everyone had heard horror stories, such as the friend whose hard drive was erased by a malicious virus hiding in that seemingly innocent freeware utility.

The antivirus companies have thrived by providing protection against viruses. So, most people understand that it's not a good idea to roam online without protection, and they pay an annual upgrade fee to an antivirus company in order to roam safely.

When users began surfing the Web, safety became an issue as soon as Web sites started to contain applets or other bits of software that made a site interactive. Essentially, it meant that users were running software written by unknown people. How many times have you found yourself at a Web site accidentally, without having any idea of the identity of the site's host or sponsor? Without that knowledge, how did you know that when your status bar displayed the message "Apple Foobar running" that you were embarking on a safe venture and not a path that lead to ruining your computer's data? Maybe because you knew applets written in Java are safe.

As you'll read in this chapter, Java was designed, from the ground up, to make it really difficult for a malicious hacker to write nasty applets. But applets are not the only bits of software users encounter on the Web. Users also encounter JavaBeans and ActiveX controls.

ActiveX Security

Microsoft believes they have found a good compromise between offering security to users and offering flexibility and power to developers. But note that it's a compromise, and some people believe that any compromises involving security automatically make the solution invalid.

Microsoft's security with ActiveX controls consists of *digital signatures*. Digital signatures are mathematically encoded files that identify who wrote the code, who is distributing the code, and information similar to that. The premise of digital signatures is that users will run software from sources they trust. Think of it this way—you'll accept an unexpected package from your local mail carrier with a return address of an acquaintance, but you might not accept a package that has an unfamiliar return address.

The problem with digital signatures is that they depend on the user to accept or reject the signature, so they're only as secure as a user's willingness to reject them. To keep up with the Joneses, or at least with Microsoft, Sun added digital signatures to JDK 1.1.1. We'll review the security structures for Java later in this chapter, as well as the newer security model included in JDK 1.2.

How Secure Are Beans?

JavaBeans are the component architecture of Java, and they are still Java at their core. So, Beans have the same security restrictions as other Java code. Applets have more restrictions than Java applications or Beans, but Beans are still bound by the security rules of Java and are therefore safe for the world.

How Java Is Made Safe For The World

The designers of Java created a security model for Java, which is popularly called the *sandbox*. The concept of the sandbox is that Java has very specific limits, and all Java programs must stay within those limits. In other words, they must stay within the sandbox. The sandbox has been criticized as too restrictive, but the designers of Java felt the ability for every user to run applets worry-free was so important that they were willing to weather the criticism. In JDK 1.2, however, Sun is implementing more flexibility with the security model.

The sandbox consists of three parts: the Byte Code Verifier, the Applet Class Loader, and the Security Manager.

Byte Code Verifier

The Byte Code Verifier is a fairly unique concept in the world of programming languages. Before running any applet, the Byte Code Verifier checks the byte codes in the class file to make sure it complies with the rules for Java. It's just like your grandmother telling you to wipe your feet on the mat outside the door before allowing you inside.

The disadvantage to the Byte Code Verifier is that it costs some time and slows down the appearance of an applet that is preparing to run. The other disadvantage is that many Java Virtual Machines (JVMs), which is the software mechanism that executes the byte codes, allow users to turn off the Byte Code Verifier to avoid the time penalty.

Applet Class Loader

As you know, all objects in Java belong to a class. The Applet Class Loader, as you might guess, checks all classes as they are loaded. For example, it verifies that the classes do not have any stack overflows or underflows, and that they do not perform any illegal data conversion. It ensures that no classes overwrite essential parts of the Java runtime system, which is the software mechanism that executes the Java byte codes, and it allows classes loaded by an applet to be identified as such with a unique name.

Security Manager

The Security Manager is the guard at the door of the store, watching as people browse the merchandise, purchase items, and leave the store. The Security Manager monitors the applet while it runs and maintains a list of suspicious activities. When the applet attempts a suspicious activity, such as writing a file to your hard drive, the Security Manager is allowed to veto the activity before it happens. A veto by the Security Manager is known as a *Security Exception*. Security Exceptions come in varying levels of warning messages.

Now that you have an idea of the mechanisms keeping Java applets in line, let's review exactly what applets can and can't do.

Applets: What They Can And Can't Do

Applets actually have two levels of restrictions, depending on whether they are local or loaded across a network. A local applet is one where the file resides on your computer, and you are running it on your computer. An applet loaded across the network is one that a user encounters while online. When a user encounters it, the applet is downloaded to the user's computer and loaded to run (after, of course, the Byte Code Verifier does its job).

With the sandbox, applets that are loaded across the network have the following restrictions:

- Cannot write or read files on the user's computer.

- Cannot make network connections except to the server hosting the applet, or to the host specified on the **CODEBASE** parameter in the **<APPLET>** tag that calls the applet.

- Cannot start programs on the user's computer.

- Cannot load libraries.

- Cannot define native method calls, which would give applets access to the user's computer.

On the other hand, applets are allowed to:

- Play sounds.

- Easily display HTML documents.

- Call public methods of applets on the same page.

NOTE

JDK 1.0.2 does not allow applications to play sounds. However, newer versions of the JDK are changing this. In JDK 1.1, the Java Media Framework allows you to play some sounds in Java applications, and the plans for JDK 1.2 include a Java Sound engine.

Local applets—applets that are not loaded over the network— don't have the same restrictions. For example, they are allowed to read and write files on your computer, and they can load libraries onto the your computer. They also bypass the Byte Code Verifier.

You now know Java's current state of security. Let's take a look at where Java security is heading.

Java Security In The Future

As mentioned earlier in this chapter, Sun added digital signatures to Java with JDK 1.1.1. In JDK 1.2, the architects are working on adding access control that works in conjunction with digital signatures. Access control would change the size of the sandbox for applets. Some applets could have very big sandboxes and be allowed to read and write virtually any file at company X, because they have the digital signature of company X's system administrator. Other applets could have medium-sized sandboxes, because they are for public consumption and they have a digital signature of a nationally known company. Still, other applets could have tiny sandboxes, because they are for public consumption, and have the digital signature of The Evil Dr. No. Access control, along with digital signatures, provides a good solution to control security at an appropriate level while remaining within the sandbox.

This concludes your tour of Java security. Please remain seated until the chapter has come to a full and complete stop. Your next stop is a look inside the designs we built in Chapter 18.

What's Wrong With The Applet Designs

You probably know why Chapter 18's applet designs didn't work. There was nothing wrong with the designs. The problem is that Java applets have more security restrictions than Java applications. Even when it appears that an applet should be allowed to perform a task, security restrictions can interfere.

In Chapter 18, we attempted to use two designs to open a network connection with the NetTransport component. As applets, the designs generated errors. As applications, they worked like champs. Let's look a little closer at the designs themselves.

The designs were very simple, and they used a NetTransport component. The NetTransport component is a little disconcerting, because all of us Java Studio geeks now expect to find input connectors on the left side of a component and output connectors on the right side of a component.

Figure 19.1
The NetTransport component has connectors that seemed misnamed.

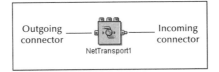

However, the NetTransport component has a connector called Outgoing on the left side, and it has a connector called Incoming on the right side, as shown in Figure 19.1. Think of it this way— the connectors are named from the perspective of the other design that is communicating with this design. The Outgoing connector receives a message that it passes to the design specified in the Remote Port field. From our view inside this design, it seems odd to us, because we send a message through the Outgoing connector.

The next question about our example is, "Why didn't we use Java Studio's Applet Viewer to view the applets after we generated them?" As you saw in Java Studio's messages, the Applet Viewer does not support JDK 1.1, and the NetTransport component uses JDK 1.1. So, we needed to avoid the Applet Viewer and, instead, use Netscape Navigator 4, Internet Explorer 4, or later versions of these browsers.

You might also be interested in the Java 1.1.1 plug-in available from Sun Microsystems. It is a plug-in for browsers, so they can use newer versions of JDK before the browsers themselves have implemented support. You can find it at **java.sun.com/products/plugin**.

Now that you know more about Chapter 18's designs, let's discuss some issues from the perspective of your users. How can you protect your users when they use your designs?

How You Can Protect Users

As a designer, you can protect users in two ways. First, you can protect users from themselves by performing error checking on any input they give to your applets or applications. Second, you can protect users from others by continuing to use Java, which is pretty hard to hack.

Of course, your users might not quite appreciate this, because it's the sort of thing that is only noticed when something goes wrong (and as long as you're using Java, nothing should go wrong). They might grumble a bit about the time it takes to load your Java applets or applications, but they'll thank you for it later, when they realize they are safe as a result.

Slow? Who Said It Was Slow?

We admit, Java has definitely suffered some reputation problems when it comes to the performance of Java applets and applications. As you saw in this chapter, some of that comes from the security built into the language. However, in Chapters 20 and 21, you'll read about some strategies for improving the performance of your designs.

Chapter 20

Improving The Performance Of A Design

As mentioned in Chapter 5, the number one rule to remember for Web interface design is that users won't tolerate sluggish designs. But, Java has a nasty reputation for being slow. As you'll see in this chapter, you can enjoy the advantages of Java and still deliver high-performance designs to your users.

Good performance is like good sailing. It's not enough to have a well-designed ship, a highly trained crew, and good-looking weather gear. You also need some elements, like the water and the wind, to go your way, and those components aren't under your control.

In Java applets, the applet is not the only component that determines performance. Other components include the speed of the user's PC and Internet connection, the general load on the Internet, the speed of the server hosting the applet, the performance of the Java Virtual Machine (JVM), and sometimes the performance of a Just-In-Time (JIT) compiler.

As you probably know, the JVM is the mechanism that actually processes the Java byte codes when an applet runs on a user's machine. Therefore, if the JVM runs slowly, your applet runs slowly as well. JIT compilers became available with Netscape Navigator 3 and Internet Explorer 3. A JIT compiler actually compiles the Java byte codes instead of allowing the byte codes to be interpreted by the JVM. The idea is that, because the applet's execution is imminent, you know which platform (PC, Unix, Macintosh, and so on) the applet will run on. Therefore, it's okay to go ahead and compile it into machine-specific code, which runs much faster than any interpreted language. Unfortunately, the main goal of JIT compilers is to quickly compile the byte codes—they do not necessarily compile the byte codes into efficient code. So again, the performance of your applet depends on the performance of the JIT compiler used by your users—something outside of your control.

So, what can you control? Your design, of course. In this chapter, we'll build a small applet and measure how quickly it downloads and runs for users. After measuring the design, we'll investigate several methods for fine-tuning the design's performance.

Build An Applet

You might recall the Hello, Indiana, Inc. company from earlier in this book. This make-believe company offers online ordering of maps for cities in the state of Indiana. The applet we are going to build in this chapter will be the opening page for the company's Web site. The Web page welcomes users to the site and offers an image map representing the four main areas of the site.

If you don't already have Java Studio running, start it now. If Java Studio is already running, save your current design. Then, build the applet by following these steps:

1. In Java Studio, open the File menu, and choose New.

2. On the GUI tab, select the Label component. Click the GUI window near the top of the window. Name the component Welcome Label, and specify the label caption as "Welcome to our home on the Web!"

3. Click the Standard tab. Look to the right of the Background field for a button with three ellipses. Click this button to display the Color Chooser window. Scroll down to the end of the list of colors, and choose White. Click OK to close the Color Chooser window.

4. Look to the right of the Font field for the button with three ellipses. Click this button to display the Font Chooser. For the family, choose SansSerif. For the style, choose bold. For the size, choose 24. Click OK to close the Font Chooser window.

5. Click OK to close the Label Customizer.

6. In the GUI window, select the Label component, and resize it so the entire caption displays. You might need to resize the GUI window to make it large enough for the Label. Make the Label a little wider than necessary. For some reason, this large label doesn't entirely display when viewing this applet in a browser unless the field is little larger than necessary, as shown in Figure 20.1.

7. Add another Label component to the design below the Welcome Label component. Name the component What Label, and specify the label caption as "What do you want to do?"

8. Click the Standard tab, and change the background of the label to white. Then, change the font to SansSerif, the style to italic, and the size to 18. Click OK to close the Font Chooser window, and then click OK to close the Label Customizer.

9. Resize the label in the GUI window so the entire caption displays.

10. Save your design.

11. To finish this design, you'll need to use the ImageMap component, as shown in Figure 20.2. But, before going any further, you need to retrieve a file from the CD-ROM that accompanies this book. Look for the file called chap20_imagemap.gif, and then copy it to the same directory as your design.

12. On the Multimedia tab on the palette, select the ImageMap component. Click the GUI window below the labels.

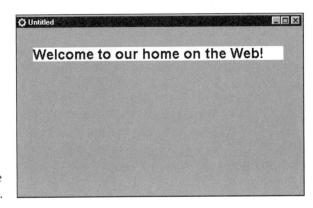

Figure 20.1
This Label component welcomes visitors to the Hello, Indiana Web site.

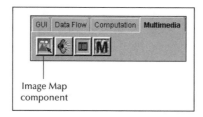

Figure 20.2
The ImageMap component on the Multimedia tab.

Image Map component

►Tip

What's An Image Map?

You might be unfamiliar with the term image map, but you already know what an image map is. An image map is a graphic element that is formatted so various areas of the image are defined as live links to other Web pages. When a user clicks a particular area on the image, the user is taken to a linked page. An image map is often used as a graphical map to a Web site, hence the term image map.

13. Leave the name of the component as Image Map1. Look to the right of the Image File field for the Browse button. Click the Browse button, and navigate in the directories until you find chap20_imagemap.gif where you copied it on your hard disk. Select the file, and click Open.

14. The Image Map Customizer offers some tools for defining the areas of the image map. Review the tools, as shown in Figure 20.3, and select the Rectangle tool.

15. With the Rectangle tool selected, click and drag a rectangle around the upper-left quadrant of the image.

16. In the Area Name field, replace Untitled Rect with "Order Maps". In the Area Value field, replace Untitled Rect with "http://www.helloindiana.com/order.html", as shown in Figure 20.4. Click Add.

17. Add three more rectangle fields around each of the images in the graphic. Use Table 20.1 to determine the values for the Area Name and Area Value fields. Remember to click the Add button after specifying the information for the fields. For reference, the information for the rectangle field you drew in the previous step is included.

Figure 20.3
The Image Map Customizer has four tools for defining areas of an image map.

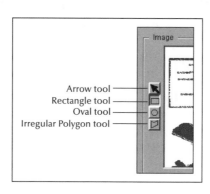

Arrow tool
Rectangle tool
Oval tool
Irregular Polygon tool

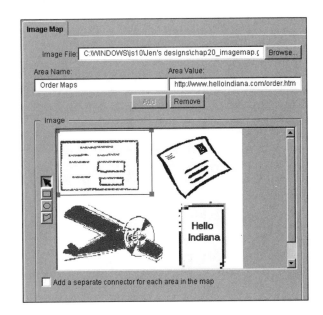

Figure 20.4
Specify values in the Area Name and Area Value fields.

Table 20.1   Values for the Area Name and Area Value fields.

Image	Area Name	Area Value
Order form	Order Maps	http://www.helloindiana.com/order.html
Envelope	Contact Us	http://www.helloindiana.com/contact.html
Airplane	Getting To Indiana	http://www.helloindiana.com/transport.html
State of Indiana	About Hello, Indiana	http://www.helloindiana.com/corporate.html

Using The Image Map Tools

After you've drawn a selection area, you can't resize it. You can change its location by using the Arrow tool, but you cannot change its size. If you draw a selection area and you don't like it, you have two choices. If you haven't clicked the Add button yet, just draw a new area, because a selection area isn't defined until you click the Add button. If you have clicked the Add button, select the selection area with the Arrow tool, and then click Remove.

If you want to change any of the values for the Area Name or Area Value fields, you need to use the techniques described in this sidebar. You cannot change the values once you click the Add button.

18. After you have added all four selection areas, click OK to close the Image Map Customizer.

19. On the Internet tab on the palette, select the URL Opener component. Click the Design window to the right of the Image Map component. Leave the default name of the URL Opener, and deselect the Automatically Display Any URL Arriving At The Set URL Connector checkbox. Click OK.

20. Connect the output connector of the Image Map component to the input connector of the URL Opener component.

21. At this point, your Design window should appear similar to Figure 20.5, with four components in it.

22. From the Customize menu, choose GUI Window. Specify the Window Title as "Welcome to Hello, Indiana". Click the Edit button to the right of the Background field, and choose white as the background color. Click OK to close the Color Chooser, and then click OK to close the GUI Window Customizer.

23. Save the file.

Your design is complete. Now, generate the design as an applet. Choose to immediately view the applet with the Java Studio browser, and choose to display the applet in the browser window.

When the applet finishes generating, and your browsing is loading the HTML file calling the applet, notice how long it takes before you see the results. Was it five or six seconds? Longer? Let's take a closer look at exactly how long this applet takes to display.

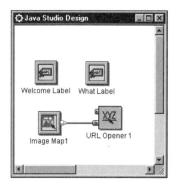

Figure 20.5
Your Design window should appear similar to this.

Measure The Applet

By far, the largest indicator of performance for an applet is the size of the files downloaded to the user's PC, because the download time is the tightest bottleneck. After the files are downloaded, applets run pretty quickly, similar to the load time you experience when you view an applet after generating it. In both cases, all the files necessary to run the applet are local on your hard disk.

To get a feel for the elapsed time for users, keep the following numbers in mind:

- A user connected using a 28.8Kbps modem typically sees a download time of 1 second for a 1K file and 10 seconds for a 34K file.

- As discussed in Chapter 5, a user needs a response from a system within 10 seconds, or they start believing the system is hung.

Table 20.2 adds up the size of the files used by this chapter's sample applet.

If you add up the file sizes in Table 20.2, you can see that the applet consists of 422K of files.

Whoa! That Sure Is A Plodding Piece Of Software

Yes, that's a lot to ask of your user, to wait for 422K of files to download. We're pleased that you're shocked—it indicates how sensitive you are to your users' burdens. Now, it's not clear that the applet needs the entire contents of the com and sunw subdirectories, but we know the applet won't work without a least some portion of it.

Table 20.2 Adding up the total size of the applet.

File	Size
HTML file generated by Java Studio that calls the applet	1K
Zip file generated by Java Studio in the classes subdirectory	220K
CLASS and DAT files in the classes subdirectory	4K
Contents and subdirectories of the com and sunw subdirectories, which are in the classes subdirectory	197K

To test which files the applet truly needs, we deleted the com and sunw subdirectories and the classes subdirectory, and generated the applet again. The structure for the classes subdirectory and the com and sunw subdirectories was generated again.

Take heart—there are some options. Let's explore how we can improve the download time for this applet.

Fine-Tune The Performance Of This Applet

Just so you have some context for the more than 420K of files for this version of the applet, let's take a look at how much the Zip file buys you. As you know, the Zip file is a file containing all the CLASS files in the classes subdirectory. By putting all the CLASS files in the classes subdirectory in a Zip file, there is less overhead time required during the download. For every file downloaded, the HTTP protocol (the protocol used by Web browsers to view Web pages) opens a new socket. When the file has finished downloading, the socket is destroyed. The setup and teardown of a socket takes time. Therefore, downloading one bigger file instead of many smaller files saves time.

A Zip file is specified by the **ARCHIVE** parameter of the **<APPLET>** tag. As noted in Chapter 7, Internet Explorer 3 and Netscape Navigator 2 don't understand the **ARCHIVE** parameter. Later versions of Explorer and Navigator support the **ARCHIVE** parameter. But, if your users are using these older versions of browsers, you need to upload the contents of the classes directory. With this applet, the contents of the classes directory, the com and sunw subdirectories, the CLASS and DAT files, and the HTML file together add up to 418K of files. However, it will take longer for a user to download, because each of the 100+ CLASS files in the classes subdirectory uses time to create 102 sockets and tear down 102 sockets, whereas the Zip file only uses 1 socket connection for the 102 files.

Well, from that perspective, the 420K of files using the Zip file isn't quite as bad. But we can do better, using one of two approaches.

Tip

Don't Delete Classes.zip

In the lib subdirectory of the JDK directory, you will find a classes.zip file. Don't delete this file—it's necessary for the JDK.

If you want to make sure you're not deleting anything important to Java Studio or the JDK, save your design in a directory completely separate from Java Studio or the JDK. When you generate the design as an applet, a classes subdirectory is created below the directory containing your design.

Approach 1: Use A JAR File

This approach has broader applications than Approach 2, but it doesn't provide as much improvement in performance. You already know that Navigator 3 and Explorer 4 support the **ARCHIVE** parameter on the **<APPLET>** tag. Up until now, you have only specified a Zip file on the **ARCHIVE** parameter, because that's how Java Studio generates the HTML file for applets.

Newer versions of Navigator 4 and Explorer 4 support JDK 1.1. With support of the JDK 1.1, you can specify a JAR file on the **ARCHIVE** parameter. A JAR file is a Java Archive file used by JavaBeans (see Chapters 10 and 11 for more information about JAR files and JavaBeans). With JDK 1.1, you can also use JAR files to compress CLASS files for applets. It's similar to using a Zip file, but Zip files are not compressed. JAR files can be compressed.

Another advantage to JAR files is that you can include the contents of the com and sunw subdirectories, further reducing the overhead download time. The following steps describe how to create a JAR file for this chapter's sample applet:

1. First, review the contents of the classes subdirectory. Look for the Zip file created when you generated the design as an applet. You need to unzip the file to get all the CLASS files.

   If you want to pare down the files as much as possible before you unzip the Zip file, delete the contents of the classes subdirectory, including the com and sunw subdirectories. Then, generate the design again as an applet.

2. Use WinZip (see **www.winzip.com** for information on how to obtain this utility if you don't already have it) to extract all the CLASS files from the Zip file into the classes subdirectory.

3. After you have extracted all the CLASS files, delete or move the Zip file so you don't accidentally include it in the JAR file. If there are any other files that are not being used by this applet, such as Zip files from previous designs, delete or move them.

4. Go to the MS-DOS prompt, and then navigate until you're in the directory containing the unzipped CLASS files.

Tip

Windows 95 Directory Names

When you're using the DOS prompt to navigate among directories, you might find yourself trying to change directories to a directory that doesn't follow MS-DOS naming conventions. In order to specify the directory's name, enclose it in quotation marks, such as:

```
cd "my designs"
```

5. Create a JAR file with the following command:

```
jar cvf chap20.jar *
```

This command calls the **JAR** command to create the JAR file called chap20.jar. All the files in the current directory, as well as all the files in subdirectories, are stored because they are specified with the asterisk. The **cvf** parameters are used to indicate the following:

- **c** means a JAR file is being created.

- **v** means that you want to see the status of the files as they are stored in the JAR file (**v** stands for verbose).

- **f** is used to indicate that the next item on the command line is the name of the JAR file.

Figure 20.6 displays the JAR file command and the beginning of the report as the files are stored in the JAR file. You can see the subdirectories are being added.

6. After the JAR file is finished storing the files, you should have a JAR file of around 250K, plus or minus a few K. The best way to test the JAR file is to upload it or move it to a separate directory so you can make sure you know exactly which files are being used for this applet.

Besides the JAR file, you need three more files, and you need to modify the HTML file. Among the three files that you need are the CLASS and DAT files generated by Java Studio.

```
:\WINDOWS\js10\Jen's designs\classes>jar cvf chap20.jar *
adding: AggToVJColumnInputTransfer.class (in=324) (out=229) (deflated 29%)
adding: AggToVJFieldValuesInputTransfer.class (in=334) (out=231) (deflated 30%)
adding: AggToVJTableInputTransfer.class (in=6842) (out=3328) (deflated 51%)
adding: BasicToBooleanInputTransfer.class (in=326) (out=227) (deflated 30%)
adding: BasicToDoubleInputTransfer.class (in=324) (out=227) (deflated 29%)
adding: BasicToFloatInputTransfer.class (in=322) (out=226) (deflated 29%)
adding: BasicToIntegerInputTransfer.class (in=326) (out=228) (deflated 30%)
adding: BasicToLongInputTransfer.class (in=320) (out=226) (deflated 29%)
adding: BasicToStringInputTransfer.class (in=2975) (out=1489) (deflated 49%)
adding: BasicToVJFieldValuesInputTransfer.class (in=338) (out=231) (deflated 31

adding: BooleanToBasicOutputTransfer.class (in=329) (out=228) (deflated 30%)
adding: chap20_imagemap.gif (in=8551) (out=8283) (deflated 3%)
adding: com/ (in=0) (out=0) (stored 0%)
adding: com/sun/ (in=0) (out=0) (stored 0%)
adding: com/sun/jpro/ (in=0) (out=0) (stored 0%)
adding: com/sun/jpro/vj/ (in=0) (out=0) (stored 0%)
adding: com/sun/jpro/vj/kernel/ (in=0) (out=0) (stored 0%)
adding: com/sun/jpro/vj/kernel/VJConnectionInfo.class (in=1714) (out=73
```

Figure 20.6
The **v** parameter on the JAR command causes all the files to be listed as they are stored.

If you look in the classes subdirectory, the CLASS and DAT files start with VJ, and it's obvious the names are generated (for example, VJad3998b50a2.class and VJad3998b50a2.dat). The third file is buried deep in a subdirectory of the com directory. Assuming you're in the classes subdirectory, the file is: com/sun/jpro/vj/components/imagemap/chap20_imagemap.gif. So if you're uploading or moving the files to a separate location, upload the JAR file, the CLASS and DAT files, and the chap20_imagemap.gif. The applet looks for the GIF file in the same subdirectory structure, so make sure you replicate it.

7. Modify the HTML file so you specify the JAR file, and add standard HTML codes around the **<APPLET>** tag. For example, Listing 20.1 displays the changes we made to chapter20_example.html.

Listing 20.1   Modify the ARCHIVE parameter, and add some HTML tags.

```
<HTML>
<HEAD>
<TITLE>Welcome to our home on the Web!</TITLE>
</HEAD>
<BODY>
<P>
<APPLET
  NAME="chapter20_example"
  CODE="VJad3998b50a2"
  CODEBASE="classes"
  ARCHIVE="chap20.jar"
  WIDTH="500"
  HEIGHT="438">
</APPLET>
</P>
</BODY>
</HTML>
```

That's it. With the vast majority of the necessary files compressed in a JAR file, the total size of all the files necessary with this technique adds up to around 260K or 270K.

The disadvantage of this approach is that it requires browsers that use JDK 1.1. The advantage is that as more and more people use the updated browsers, this approach will become more widely used.

The next approach uses a completely different viewpoint to maximize your users' time.

Approach 2: Use Plain HTML

We point out this approach so that you can remember to take a step back and occasionally consider if you really and truly need to write an applet to accomplish what you want. Take a look at Listing 20.2. The results are very similar to the results we achieved with the applet.

Listing 20.2   This HTML code accomplishes the same result as the applet.

```
<HTML>
<HEAD>
<TITLE>Welcome to our home on the Web!</TITLE>
</HEAD>
<BODY>
<H1>Welcome to our home on the Web!</H1>
<P>What do you want to do?</P>
<IMG
  SRC="chap20_imagemap.gif"
  WIDTH=318
  HEIGHT=270
  USEMAP="#image1"
  BORDER="0">
<MAP NAME="image1">
<AREA
  SHAPE="rect"
  ALT="Order maps"
  COORDS="1,2,153,114"
  HREF="order.html">
<AREA
  SHAPE="rect"
  ALT="Contact us"
  COORDS="158,1,310,114"
  HREF="contact.html">
<AREA
  SHAPE="rect"
  ALT="Getting to Indiana"
  COORDS="1,127,192,237"
  HREF="transport.html">
<AREA
  SHAPE="rect"
  ALT="About us"
  COORDS="195,127,310,264"
```

```
   HREF="corporate.html">
<AREA SHAPE="default" nohref>
</MAP>
</BODY>
</HTML>
```

Okay, the HTML file is still only 1K, and the GIF file is 9K, giving us a grand total of 10K in file size. It doesn't take a brain surgeon to know this makes much more sense than the applet. Don't worry if you aren't comfortable figuring out the **<MAP>** HTML tags and the coordinates of the regions in the graphic. There are several tools easily available to make this a snap. For example, MapEdit from Boutell.com (at **www.boutell.com**) offers a 30-day demo, and then it's only $25 to license.

But obviously, you can't transform many of your Java Studio designs into HTML-only pages. That's why we reviewed the JAR file technique first, because it is applicable to more Java Studio designs. But Approach 2 represented such huge savings in terms of file size that we had to present it.

Give Me More Performance

Ready to dig a little deeper in the wonderful world of performance issues? In Chapter 21, we'll discuss the minimum size for a Java Studio applet and the reasons why Java is slow. We'll also review which components in Java Studio can be more efficiently presented outside of Java Studio.

Chapter 21

Understanding Performance

"Premature optimization is the root of all evil," said Donald Knuth, a pioneer in computer programming. Focus on other design aspects before you obsess about performance. This chapter looks at improving designs before and after code is generated.

Because Java Studio is a visual development environment, you have no control over the specific code generated. Therefore, this chapter focuses on planning appropriate strategies for efficient delivery to users and on minimizing the file size of the delivered files. In this chapter, we'll discuss how to measure performance, review why Java is slow, determine the size of the files generated by various Java Studio components, and explore three methods of improving performance.

How To Measure Performance

As discussed in Chapter 20, the performance of your applet depends on several factors that are beyond your control. The advantage of this is that those beyond-control components might be able to improve without any effort on your part. For example, the performance improvement from JDK 1.02 to JDK 1.1 is fairly significant.

In Chapter 20, we performed another measurement of performance—file size. We added the sizes of all the files needed by the applet. If you decrease your file size, then you decrease the time your users need to load the applet.

Besides reviewing the improvement in performance offered by newer versions of the JDK and counting kilobytes, how can you determine the actual burden on your users? By simulating your users' environments, of course.

CaffeineMark JDK Benchmark

If you are interested in the details of the performance improvement from JDK 1.02 to JDK1.1, see Sun's report on the results of a benchmark test called CaffeineMark at **java.sun.com/products/jdk/ 1.1/performance/caffeinemark.html**. CaffeineMark was developed by Pendragon Software, and it measures the performance of a Java system. The test includes evaluating performance of Just-In-Time (JIT) compilers, Java byte code interpreters, and applet viewers. You can learn more about CaffeineMark at **www.webfayre.com/pendragon/cm2/index.html**.

User Tests

As far as testing goes, nothing beats uploading an applet to a Web site and trying to load the Web page from another machine. When you test your applet this way, you should use another machine, because undoubtedly, your PC has all the necessary files in the path and the applet might still be in your hard disk cache. If you use your own machine, you might not really know if you're downloading all the files or not. For a variety of test results, upload the files, and then call your friends, siblings, parents, children, and other relatives. Ask them to view the Web page and time how long it takes them to download the applet. After all, the proof is in the pudding.

Other tools exist to improve the performance of Java applets and applications, but they are not necessarily very helpful to us.

Profilers And Optimization Tools

Tools called *profilers* measure where your applet or application spends most of its time, so you can focus on improving the parts of your design that have the biggest impact on total performance. Profilers are included with Sun's Java Workshop 2 and with the JDK. Profilers are available from other vendors that help interpret the often hard-to-read results from the Java profiler. See Appendix B for vendor specifics.

But profilers are mostly useful if you can change the code. Which, of course, we can't, with Java Studio. If you are determined to optimize the heck out of an applet or application, you can use these tools and work on the design in Java Workshop or another Java development environment and focus on the code itself.

Another set of tools are *optimization tools*. Optimization tools actually modify your Java applet or application to make it more efficient. The vendors who offer optimization tools cite some pretty impressive numbers that indicate they can dramatically improve the performance of your design. However, these optimization tools are fairly pricey. One, called DashO from Preemptive, lists for $1,145 and is on sale at press time for $895. This appears to be typical for optimization tools. So, you need to be fairly serious about your optimization efforts to justify the cost. If you are churning out a fair number of applets and applications, then an optimization tool could pay for itself pretty quickly in terms of time savings for your users. For more information on optimization tools, see Appendix B.

We've spent a little time discussing the outside forces that impact your applet's performance, how to measure it, and other tools to explore if you want to work on the code. Now, let's take a look at exactly why Java is slow.

Why Java Is Slow

There are several reasons why Java is slow. Mostly, Java is slow as a result of certain features that make it such an appealing language: strong security and cross-platform compatibility. The reasons for Java's slowness include the Byte Code Verifier, the Security Manager, and the interpreted nature of Java.

The Byte Code Verifier checks all byte codes before loading an applet. It is one of the prongs of the security mechanism built into Java that prevents malicious code from sneaking into an applet before it is executed by the user. It's vital to Java security, but users pay for it by spending a little extra time as their byte codes are verified.

The Security Manager monitors what happens while the applet runs. It is also part of the security mechanism of Java. Before performing any potentially dangerous operation, the applet checks with the Security Manager to see if it's okay. Again, this is good for security, but tough on performance.

Java is essentially an interpreted language, interpreted by the Java Virtual Machine (JVM), and interpreted languages are slower than compiled languages. What does this mean? Think of it as the difference between hearing someone speak your native language, and hearing someone speak a language you've been studying for a couple of months. It takes you a lot longer to process the foreign language, because you translate each word into your native language, and then you understand the meaning of each word. On the other hand, when you hear your native language, you understand it immediately without need for intermediate translation.

Hearing the foreign language is similar to what's happening with an interpreted language, such as Java. Hearing your native language is similar to running a compiled program, such as those written in C or C++.

However, the impact of Java being an interpreted language is lessening with newer versions of browsers. Navigator 3 and Internet Explorer 3 include JIT compilers, which improve the performance of Java. As noted in Chapter 20, JIT compilers kick in when an applet is about to be interpreted by the JVM and compile an applet into faster-executing machine code.

Now you understand why Java is slow, but exactly what can you do in Java Studio to improve the performance of applets? Let's take a look at the impact of choosing various components on file size.

Measure Up: Component Sizes

We've already discussed that one of the best ways to improve the performance is to keep an eye on the size of files for applets. Are you curious whether any components are space hogs? We tested each component by creating a design containing just that one component. We generated the design as an applet and as a JavaBean. Then, we repeated the test for every component on the component palette. The results of our tests are shown in Table 21.1.

Table 21.1   Size of components, generated as applets and Beans.

Tab	Component	Size Of Zip File (Applet)	Size Of JAR File (Bean)
GUI	Label	173K	104K
	Button	181	109
	Checkbox	182	109
	Choice	189	113
	Text Field	183	110
	Text Area	181	109
	List	190	113
	Scrollbar	187	112
	Slider	187	111
	Menu	187	111
	Ticker Tape	193	116
	Label3D	191	114
	Spin Control	218	128
	Floating Text Field	197	118
	Direction Button	202	120
Data Flow	Distributor	181	109
	Merger	177	107
	If	181	109
	Switch	173	105
	Multiplexor	170	103
	External Connector	164	100
	Adapter	170	103
	Memory	171	103
	Sequence Generator	177	107
	Timer	183	110
Computation	Arithmetic	180	109
	Logical	182	110
	Relational	184	110
	String Function	187	112
	Math	174	106
	Expression Evaluator	177	107

(continued)

Table 21.1 Size of components, generated as applets and Beans *(continued)*.

Tab	Component	Size Of Zip File (Applet)	Size Of JAR File (Bean)
	Logic Evaluator	180K	109K
	Stack	173	104
	Constant	174	105
Multimedia	Image Map	193	116
	Sound Player	178	107
	Animator	182	110
	MontageLite	241	143
Internet	URL Opener	182	109
Database	Simple DBAccess	393	208
	TableOutput	287	163
	Validation Text Field	216	127
Debug	Debug	174	105

Interesting, isn't it? With the exception of some of the components on the Database tab, each component generates files that are pretty much the same size. So, the next logical question is, "How much does the file size change with the addition of more components?" See Table 21.2 for the results of our tests.

Table 21.2 File sizes of various designs.

Description Of Design	Size Of Zip File (Applet)	Size Of JAR File (Bean)
1 Label and 1 Button	190K	104K
2 Labels and 1 Button	190	114
10 Labels and 1 Button	191	114
10 Labels, 1 Button, and 1 Simple DBAccess	414	219
10 Labels, 1 Button, 1 Simple DBAccess, with all connectors selected for all 10 Labels	418	221
1 Label and 1 Button, but label text is 32 points, with Zapf Dingbats as the font	190	104

As you can see in Table 21.2, adding more components only changes the file size in fairly small increments. In designs with Database tab components that are larger, the file size is also only incrementally larger than if the Database component was the only item in the design.

We also tested what happens to file sizes by changing the size of the GUI window to be very large and very small. It did not seem to affect the size of the Zip file.

Our conclusion is that it matters very little:

- Which components you choose, except for the Database tab components.

- How many components you use.

- How many connectors you choose on the components.

- Which characteristics the components have, such as the font family or font size.

- What size the GUI window is.

If these choices, internal to Java Studio, don't significantly affect file size, then we are left with external methods to improve performance.

The Most Bang For Your Buck: Three Ways To Improve Performance

First of all, it's clear that if you use Java Studio, the size of the Zip file or JAR file doesn't vary much, except if you use one or two big components. So, let's review the methods you *can* use to improve performance:

- Use JAR files.

- Don't use components that can be coded in plain HTML.

- Change the users' perception of download time by telling them ahead of time about the applet load time.

In the next few sections, we'll review each of these methods.

Method 1: Use JAR Files

Using JAR files is the technique we used in Chapter 20 for the first revision. JAR files allow compression, whereas Zip files do not. Of course, you already know that you can only use JAR files for users who are running Navigator 4 or Internet Explorer 4. So, what can you do for users running earlier browsers?

You can continue to use Zip files for Navigator 3 or something called CAB files for Internet Explorer 3. CAB files are Cabinet files (think of storing objects in a cabinet). For more information on CAB files, see **www.microsoft.com/workshop/management/ cab/overview.asp**.

When you write the applet code, remember to accommodate older versions of browsers that don't understand applets. For example, Listing 21.1 displays HTML code that offers a message for users with browsers that don't understand the **<APPLET>** tag.

Listing 21.1   HTML code for older browsers.

```
<HTML>
<HEAD>
<TITLE>Welcome to our home on the Web!</TITLE>
</HEAD>
<BODY>
<H1>Welcome to Hello, Indiana!</H1>
<APPLET
  NAME="chapter20_example"
  CODE="VJad22ecc93bc"
  CODEBASE="classes"
  ARCHIVE="chapter20_example.jar"
  WIDTH="403"
  HEIGHT="378">
</APPLET>
<P>This applet displays an image map
for the Hello, Indiana site. I'm sorry,
but your browser does not understand applets,
so you won't be able to use this applet.</P>
</BODY>
</HTML>
```

Note that this primarily affects Internet Explorer 2 and the very earliest version of Navigator. So, we hope only a small percentage of users will be affected.

If your users have the Navigator 3 or Explorer 3 browsers, which do not support JAR files on the **ARCHIVE** parameter, the browsers will discard the **ARCHIVE** parameter. Then, the browsers will look for the necessary CLASS files on the applet's server in the subdirectory specified by the **CODEBASE** parameter. To accommodate users with Navigator 3 and Explorer 3 browsers, make sure you upload all the needed CLASS files, in addition to the JAR file, so the applet will run for those users.

Method 2: Don't Use Some Components

This may seem a little inelegant, but it's a basic truth. Don't use Java Studio to do something that can be done in plain HTML. For example, you already know that you should use HTML to include an image map in your Web site, and you've seen the HTML code at the end of Chapter 20.

If you only want headings, don't use the Label component. Use HTML tags, such as **<H1> Heading1</H1>** and **<H2>Heading2</H2>**. Of course, using the Label components within a design to document the use of fields is not only appropriate but also necessary. And, as we've seen, it doesn't really cost you anything in terms of file size.

One of the components available in the contrib directory is called Lines Rounded. It displays a nice horizontal rule in your design. If you can break your design into pieces, you can use the HTML horizontal rule tag instead, such as **<HR SRC="colorfulrule.gif">**.

Method 3: Provide Feedback

You can improve a user's perception of load time by providing feedback before the applet loads and while it's processing information. For example, the code in Listing 21.2 displays the image of an hourglass and a text warning that an applet is loading. This keeps your users from wondering what the gray box is and why the page appears frozen.

Listing 21.2   HTML code to let users know an applet is going to load.

```
<IMG SRC="hourglass.gif" ALIGN=left>
<P>Please wait while the applet loads...</P>
```

Even better, give your users a choice whether they want to load an applet or not.

The Need For Speed

Now that you're aware of the options, use them to improve the performance of your Java Studio designs. Users have a deep-seated need for speed, and you now have techniques to satisfy them. With Java Studio, you won't be ready for the race-car circuit of the programming world, but you can improve results for your users.

In the next two chapters, we explore debugging Java Studio designs. That is, if you haven't already skipped ahead to those chapters. As you'll read, we share your frustrations with Java Studio.

Chapter 22

Testing And Debugging Java Studio Designs

My five-year-old calls this the ladybug chapter, because the Debug component looks like a ladybug. You might call the Debug component your saving grace, because that ladybug helps uncover some of the mysteries of Java Studio.

You might be reading this chapter out of order, because you are confounded by some of Java Studio's behaviors. Fortunately, the Debug component offers a lot of information. It doesn't tell you how to solve problems, but at least you can decipher what is happening to your design.

In this chapter, we'll build one of the more complex designs presented in this book. We do this partly because complex designs seem to engender the need for debugging and because it seems an appropriate ending for this book.

The design converts a decimal number to hexadecimal. This is handy for specifying the background color on Web pages and matching it to the background color you choose for your applets. When you customize the background of the GUI window (using the Customize|GUI Window command), the colors are shown in the Color Chooser window specified with decimal numbers for the red, green, and blue values, as shown in Figure 22.1.

Now, you might be asking, "Why do I need to know the hexadecimal version of these numbers?" You need the hexadecimal versions of numbers because that's how you specify them as the background color in HTML code. Listing 22.1 displays typical HTML code in which the background color is specified as sky blue, which has the decimal number value of red=135, green=206, and blue=205. In hexadecimal, that's red=87, green=ce, and blue=fa.

Figure 22.1
The Color Chooser defines colors with decimal values for red, green, and blue.

Listing 22.1   This Web page has a sky blue background.

```
<HTML>
<HEAD>
<TITLE>A Sky Blue Background</TITLE>
<BODY
    BGCOLOR="87cefa"
    TEXT="000000"
    LINK="8a2be2"
    VLINK="ff00ff">
</HEAD>
```

By having a tool that easily converts decimal numbers to hexadecimal, you can leisurely choose a pleasing background color in the Color Chooser window, and then modify the code on your Web page to match. You don't have to struggle to find the exact color in the Color Chooser that matches the background of your Web site.

Knowing you'll have the power of this in your hands just makes your head spin, doesn't it? Well, okay—maybe it's not *that* exciting, but it will at least be an interesting design.

In this chapter, we'll first plan our design. Then, we'll work on building a Packaged Design that takes a number from 10 through 15 and converts it to the hexadecimal equivalent, which is A through F. After generating the Packaged Design, we'll work out some problems in one section of the main design, and then we'll complete the design.

Plan Dec2Hex

Let's talk through the design, which we'll call Dec2Hex. We know that users will enter numbers from 0 through 255, because the values for the colors in a red/green/blue palette are only valid from 0 through 255.

The resulting hexadecimal number is a maximum of two digits, between 00 and FF. For those of you who might feel a little rusty with hexadecimal, the first digit represents how many sets of 16 are in the number, and the second digit represents how many 1s are in the number. As mentioned earlier, 10 is represented by the letter A, 11 is represented by the letter B, and so on, until 15 is represented by the letter F.

A Shortcut

For those of you lacking the energy right now, you can skip this section. Go ahead and grab the design from this book's companion CD-ROM. The design is called chapter20_ convert.vj. Copy the design to your hard disk, open it in Java Studio, and generate it as a Packaged Design. Then, you can skip to the section, "Build A Truncate Design."

To obtain the first digit in a hexadecimal number, you divide the input by 16 to determine the number of whole sets of 16 in the input number. If the result is from 10 through 15, it needs to be truncated and then converted to values A through F. For example, if the number is 10.125, it needs to be truncated to 10 and converted to A. If the number is 15.55, the number needs to be truncated to 15 and converted to F.

If the resulting number is less than 10, the number needs to be truncated. For example, if the number is 4.25, you need to truncate it to 4. So, your first digit has been converted to a digit from 0 through 9 or a letter from A through F.

For the second digit, you need to determine the remainder after dividing by 16. With the remainder, you can go through the same evaluation and conversion process as for the first digit. That is, if the number is greater than 10, it needs to be truncated and converted to A through F. If the number is less than 10, it needs to be truncated. Then, you have your second digit.

This quick review provides the basis of how the Dec2Hex design will work. In the next section, we'll build a Packaged Design to handle some of the function of the design.

Build A Convert Design

Why are we slicing off a chunk of the design into a Packaged Design? For two reasons:

- The conversion is performed twice—once for the first digit and once for the second digit.
- If all the work is done in the main design, the Design window wouldn't be big enough to include everything, unless you have a mondo monitor.

The Convert design has many components in it, but it's not a complex design. It repeats the same steps six times, for the resulting values A through F. The first section describes the basic design. Then, the next section tells you how to duplicate the design five more times. After that, we'll finish the design and generate it as a Packaged Design.

The Basic Design

In this part of the design, we'll check if the number is greater than or equal to 10 and if the number is less than 11. If the result of both evaluations is true, then the letter A is sent to output.

If you don't already have Java Studio running, start it now.

1. On the Computation tab on the palette, select the Relational component and place it in the Design window. Name the component ">=10", and in the Function area, select the Is Greater Than Or Equal To function. Then, select the Set The Right Value To A Constant checkbox. Specify 10 in the checkbox's field, as shown in Figure 22.2. Click OK to close the customizer.

2. Add another Relational component called "<11". In the Function area, select the Is Less Than function. Select the Set The Right Value To A Constant checkbox, and specify 11 in the field after the checkbox. Click OK to close the customizer.

3. Add a Logical component, and name it "AND". In the Function area, select the AND function, as shown in Figure 22.3. Click OK to close the customizer.

4. Add a Constant component, and click in the Design window to the right of the components. Name the component "Const A", and specify "A" in the Value field, as shown in Figure 22.4. Click OK to close the customizer.

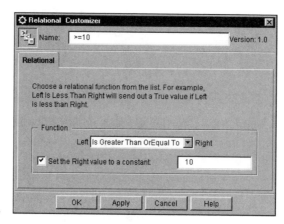

Figure 22.2
Add a Relational component called >=10.

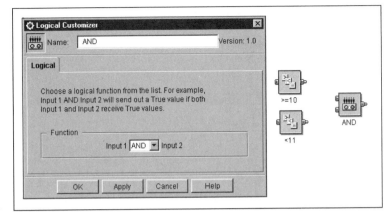

Figure 22.3
Add a Logical
component called AND.

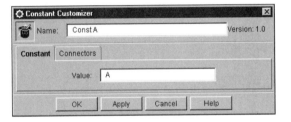

Figure 22.4
Add a Constant
component named
Const A.

5. On the Data Flow tab, select the If component, and click in the Design window to the right of the components. Name the component "If 10", and click OK to close the customizer.

6. Add a Distributor component to the left side of the components. Leave the default name, and add one more connector for a total of three output connectors.

7. Add a Text Field component on the left side of the Distributor component, and add another one on the right side of the components. It doesn't matter what you name them, because we're only using them temporarily.

8. Connect the components using the information in Table 22.1.

   Your design should appear similar to Figure 22.5. Note that the bottom output connector of the If component is not connected to anything.

9. Save your design as chap22_convert.

10. Now, you can test this little piece of design. Switch to the GUI window, and make sure you know which is the input

Table 22.1   Connect the components.

Connect This Connector	To This Connector
Output connector of the first Text Field	Input connector of the Distributor component
First output connector of the Distributor component	Input connector of the >=10 Relational component
Second output connector of the Distributor component	Input connector of the <11 Relational component
Third output connector of the Distributor component	Trigger connector of the Const A Constant component
Output connector of the >=10 Relational component	Top input connector of the AND Logical component
Output connector of the <11 Relational component	Bottom input connector of the AND Logical component
Output connector of the AND Logical component	Top (north) input connector of the If 10 If component
Output connector of the Const A Constant component	Left input connector of the If 10 If component
Top output connector of the If 10 If component	Input connector of the last Text Field component

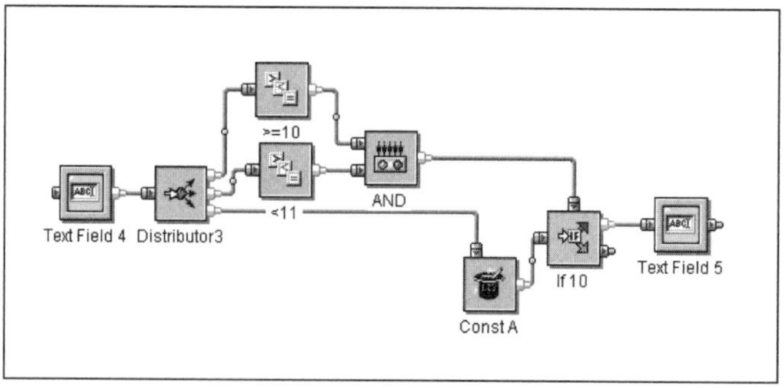

Figure 22.5
Your Design window should appear similar to this.

Text Field and which is the output Text Field. If you're not sure, switch to the Design window, select the input Text Field, and then switch to the GUI window. The selected field is the input Text Field.

Enter a number in the input text field that is somewhere from 10.0 through 10.999, and press Enter. The result should be A. After you test a number, clear both Text Field components before testing another number. You can also test numbers less than 10 and more than 10.999, so you can see that the output field remains blank.

11. When you are done testing, disconnect the Distributor component from the two Relational components, and move the Distributor and the input Text Field out of the way for now. Disconnect the If component from the output Text Field, and move the Text Field out of the way for now.

With this part of the design working satisfactorily, we can propagate it five more times.

Five More Times

The basic design for our Convert design is repeated five more times, because we are evaluating numbers that can fit through six gates. If the number passes through the first gate, the design generates an A. If the number passes through the second gate, the design generates a B, and so on until we reach the letter F.

In the basic design in the previous section, we created a gate that evaluated whether a number was greater than or equal to 10 and if it was less than 11. The second gate evaluates whether the number is greater than or equal to 11 and if it is less than 12, and so on. For the purposes of creating this design, we are going to name each gate after the result. So, the first gate is called the A Gate, the second gate is called the B Gate, and so on.

Use Table 22.2 to create the components for B Gate through F Gate, just as you did for A Gate. (You might want to take a peek at Figure 22.7, so you can get a visual goal in mind.)

You can connect the gate components as you go along, or you can wait until you've placed all the gate components and then connect them all at once. For now, there are no connections to the input connectors of the Relational components nor is there a connection to the trigger connector of the Constant component. Figure 22.6 displays the connections you can make now within the gate components.

When the gate components are in place and internally connected, then you're ready to finish the design.

Table 22.2 Create the components for B Gate through F Gate.

Gate	Component	Name Of Component	Values To Set In Customizer
B	Relational	>=11	Is Greater Than Or Equal To; set the right value to 11
	Relational	<12	Is Less Than; set the right value to 12
	Logical	AND	AND
	Constant	Const B	B
	If	If 11	(no values to set)
C	Relational	>=12	Is Greater Than Or Equal To; set the right value to 12
	Relational	<13	Is Less Than; set the right value to 13
	Logical	AND	AND
	Constant	Const C	C
	If	If 12	(no values to set)
D	Relational	>=13	Is Greater Than Or Equal To; set the right value to 13
	Relational	<14	Is Less Than; set the right value to 14
	Logical	AND	AND
	Constant	Const D	D
	If	If 13	(no values to set)
E	Relational	>=14	Is Greater Than Or Equal To; set the right value to 14
	Relational	<15	Is Less Than; set the right value to 15
	Logical	AND	AND
	Constant	Const E	E
	If	If 14	(no values to set)
F	Relational	>=15	Is Greater Than Or Equal To; set the right value to 15
	Relational	<16	Is Less Than; set the right value to 16
	Logical	AND	AND
	Constant	Const F	F
	If	If 15	(no values to set)

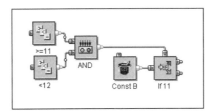

Figure 22.6
Internally connect the
gate components.

Finish The Convert Design

To finish the Convert design, you need to modify the existing
Distributor component, add a Merger component, and complete
the remaining connections. Then, you can test the design.

1. Move the Distributor component and the connected Text
   Field component to the middle of the Design window along
   the left border.

2. Right-click the Distributor component, and choose Customize. The Distributor component currently has three
   connectors: two default connectors and one connector that
   you added earlier. Add 15 more connectors, and then click
   OK to close the customizer.

3. On the Data Flow tab on the palette, select the Merger
   component. Click the Design window on the right side of the
   design. Add four more connectors to the two connectors that
   come with the Merger, for a total of six output connectors.

4. Find the orphan Text Field component you used during
   testing as the output Text Field. Move it next to the Merger
   component, and connect the output connector of the
   Merger component to the input connector of the Text Field
   component.

5. Now, you need to connect the 18 output connectors of the
   Distributor component. Each of the six gates gets three output
   connectors—one for each of the Relational components, and
   one for the trigger connector on the Constant component.
   Connect the output connectors of the Distributor component
   to the appropriate input connectors, as shown in Figure 22.7.

6. Connect the top output connector of the If component in
   each gate to an input connector on the Merger component.

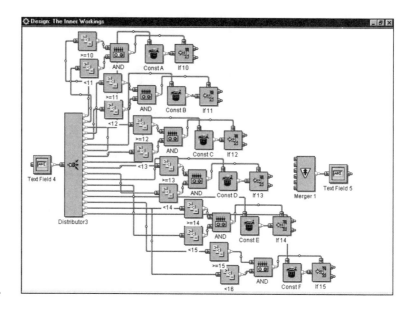

Figure 22.7
Connect all the output connectors of the Distributor component.

7. All the connections are now complete. Switch to the GUI window, and experiment by specifying a variety of numbers from 10 through 15.999. Make sure you test floating-point numbers, such as 10.125, in addition to integers, such as 10.

Prepare To Generate A Packaged Design

Is your testing complete? Okay, let's prepare the design for generation as a Packaged Design.

1. Delete both Text Field components.

2. On the Data Flow tab, select the External Connector component. Click the Design window on the left side, next to the Distributor component. Select the Imports Messages radio button, as shown in Figure 22.8.

3. Connect this External Connector to the input connector of the Distributor component.

4. Add another External Connector component on the right side of the design. This time, select the Exports Messages radio button. Connect the output connector of the Merger component to the input connector of the External Connector component.

Now, the Convert design is complete, so we can generate it as a Packaged Design.

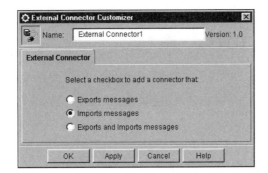

Figure 22.8
Add an External
Connector component
that imports messages.

Generate A Packaged Design

We're going to generate the Convert design as a Packaged Design, because we want to encapsulate it for use in another Java Studio design. And, for now, we don't intend to share it with anyone else or to use it in another development environment. If that was true, then we might generate it as a Bean. But, because we're only using the Convert design internally, generating it as a Packaged Design is easier and faster.

1. Save your design.

2. From the Generate menu, choose Packaged Design.

3. You can use the default names, if you like. Click Next.

4. Choose a name for the component, such as Convert. Specify a description, such as "Convert 10 through 15 to A through F", as shown in Figure 22.9. Click Next.

5. You can leave the default image for the icon. Click Next.

6. Leave the default and allow the component to be automatically imported on to the User tab. Click Next.

7. Because you have External Connector components, you can choose where the connectors they represent appear on the component. The defaults should show the first External Connector appearing on the West side of the component, and the second External Connector appearing on the East side of the component. Click Next.

8. Click Finish.

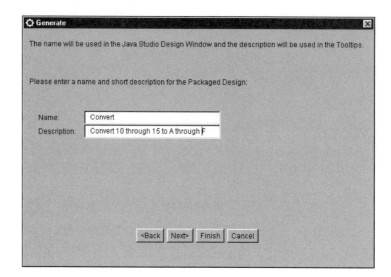

Figure 22.9
Choose a name and a description for the component.

When Java Studio finishes generating the design, it appears as a component on the User tab. When this is complete, you can proceed to the next section to work on a piece of the Dec2Hex design.

If you are experimenting with the Convert design and end up generating multiple versions of the component, you may be interested in a few tips:

- Every time you generate a Packaged Design, Java Studio needs a unique JAR file name. By default, Java Studio changes the JAR file names by incrementing a number and appending it to the design file name.

- After you have added two or three new components to the User tab, delete some. Too many components on the User tab seem to cause problems, such as slowing down Java Studio's performance or even crashing.

- After you delete a component, you need to restart Java Studio before importing a component by the same name.

With those tips tucked in your head, you are now ready to work on the Dec2Hex design.

Build A Truncate Design

The Dec2Hex has a portion of the design that truncates a floating point number to an integer. For example, the number 3.14159 truncates to 3. We could use the Math component and choose the Floor function, which always rounds a number down to the nearest integer that is less than the current number. The concept is the same, but it's not quite right for our purposes, because the Floor function always returns a number with a decimal point and a zero. For example, **Truncate(3.94159)** returns **3.0**. We need just the first digit, because we want to slide the digit into the resulting hexadecimal number, and we need a single digit to represent each place in the hexadecimal number.

To build the truncate portion of the Dec2Hex design, follow these steps:

1. If you haven't already done so, open the File menu, and choose New. If asked, save your current design.

2. On the GUI tab on the palette, select the Text Field component. Place one in the Design window on the left. Name it "Input TF". Click OK to close the customizer.

3. On the Data Flow tab, select the Distributor component. Place it to the right of the Input TF component. Leave the default name, and add one more connector to the two default connectors. Click OK.

4. On the Computation tab, select the Constant component. Place it to the right of the Distributor component. Name it "Const 0", and leave the default value 0 in the Value field. Click OK.

5. Add another Constant component, and place it below the Const 0 component. Name this one "Const 1", and specify 1 in the Value field. Click OK.

6. On the Computation tab, select the String Function component. Place it to the right of the Constant components. Name it "String Substring", and open the drop-down field to find the Substring function. Select the Substring function, and click OK.

7. On the GUI tab, select the Text Field component. Place it to the right of the String Substring component, and name it "Output TF". Click OK.

8. Use Table 22.3 to connect the connectors.

Your design should appear similar to Figure 22.10.

Time to test the design. Enter numbers such as 10.2, 1.0345, 15.99, and so on. Working okay? Then, let's forge ahead with more of the Dec2Hex design.

In the next part of the design, we use the Input TF component as the field to collect the decimal number to convert to hexadecimal. We distribute the number to two areas—one area evaluates

Table 22.3   Connect the components of the truncate portion of the design.

Connect This Connector	To This Connector
Output connector of the Input TF component component	Input connector of the Distributor
Top output connector of the Distributor component	Top input connector of the String Substring component
Middle output connector of the Distributor component	Trigger connector of the Const 0 component
Bottom output connector of the Distributor component	Trigger connector of the Const 1 component
Output connector of the Const 0 component	Middle input connector of the String Substring component
Output connector of the Const 1 component	Bottom input connector of the String Substring component
Output connector of the String Substring component	Input connector of the Output TF component.

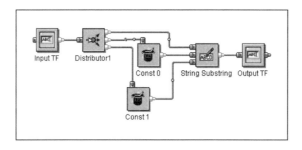

Figure 22.10
The truncate portion of the design.

the number for the whole sets of 16 in the number, and the other area evaluates the number for the singles in the number. For now, we're just focusing on the first area.

After distributing the number to the first area, we divide it by 16 and display the results. Then, we evaluate whether the number is less than 10. If it is, then it is sent to the truncate portion of the design we built earlier in this section. If the number's not less than 10, then we can send it to our Convert component to convert to a letter.

Follow these steps to build the first area of the design:

1. Disconnect the Input TF component from the Distributor component. Move the Input TF component to the far left side of the Design window.

2. On the Data Flow tab, select the Distributor component. Add a new Distributor component to the right of the Input TF component. Add one more connector for a total of three output connectors, and click OK.

3. On the Computation tab, select the Relational component. Add it to the right of the Distributor component. Name the component "Divide by 16". In the Function area, open the drop-down box, and select the slash (/). Select the Set The Right Value To A Constant checkbox, and enter 16 in the field, as shown in Figure 22.11. Click OK.

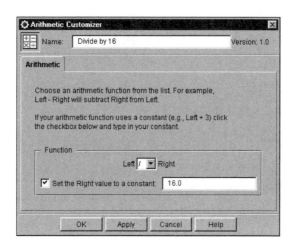

Figure 22.11
Add a Relational component called Divide by 16.

4. On the GUI tab, select the Text Field component. Place the Text Field component to the right of the Divide by 16 component. Leave the default name, because we're only going to use it to test the design along the way. Add a connector to trigger the component, and then click OK.

5. On the Data Flow tab, select the Distributor component. Place it to the right of the new Text Field component, and leave the default number of connectors. Click OK.

6. On the Computation tab, select the Relational component. Place it to the right of the newest Distributor component, and name it "Less Than 10?" In the Function area, display the drop-down field, and select Is Less Than. Select the Set The Right Value To A Constant checkbox, and enter 10 in the field. Click OK.

7. On the Data Flow tab, select the If component. Place it below the Less Than 10? Relational component. Name it "If < 10", and click OK.

8. Use Table 22.4 to connect the components. See Figure 22.12 for a view of the Design window.

Now, we can test this part of the design. We only have it hooked up to evaluate numbers from 0 through 159, so switch to the GUI window and try entering some numbers within the appropriate range. You should see the results of the Divide By 16 function appear in the temporary Text Field component. But, the Output TF component doesn't seem to be getting the signal. What's wrong? Let's take a look at how we can use the Debug component to help us pinpoint the problem.

Using The Debug Component

The Debug component is the only component on the Debug tab. Place the Debug component at key points in your design to determine the answers to several questions, such as:

• Does the signal get to the Debug component?

• If the signal arrives, what is the content of the signal?

Table 22.4   Connect the components.

Connect This Component	To This Component
Output connector of the Input TF component	Input connector of the Distributor component
Top output connector of the Distributor component	Input connector of the Divide by 16 component
Output connector of the Divide by 16 component	Input connector of the temporary Text Field component
Output connector of the temporary Text Field component	Input connector of the next Distributor component
Top output connector of the Distributor component	Input connector of the Less Than 10? component
Bottom output connector of the Distributor component	Input connector of the If 10 component
Output connector of the Less Than 10? component	Top (North) connector of the If 10 component
Top output connector of the If 10 component	Input connector of the Distributor component that starts the truncate portion of the design

Figure 22.12
The first area of the design is built and connected to the truncate portion of the design.

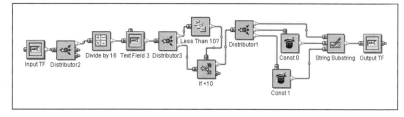

Use the Debug component to debug the Convert design by following these steps:

1. On the Debug tab, select the Debug component. Click anywhere in the Design window. The customizer for the Debug component displays, as shown in Figure 22.13. Leave the default choice to send debug messages to the Java Console window. Click OK.

2. Insert the Debug component between the temporary Text Field component and the Distributor component, as shown in Figure 22.14.

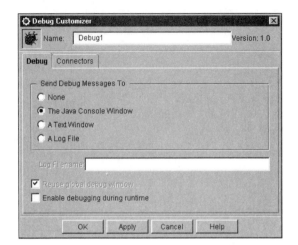

Figure 22.13
The Debug component has several choices enabling you to specify where to send debug messages.

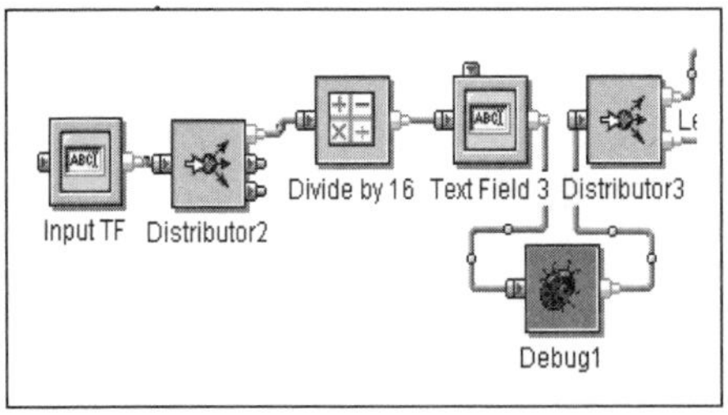

Figure 22.14
Insert a Debug component.

3. Switch to the GUI window, and test another number from 0 through 159. What happened? Again, the temporary Text Field displayed the results of the Divide by 16 component, and, of course, no change in the Output TF component. But another event didn't happen. We didn't see the Java Console window appear. The Java Console window appears any time it receives input, so it means that the signal never left the temporary Text Field component, and it never got to the Debug component.

4. Go to the first Distributor component in the design, the one connected to the Input TF component, and connect one of the output connectors to the trigger connector on the temporary Text Field component. Now, switch to the GUI window and test a number from 0 through 159.

This time, the Java Console window should appear, as shown in Figure 22.15. As you can see in the figure, the Debug component called Debug1 received a message from the

Figure 22.15
The Java Studio Java Console displays the message intercepted by a Debug component.

component called Text Field 1. Debug1 then sent the message to the Distributor 2 component, and the contents of the message were 2.5 \r. In the console window, the \r represents when a user has pressed Enter or Return.

5. Continue to test a few more numbers. Every time you do, another set of debug messages is appended to the existing debug messages in the Java Console window. You can scroll in the Java Console window to see all of the messages.

   It appears that the signal is now getting through all the way to the Output TF component. Great!

6. We don't need the temporary Text Field component any more, because the Debug component is performing the same function for us. Delete the temporary Text Field, and leave the Debug component in place. Also, modify the first Distributor component to remove one output connector. You only need a total of two output connectors.

Now that we have this problem shaken out of our design, we can finish the rest of the design.

Finish Dec2Hex

In this section, we'll first finish the work we started by filling in the components that deal with the number if it is greater than 10. Then, we'll start working on the second area, which is where the design evaluates and processes the number that goes in the singles place in the resulting hexadecimal number. After we obtain the digit, it goes through the same process as the first area, where we determine if it's less than 10. If so, we'll truncate the number. If not, we'll send the number to the Convert component to change it to an alphabetic letter. After that, we'll merge the resulting digits, in the correct order, and send it to the Output TF. Finally, we'll slap on a few labels to document our fields, and the design will be done.

First, let's finish the first area of the design by following these steps:

1. Disconnect the Output TF component from the String Substring component. Move the Output TF component to the far right side of the design.

2. Look for the If 10 component. Place a Convert component to the right of the If 10 component. The Convert component should be on your User tab, if you imported the Packaged Design you built at the beginning of this chapter. Leave the default name for the Convert component, and click OK.

3. On the Data Flow tab, select the Merger component, and place it to the right of the Convert component.

4. Use Table 22.5 to connect these components. Figure 22.16 displays this area of the Design window after connecting these components.

Table 22.5   Connect the newest components.

Connect This Connector	To This Connector
Bottom output connector of the If 10 component	Input connector of the Convert component
Output connector of the String Substring component	Top input connector of the Merger component
Output connector of the Convert component	Bottom input connector of the Merger component

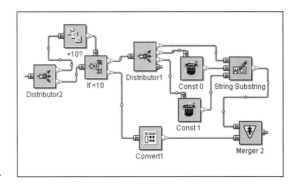

Figure 22.16
The first area is finished.

Now, we can process the number that represents the singles in the hexadecimal number.

5. Look for the first Distributor component on the left side of the Design. On the Computation tab, select the Expression Evaluator component, and place it to the right of the Distributor component. Name the component "Remainder", and in the Expression To Evaluate field, specify "a%16", as shown in Figure 22.17. The percent sign represents a MOD function, or a remainder function. The result is the whole number that is left over after performing division by the number to the right of the percent. For example, 16%16 is 0; 18%16 is 2, and 33%16 is 1.

6. Add a Debug component to the right of the Remainder component.

7. Connect the bottom output connector of the Distributor component to the input connector of the Remainder component.

8. Connect the output connector of the Remainder component to the input connector of the Debug component.

9. For the rest of this area, go back and review Figure 22.16. Repeat every component displayed in Figure 22.16 for the second area of the design. Figure 22.18 displays the Design window after you complete this task.

Figure 22.17
Add an Expression Evaluator component, and specify an expression to get the remainder after dividing by 16.

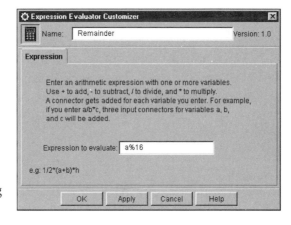

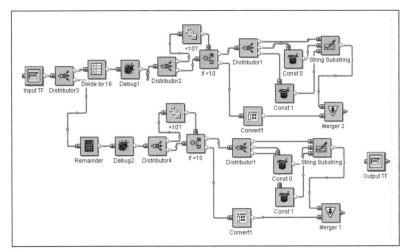

Figure 22.18
The Design window, after the second area has been added to the design.

Hold on, we're almost done. We only have three more components to add—one String component, and two Label components.

10. On the Computation tab, select the String component. Place it on the right side of the design, near the Output TF component. Name the component "String Prepend". In the Function area, open the drop-down field, and choose the function Prepend(a,b). Click OK.

11. Connect the output connector of the Merger component for the top area to the top input connector of the String Prepend component. Then, connect the output connector of the bottom Merger component to the bottom input connector of the String Prepend component.

12. Connect the output connector of the String Prepend component to the input connector of the Output TF component.

13. Add two labels to the GUI window for each of the Text Field components. Specify the label text for one as "Enter a decimal number (0-255)". Specify the label text for the second field as "Hexadecimal".

Whew! That was a chunk of work, wasn't it? Well, now we have a useful little utility to help us figure out the hexadecimal equivalents of numbers.

Call Yourself An Exterminator

You're now well qualified to use the Debug component to track down and destroy any bugs in Java Studio designs. But, as you may have already learned, sometimes the Debug component isn't enough to fix problems in Java Studio designs. Chapter 23 offers some tips and techniques for shaking out the bugs in just about any design.

Chapter 23

Understanding Debugging Java Studio Designs

Unless you have some deep-seated, karmic understanding of how Java Studio works, using the Debug component is just the beginning. This chapter offers you several tips on how to force a stubborn design to work.

This chapter starts by reviewing the more interesting aspects of the Dec2Hex design. Then, it goes into more detail on how to use the Debug component. Finally, this chapter reveals our hard-earned tips and tricks for Java Studio.

About Dec2Hex

There are a few areas in the Dec2Hex design we built in Chapter 22 that we want to review. The next few sections discuss a minor testing technique that we used when building the Convert Packaged Design, review why we deleted Text Field components and replaced them with External Connector components in the Convert Packaged Design, and look at more details of the Substring function in the String Function component.

Clearing Text Fields

After building the first piece of the Convert Packaged Design, we started testing the design. You were instructed to enter a number in the input text field from 10.0 through 10.999 and to press Enter. Then, after you tested a number, you were told to clear both text fields before testing another number. Why? Because you need to know the results of each test. The way we set up the design meant that the output text field is not cleared before or after displaying a result. So, if you enter a number less than 10.0 or greater than 10.999, the field will still appear to have an A in it because the results of the previous test (presumably using an in-bounds number) have not been cleared. The output text field should be blank, because, if a number falls outside the bounds, the False path is taken in the If component and it doesn't lead anywhere.

Deleting Both Text Field Components

At the end of building the Convert Packaged Design, we instructed you to delete both text fields. Why? Because when you use the Convert component in the Dec2Hex design, you want to send a number to the Convert component and receive the correct letter in return. You don't want to see any text fields appear in the GUI window when you add the Convert component to your design. The Convert component is just a processing component—it doesn't need to (and shouldn't) have any elements visible in the GUI window.

On the other hand, when we developed and tested the design, we left the text fields in the design when we generated it as a Packaged Design. You may find this helpful when you are working on a new design. This technique allowed us to see what was actually happening as a message was passed to the Convert component and then processed. But after we were satisfied that the Convert design was working as expected, we deleted the text fields and replaced them with External Connectors, as shown in Figure 23.1.

Using External Connectors allows us to control the connectors on the component. By adding an External Connector that imports messages, we defined an input connector. The second External Connector, which exports messages, became an output connector.

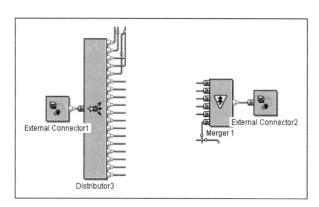

Figure 23.1
Both Text Field components were replaced with External Connector components.

Using The Substring Function

The Dec2Hex design is the first time we used a String Function component, as shown in Figure 23.2. For a complete description of the functions of the String Function component, see Appendix A.

The Substring function of the String Function component is relatively easy, once you understand how to use it. The purpose of the Substring function is to extract a substring from a specified string. You specify the substring by sending the index of the substring and the length of the substring. The index starts at zero. So, Substring(hello, 0, 2) returns *he*, because the index is set to 0 and the length of the substring is set to 2. For our use, we know we want only the very first digit of a floating-point number. So, we called it the truncate function, because that's how we adapted the Substring function for the purpose of this design. The truncate function is displayed in Figure 23.3. We set up constants using the number 0 to specify the index and 1 to specify the length of the substring.

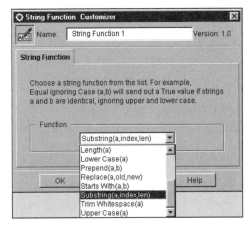

Figure 23.2
The String Function component has a variety of functions, including Substring.

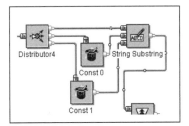

Figure 23.3
The truncate portion of the Dec2Hex design.

Of course, this worked only because we knew the only numbers to be truncated were less than 10. If a number was greater than 10, then it was sent to the Convert component for processing. To adapt the truncate portion of the design for broader purposes, you could specify the index and the length instead of setting up constants. Notice that we triggered the constants in the truncate portion. If you don't send a trigger message to a Constant component, it never sends out the value.

Using The Debug Component

The Debug component can be a lifesaver or, at least, a stress saver. When a design isn't working and it appears that the logic is valid, then insert several Debug components and learn exactly what is happening inside the design.

The Debug component gives you a variety of choices for the destination of the debug messages, as shown in Figure 23.4. In Chapter 22, we kept the default choice of sending messages to the Java Console window. Following is a brief explanation of each choice.

None

You use the None option when you don't want to remove the Debug component yet, but you don't want any debug messages

Figure 23.4
The Debug component offers you choices in the customizer.

▶Tip

No Java
Console Window?

If you add Debug components to watch and you don't see any debug messages pop up in a Java Console window, you might have accidentally deselected the Pop-up On Any Output checkbox on the Java Console window. To view the Java Console window, open the View menu, and chose Java Console.

sent. For example, if you have many Debug components, and you're trying to narrow down the problem, you might turn off the debug messages on some components while you focus on other Debug components.

Java Console Window

The Java Console Window option is used for light debugging, because you can't print the contents of the window unless you copy the text into another application for printing. The messages appear in the Java Console window as soon as any debug messages are received. Until you click the Clear button on the Java Console window, the messages accumulate. Even if you close the Java Console window, the messages remain and appear when the Java Console window appears again.

Text Window

You should use the Text Window option for a variation of using the Java Console window. The text window functions similarly to the Java Console window, except the text window does not offer buttons to clear the window. Also, the text window continues to accumulate messages until you close it. Figure 23.5 shows a typical text window. When you open it again, the file is cleared. When you deselect the Reuse Global Debug Window checkbox, the contents of the messages change in the text window. Instead of appearing in the same format that you see in the Java Console window, only the messages appear. The information specifying the sending component and the receiving component do not appear.

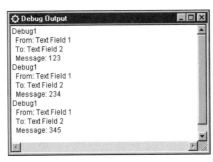

Figure 23.5
The text window messages appear similar to the Java Console window messages.

Log File

The Log File option should be used for more serious debugging. This option sends the debug messages to the file you specify. When you close Java Studio, the file is closed. This is particularly useful when your design is going in an infinite loop. If you think you're having problems with a loop that doesn't end, add Debug components where you have selected to send the messages to a log file. When the design goes infinite, shut down Java Studio (using Ctrl+Alt+Delete, if necessary) and then study the contents of the text file. Most likely, you will be able to pinpoint the source of the problem.

When you specify a log file name, the file is stored in a subdirectory of your Java Studio directory, such as Java-Studio1.0\JS\intel-win32\bin. Figure 23.6 displays the contents of a typical log file.

If you don't specify a log file name, the log file is named VJlog and contains slightly different messages, as shown in Figure 23.7. VJlog is stored in c:\windows\js10\vj\vjlog. If you can't find it, click the Start button, choose Find, click Files Or Folders, and look for the VJlog file. The log file, in this case, doesn't appear to collect debug messages, just Visual Java warnings.

Reuse Global Debug Window

The Reuse Global Debug Window option, as mentioned earlier, allows you to specify whether the template used by the Java Console window for displaying debug messages is used. If you

Figure 23.6
The log file formats the debug messages a little differently than the Java Console window.

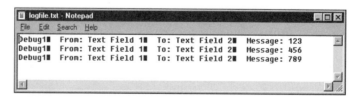

Figure 23.7
The log file appears to log Visual Java messages.

select this checkbox, each debug message includes the name of the Debug component, the names of the sending and receiving components, and the contents of the message. If you deselect this checkbox, the debug message only includes the message and lacks any component information.

Enable Debugging During Runtime

You should select the Enable Debugging During Runtime checkbox if you want to see debug messages after the design has been generated as an applet, application, JavaBean, or Packaged Design. The debug messages appear in whatever container you selected in the Send Debug Messages To area.

And now, finally, you're ready to read our tips and tricks for trying to make Java Studio designs behave.

Tips And Tricks

Before we reveal our tips and tricks, we want you to be aware that we gained a few gray hairs courtesy of Java Studio. There were times when we were ready to throw our laptops out the window, because we were so incredibly frustrated. We know we're not alone in feeling this way, because our technical reviewer has reported problems as well.

The point is that we understand if you've been frustrated. The tips we offer here are not guaranteed fixes—they're ideas for you to try when you're stymied. The Debug component can go a long way toward revealing what is actually happening in your design, but sometimes the information just adds to the confusion.

For example, when creating a Java Studio design for a chapter, we build it and work on it until the bugs are gone. Then we build it again while we write the chapter. While building the Dec2Hex design for the second time, we had problems. This was frustrating because we had a working example that was almost identical, except that some of the component names were slightly different. So, we threw a lot of Debug components into the nonworking design. We discovered that messages were being received at the end of the design before they had entered the design, which didn't make sense. In this case, we solved the problem by starting over, our third and final tip in this chapter.

Our tips include the following:

- It seems that one of the most common problems is that the message being sent through a design stops before it reaches the end of the design. We call this the *Stuck Electrons Syndrome*. If you have this problem, be suspicious of any component that has the possibility of a trigger connector, such as Text Field components and Constant components. They seem to be likely stopping points. Place Debug components before and after suspicious components and see if the message goes through them. If not, add a distributor before the suspicious component so you split the message. Connect one output connector to the input connector to send the message, and connect one output connector to the trigger connector to trigger the message.

  If you have inserted Text Field components to display the progress of the message, and you're having problems with Stuck Electrons Syndrome, try deleting your Text Field components. Sometimes, your design starts working when you remove them.

- Try using the Adapter or Memory components. Both of these components control messages. The Adapter component collects input and sends out its contents whenever any of the input messages change. The Memory component collects input and sends out its output when all the inputs have changed, or you can trigger the Memory component to send out its contents.

- If something just doesn't make sense, delete the components and start over. We've only used this tactic in drastic cases, but amazingly, it works. When you've studied your design and know that the logic is sound, and the Debug components are reporting debug messages that are illogical, it might be time to try this drastic measure. Perhaps, the root of the problem is some small renegade keystroke and rebuilding the design from scratch eliminates the problem. Whatever it is, leave this option as a last resort, but give it a try when you're almost ready to give up hope.

A Fond Farewell

That's it! That's the whole kit and caboodle. We have emptied our brains on Java Studio and related topics, and you now have the contents in your hands. We wish you designs that always work, users who appreciate your efforts, and a more rigorously tested Java Studio 2.

Appendix A

Components Reference

This reference section offers further details on the predefined components that are provided with Java Studio. It's designed to help the developer-in-a-hurry who wants to quickly:

- Decide which component to use
- Identify what input and output connectors a component requires or supports
- Determine if and how a component can be modified to meet current needs
- Grasp what kinds of content or resources a component requires or supports
- Verify what appearance controls are available for a component

NOTE

Additional component descriptions are available in the Java Studio Components online help section, where they are organized alphabetically and by palette tab. To open the help section for a specific component placed in your design, right-click its icon in the Design window, and select Help.

Components in this reference are grouped into the following four sections and listed alphabetically within each section:

- *Form Components*—Used to create input forms and other formlike functions.
- *Math And Logic Components*—Used to perform specific logical functions or mathematical operations.
- *Show And Go Components*—Used to create visual effects, formatted output, and navigation functions.
- *Toolbox Components*—Used with other components to build applets or applications.

A Terminology Refresher

Just for insurance, let's review some of the basic terminology and concepts you'll see in the component descriptions that follow.

Disable, Enable, And Editable

Many of these components have *disable* and *enable* properties that you can select in the component's customizer dialog box. Don't confuse these with the occasional *shown* and *not shown* properties. Here are a few illustrations of what we mean:

- *If a component is disabled and shown*—For example, it is visible in the GUI window, but you can't use it. It displays with a grayed-out appearance familiar to most GUI users, indicating that this particular component is there, but not usable. For example, you might have a checkbox component for Gift-Wrapping on an order form. Your applet or application should disable that component if the user has indicated that the current purchase is not a gift.

- *If a component is enabled, it can be used (whether it's shown or not)*—For example, let's go back to your order form, where there's another checkbox component for Enclose A Gift Message. If the user selects this checkbox, a handy gift message text field becomes enabled and shown.

- *When setting a component's editable property*—A yes or true setting allows the user to edit the value of that component. If editable is set to no or false, the component's value is displayed, but the user can't edit it.

Triggers

Triggers are messages that tell the receiving component to initiate or launch its intended action or function. (Think of it as a green traffic light or a "go" signal.) Triggers can contain any message content—logical values, strings, numbers, or anything.

True/False Values

When you send true or false messages—typically regarding the enable/disable or shown/not shown states of a component—the message value itself is case-insensitive. In other words, True, true, and TRUE have the same value, just as False, false, and FALSE do.

Form Components

This section describes the Java Studio components that you use to build Java-based forms for user input and data display. Most components function in ways similar to their HTML counterparts—if you've built forms in HTML before, the form components will be fairly familiar.

Checkbox

Palette icon Design icon

| **Usage** | Sends either of two values, depending on its checked or unchecked state, when it is triggered to send output. Use this component to store and send "either/or" values to other components, such as an Arithmetic or Expression Evaluator component, an If component, or a Logical component. The two values can express any two alternative states or conditions, such as on/off, Unix/PC, or domestic/international. You can output (case-insensitive) true/false values to If, Logical, Logic Evaluator, or Stack components. You can output string or numeric values to Arithmetic, Expression Evaluator, Relational, String, Math, Constant, or Stack components. |

Output

Sends the value of the checkbox—as determined by its checked or unchecked state—when triggered.

Custom Connectors

Add custom input connectors to:

- Trigger the component to send the value associated with its current state.
- Hide or show the component when it receives a message with a true (hide) or not-true (show) value.
- Enable or disable the component when it receives a message with a true (enable) or not-true (disable) value.
- Specify the name of the checkbox.
- Set the component's state to checked when it receives a true value, and unchecked when it receives a false value.
- Set the value associated with the component's checked or unchecked state.

Content

Use the Checkbox tab to:

- Enter the name and caption for the component.
- Specify the value sent by the component when in a checked state.
- Specify the value sent by the component when in an unchecked state.

Looks

Use the Standard tab to define the appearance of the component:

- Height and width
- Enabled
- Foreground (color)
- Background (color)
- Font
- Show

Choice

Palette icon Design icon

Usage

Displays a series of items in a drop-down list of choices. Each item is associated with a value. When a user selects an item, the Choice component sends either the item's name or the item's value to the output connector. If the receiving component can handle both values, the Choice component sends both the item name and its value. For example, if you connect your Choice component to the AddString connector of a second Choice component, then any selection in the first Choice component passes the item's name and value to the second Choice component. On the other hand, if you connect the first Choice component to the Select Item connector of the second, then selecting an item from the first Choice component causes any matching item in the second to be selected.

Use this component to give users a selection from among predefined values, especially in situations where a data entry field would invite misspellings or inconsistencies. (Note that the Design window and the final page display show only the selected or first item in the Choice component.)

Output

Sends the name of the selected item and/or its value, depending on the receiving component.

Custom Connectors

Add custom input connectors to:

- Trigger the component to send the value associated with the currently selected item.
- Hide or show the component when it receives a message with a true (hide) or not-true (show) value.
- Enable or disable the component when it receives a message with a true (enable) or not-true (disable) value.
- Add the incoming string (containing an item name and value) to the component.
- Select an item in the list that matches the string value. (Does not automatically trigger the component to send the corresponding value—use a trigger connector to do this.)

Content

Use the Choice tab to:

- Enter the name for the Choice component.

- Enter the name of an item and the value sent when that item is selected.
- Add, remove, or modify an item and/or its value.

Looks   Use the Standard tab to define the appearance of the component:
- Height and width
- Background (color)
- Enabled
- Font
- Foreground (color)
- Show

Note: *For information related to the Choice component, see the List and Menu components.*

Floating-Point Text Field

Palette icon Design icon

Usage   The Floating-Point Text Field component displays a floating-point decimal number in a text field. Use this component to display, accept input of, or send a floating-point number. All floating-point numbers require a minimum of two decimal places.

Note: *You can't send a number to the Floating-Point Text Field from another component. Because the component is, for all intents and purposes, a text field with special formatting, the user needs to enter the number.*

Input   Accepts an input that triggers the component to send its value in text format.

Output   Displays the value of the field in text format.

Custom Connectors   Add custom input connectors to:
- Hide or show the component when it receives a message with a true (hide) or not-true (show) value.
- Enable or disable the component when it receives a message with a true (enable) or not-true (disable) value.

Content   Use the Floating-Point Text Field tab to:
- Enter the name for the floating text field.
- Enter the number text in the field.
- Specify the length and the precision (number of decimal places) for the field.
- Specify the font name, size, and style (bold or italic) used to display text in the field.

Looks   Use the Standard tab to define the appearance of the component:
- Height and width   • Background (color)
- Enabled   • Foreground (color)
- Show

List

Palette icon Design icon

Usage   Displays a series of selectable items in a visible list of choices. Each
list item is associated with a value. When a user selects an item, the
List component sends either the item name or its value to the
output connector. Or, if the receiving component can handle both
values, the List component sends both the item name and its value.

Use the List component to give users a selection from among
predefined values, especially in situations where a data entry field
would invite misspellings or inconsistencies. Note that the List
component shows as many of its items as the size of the
component allows—as compared to the Choice component, which
only displays the first item until you open its drop-down list. You
can also use the List component as a temporary container for such
things as messages to the user or data entry by the user.

Input   Accepts input connectors for item name and item value, and adds
them to the list of choices.

Output   Sends the value of the selected item when triggered.

Custom Connectors   Add custom input connectors to:
- Hide or show the component when it receives a message with a
true (hide) or not-true (show) value.
- Enable or disable the component when it receives a message
with a true (enable) or not-true (disable) value.
- Add the incoming item name and value to the component.
- Select an item in the list by name or position, and remove it
from the list.
- Clear all choices from the list.
- Select an item in the list by name or position. (Does not trigger
the component to send the corresponding value—use a trigger
connector to do this.)

Content

Use the List tab to:

- Enter the name of the List component.
- Enter the name of an item and its value to be added to the list. (If Value is undefined, Java Studio uses the name of the item as its value.)
- Add, remove, or modify a list item name and/or its value.

Looks

Use the Standard tab to define the appearance of the component:

- Height and width
- Enabled
- Foreground (color)
- Background (color)
- Font
- Show

Note: *For information related to the List component, see the Choice and Menu components.*

Menu

Palette icon Design icon

Usage

Displays a series of selectable items in a menu of choices, available from the window's menu bar. Each menu item is associated with a value. When a user selects an item, the Menu component sends either the item name or its value to the output connector. Or, if the receiving component can handle both values, the Menu component sends both the item name and its value.

Use the Menu component to give users a selection from among predefined values, especially in situations where the selections resemble commands or functions that users expect to find in the menu bar. Each item in the menu has its own input and output connectors.

Note: *If your design doesn't have a Menu component and you try to generate an application, Java Studio asks you, by default, if you want to add one—because it assumes you at least want to provide a File|Exit function for your application.*

Input

Accepts an Enable input connector to enable (true) or disable (false) the component.

Content

Use the Menu tab to:

- Enter the name for the Menu component (as shown in the Design window).
- Enter item names and values.

- Add or remove an item and its value to/from the menu.
- Add a separator line to the menu, to visually group menu items for usability.

Note: *For information related to the Menu component, see the Choice and List components.*

Text Area

Palette icon Design icon

Usage

Displays or accepts multiple lines of text. Use the Text Area component to display extended text results or to allow the user to enter extended text. You can control whether entered text is appended to, prepended to, or overwrites existing text.

Input

Accepts text input messages, and appends incoming text to the end of existing text.

Custom Connectors

Add custom input connectors to:

- Hide or show the component when it receives a message with a true (hide) or not-true (show) value.
- Enable or disable the component when it receives a message with a true (enable) or not-true (disable) value.
- Clear all text from the text area.
- Toggle the component's edit configuration on (editable by user) or off.
- Replace existing text with new text.
- Prepend new text by adding text to the beginning of existing text.
- Add an output connector and trigger the text field to output its content text through that connector.

Content

Use the Text Area tab to:

- Enter a name for the component.
- Configure the text area as editable by the user.

Looks

Use the Standard tab to define the appearance of the component:

- Height and width
- Enabled
- Foreground (color)
- Background (color)
- Font
- Show

Note: *For information related to the Text Area component, see the Text Field and Label components.*

Text Field

Palette icon Design icon

Usage

Displays a single line of text, accepts input from the user, and sends the entered text to the output connector when triggered by the Return key or some other connector. If a user enters text, the field value can be sent to any component that accepts text. If a user enters a number, the value can be sent to any component that accepts numeric input. If a user enters "true" or "false", the field value can be sent to any component that accepts logical input.

Use this component to collect or display text, numeric, or logical data.

Input

Accepts input to set text by replacing the existing text field contents.

Output

Sends text when triggered by a message or by the user pressing the Return (Enter) key.

Custom Connectors

Add custom input connectors to:
- Add an output connector and trigger the text field to output its content text through that connector.
- Hide or show the component when it receives a message with a true (hide) or not-true (show) value.
- Enable or disable the component when it receives a message with a true (enable) or not-true (disable) value.
- Toggle the component's edit configuration on (editable by user) or off.
- Clear all text from the text field.
- Insert new text at the current cursor position in the text field.
- Prepend new text by adding text to the beginning of existing text.

Content

Use the Text Field tab to:
- Enter a name for the component.
- Configure the text field as editable by the user.

Looks	Use the Standard tab to define the appearance of the component:

- Height and width
- Enabled
- Foreground (color)
- Background (color)
- Font
- Show

Note: For information related to the Text Field component, see the Text Area and Label components.

Validation Text Field

Palette icon Design icon

Usage	Provides data entry validation for databases connected via the Simple DBAccess component. The ValidationTextField component connects to the Simple DBAccess component, and retrieves the label and value of a single column in the specified database table.
	Use this component to display the label and value of a specific database column. To access multiple columns, use multiple Validation Text Field components.

Input	Accepts input connectors to:

- Set or get the text field's name or value (a bidirectional input).
- Trigger a clear action that deletes the current contents of the Validation Text Field component.

Content	Use the Validation Text Field tab to:

- Enter a name for the component.
- Configure the validation text field as editable by the user.

Looks	Use the Standard tab to define the appearance of the component:

- Height and width
- Enable
- Foreground (color)
- Background (color)
- Font
- Show

Note: For information related to the Validation Text Field component, see the Simple DBAccess and TableOutput components.

Math And Logic Components

Use the following Java Studio components to perform logical functions, math calculations, and math operations. When using math and logic components, remember that the result of your calculation or logical statement is always assigned to the component output. That is, when you're thinking in terms of equations, remember that the **=result** part is always implied to be the *output* of the calculation, and you don't need to include it in your statement.

Arithmetic

Palette icon Design icon

Usage	Performs basic arithmetic functions—addition, subtraction, multiplication, and division—on two input values. Input values are designated *left* and *right*, depending on their position in the calculation relative to the operand. They can be either integers or floating-point values. (You can set the right value to a constant.)
	Use the Arithmetic component to take two input values, perform simple arithmetic calculations on them, and pass the result to another component. (To perform a calculation with more than two values, use the Expression Evaluator component.)

Note: *The division function of the Arithmetic component will produce decimal numbers as needed; there is no automatic rounding of division results.*

Input	Accepts inputs that define the left and right value of the Arithmetic operation.

Output	Sends as output the result of the Arithmetic operation.

Content	Use the Arithmetic tab to:
	• Enter a name for the component.
	• Specify the arithmetic operation to apply to the two input values—add, subtract, multiply, or divide.

Note: *For information related to the Arithmetic component, see the Expression Evaluator component.*

Constant

Palette icon Design icon

Usage	Stores a constant value that can be a number (real or integer), string, or logical value (yes/no). The original default value of a constant is zero, but you can set a new default.
	Use this component to store a value and send it "on demand" to another component. The component sends out that value when—and not until—it receives a trigger message.
Input	Accepts a trigger message.
Output	Sends outs the current stored value.
Custom Connectors	Add a custom input connector that accepts a new value for storage in the component.
Content	Use the Constant tab to enter the name and initial value of the component.

Expression Evaluator

Palette icon Design icon

Usage	Evaluates an arithmetic expression and outputs the calculated result. Each variable you define in the expression gets its own input connector and assumes the value set by a message to that connector. When you create an expression, include only the calculation elements—the result is always sent to the component's output. In other words, when you type in a formula, don't include an equal sign, because it's already assigned to the output result. (For example, simply enter "(x + y) * z" as your expression. The calculated result will be output by the component.)
	The Expression Evaluator component applies operators in this order: multiplication, division, remainder, addition, and subtraction.

The component must receive input that sets values for all variables. After it calculates the result, the component clears the variables. To evaluate the expression again, you must send new values. (You can also store some or all of the values, using the Adapter component.)

Use this component for expressions and calculations that have more than two elements, or if you want to perform a calculation that generates a remainder.

Note: *The Expression Evaluator is the only math component that generates a remainder value.*

Output   Sends out the calculated result for the evaluated expression.

Custom Connectors   The component creates an input connector for each variable defined in the expression.

Content   Use the Expression tab to:
- Enter the name of the component.
- Enter the expression to be used. Use any alphabetic characters or (text) words for variables. Separate variables by a space or an operator. Any characters/words that are not numbers or an operator are assumed to be variables. Use parentheses to group parts of the expression as needed. Use standard symbols for operations: multiplication (*), division (/), subtraction (-), addition (+), and remainder (%).

Note: *For information related to the Expression Evaluator component, see the Arithmetic and Adapter components.*

If

Palette icon   Design icon

Usage   Receives data and directs it to a unique output based on its true or false condition. This component accepts data in one input connector and a true/false value in another input connector. It then directs that data to either the "if true" output or the "if false" output connector, depending on the true/false value received.

Use this component as a "gate" switch to evaluate the true/false value of a message or data stream, and then select which output path to send it along.

Input	Accepts a data message in the left input connector and a corresponding true/false value the top input connector. This data message can be a string, a number, or a logical value (such as true/false).
Output	Outputs the data message to the corresponding "true" or "false" output connector.
Content	Enter a name for this component.

Note: *For information related to the If component, see the Logical and Relational components.*

Logical

Palette icon Design icon

Usage	Evaluates one or two input values and outputs the result. To evaluate one value, select NOT. To evaluate two input values, apply an AND, OR, or XOR condition between them. When all active input connectors have received a value, the component will calculate a true/false result and send the appropriate output to the next component. After outputting the results, the component clears all input values. To store these values, use an Adapter component.
	Use this component to resolve an input message to true or false and forward the results.
Input	Accepts up to two true/false input connectors (the second value requires an AND, OR, or XOR condition in the expression).
Output	Sends out a true or false value, resolved from the input data.
Content	Use the Logical tab to:
	• Enter a name for the component.
	• Choose the appropriate operator: AND, OR, XOR, or NOT.

Note: *For information related to the Logical component, see the If, Logic Evaluator, and Relational components.*

Logic Evaluator

Palette icon Design icon

Usage

Evaluates a complex logical expression and outputs a true or false value. This component accepts multiple variables (in which their values can themselves be expressions) as input, resolves them in a logical expression, and outputs a true or false result. For each variable in your expression, Logic Evaluator creates a separate input connector, which you connect to the source of that variable's value.

Use this component for complex logical expressions that would otherwise require complicated chains of multiple If, Logical, or Relational components.

This component deals with (or, more formally, "resolves") logical operators in the following priority or sequence: NOT (!), AND (&), OR NOT/XOR (^), and OR (|). All operators associate to the left. You can use parentheses to control operation precedence.

Input

This component creates input connectors as needed for each variable in the expression.

Output

Sends out a true or false value calculated from the input and the selected operator.

Content

Use the Logical Evaluator tab to:

• Enter a name for the component.
• Specify a complex logical expression using one or more variables and symbols for one or more of the logical operators: AND (&), OR (|), NOT (!), or XOR/OR NOT (^).

Note: For information related to the Logic Evaluator component, see the Logical and If components.

Math

Palette icon Design icon

Usage

Calculates a mathematical or trigonometric function, and outputs the result. Based on the function you choose, this component adds input connectors and a trigger connector as necessary. Use this component to generate advanced mathematical and trigonometric functions that are not available with the Arithmetic or Expression Evaluator, such as random or sin/cos functions.

Input

This component creates input connectors as needed for each variable in the expression.

Output

Sends out the calculated result of the math function applied to the input value.

Content

Use the Math tab to:
- Enter a name for the component.
- Select a math function from the following list. Functions with multiple variables will create multiple input connectors.
  - Abs(x) returns the absolute value of a x. (The number without its positive or negative sign.)
  - Acos(x) returns the arccosine of x—that is, the angle whose cosine is x—expressed in radians between zero and pi.
  - Asin(x) returns the arcsine of a x—that is, the angle whose sine is x—expressed in radians between -g/2 and g/2.
  - Atan(x) returns the arctangent of x—that is, the angle whose tangent is x—expressed in radians between - g/2 and g/2.
  - Atan2(x,y) returns the arctangent of the specified x- and y-coordinates. The arctangent is the angle from the x-axis to a line containing the origin (0,0) and a point with coordinates (x,y), expressed in radians between - g and g, excluding -g.
  - Ceil(x) takes the floating point number x and rounds it up to the nearest whole number. Compare with Floor(x) and Round(x).
  - Cos(x) returns the cosine of the given angle x.
  - E() generates the constant E to the power of 1 (a value of 2.718281828459045). E is the base of natural logarithms.
  - Exp(x) generates the value of the constant E to the specified power x.
  - Floor(x) takes a floating point number and rounds it down to the nearest whole number. Compare with Ceil(x) and Round(x).
  - IeeeRemainder(x,y) returns the whole number remainder of x divided by y. For example IeeeRemainder (2,3) is 2/3, which is 0 with 2 left over so the result is 2.
  - Log(x) returns the logarithm of a number to the base you specify.
  - Max(x,y) returns the greater of the two values.
  - Min(x,y) returns the lesser of the two values.

- Pow(x,y) returns the value of x raised to the power y.
- PI() generates the number pi to 15 decimal places: 3.141592653589793.
- Random() generates a random number, typically one that is 15, 16, or 17 decimal places, such as 0.1234567890123456.
- Rind(x) rounds x to the value of x with one decimal place.
- Round(x) rounds x to a whole number. If x is closer to the next highest whole number, then it rounds up. If x is closer to the next lower whole number, then it rounds down. Compare with Ceil(x) and Floor(x).
- Sin(x) returns the sine of the given angle x.
- Sqrt(x) returns the square root of x.
- Tan(x) returns the tangent of the given angle x.

Note: *For information related to the Math component, see the Arithmetic and Expression Evaluator components.*

Relational

Palette icon Design icon

Usage

Tests two numeric values in a relational statement, and sends out true or false as a result. This component uses the following relational operators to express the relationship between two variables:

=	equals	!=	does not equal
>	greater than	=>	greater than or equal to
<	less than	<=	less than or equal to

The Relational component then accepts input from other components to define the value of those variables and outputs the logical evaluation of that statement. The right value can be set to a constant.

Use this component to test two values and output the result as a logical value.

Input

Accepts input connectors that supply the left and right values for testing in the expression.

Output

Sends a true or false value based on the input values and the selected operator.

Content	Use the Relational tab to:
	• Enter a name for this component.
	• Specify the relational operator to express the relationship between this component's left and right values.
	• Set the right value of the expression to a constant (which removes the input connector for that value). The default value for the right value constant is zero, but you can set that value as needed.

Note: *For information related to the Relational component, see the Logical and Logic Evaluator components.*

Show And Go Components

Use the following Java Studio components to create visual effects (that's the show part), page formatting controls, and user navigation (get-up-and-go) functions.

Animator

Palette icon Design icon

Usage	Adds an animated object to your page. Use this component to embed a GIF file containing multiple images. Use one of the preset animations provided with Java Studio, or create a GIF file of your own that contains images of equal width and height, placed next to each other with no gaps. (The image sequence determines the animation display sequence.)
Input	Accepts input connectors to:
	• Start or stop the animation.
	• Control the animation speed.
Custom Connectors	Add a custom input connector to hide or show the component when it receives a message with a true (hide) or not-true (show) value.
Content	Use the Animator tab to:
	• Enter the name of the component.
	• Specify the animation source file to display (from external sources).
	• Identify preset animations to display (from those supplied with Java Studio).

- Configure the animation speed setting between 1 (slowest) and 100 (fastest).
- Specify the loop animation selection for continuous looping (yes) or one-time only (no).
- Specify the run animation setting to enable (yes) or disable (no) the animation.

Looks

Use the Standard tab to define the appearance of the animation:

- Height and width
- Enabled
- Foreground (color)
- Background (color)
- Font
- Show

Button

Palette icon Design icon

Usage

Adds a clickable button to your page that can launch a link or trigger another component. When clicked, the Button component sends its label text as output. This label text usually serves as the trigger message for the receiving component.

Use this component to let users trigger other components on demand, such as the MontageLite, Sound Player, or Text Field components.

Input

Accepts input connectors to set the label of the button.

Output

Sends the label of the button as a text message.

Custom Connectors

Add custom input connectors to:

- Trigger the component to send its label to another component.
- Enable or disable the component when it receives a message with a true (enable) or not-true (disable) value.
- Hide or show the component when it receives a message with a true (hide) or not-true (show) value.

Content

Use the Button tab to define the component's name and button caption.

Looks	Use the Standard tab to define the appearance of the component:

- Height and width
- Enabled
- Foreground (color)
- Background (color)
- Font
- Show

Direction Button

Palette icon Design icon

Usage	Displays a clickable button with a directional arrow on it. Use this component to provide a button that directs users in a particular navigational direction.

Output	Sends a message that the button was clicked.

Custom Connectors	Add custom input connectors to:

- Hide or show the component when it receives a message with a true (hide) or not-true (show) value.
- Enable or disable the component when it receives a message with a true (enable) or not-true (disable) value.

Content	Use the Direction Button tab to:

- Enter the name for the direction button.
- Set the arrow direction as left, right, up, or down.
- Configure the component to indicate when it has the window focus with yes (enable) or no (disable).
- Set check button mode on (yes) or off (no). When on, the clicked button appears depressed, and the unclicked button appears raised.

Looks	Use the Standard tab to define the appearance of the component:

- Height and width
- Font
- Enabled
- Show
- Enabled button background
- Disabled button background
- Enabled button foreground
- Disabled button foreground

ImageMap

Palette icon   Design icon

Usage

Creates a clickable image map from a GIF file. This component superimposes clickable hotspots onto an image and allows you to link specific URLs, descriptive messages, or other resources to each hotspot.

Use this component to add active images to your Web page or to provide image-based navigation mechanisms.

Output

No default outputs. Java Studio adds outputs as you add hotspots.

Content

Use the ImageMap tab to:

- Enter or browse to the image file name in the Image File field.
- Define clickable areas using the oval, rectangle, or irregular polygon drawing tools.
- Enter a target URL, and relate it to a clickable area.
- Move or resize a clickable area with the arrow tool.
- Delete an area with the arrow tools and the Remove button.
- Add a separate connector for each clickable area in the map, to launch other components from the clicked area.

Label

Palette icon   Design icon

Usage

Displays predefined text. You can also customize a Label component to display text that is passed to it from another component or to accept a trigger message that causes the Label component to pass its own text to another component. Use this component to add description or explanatory text to your Web page or to create text containers that can be updated or changed by other components.

Custom Connectors	Add custom input connectors to:
	• Enable or disable the component when it receives a message with a true (enable) or not-true (disable) value.
	• Set the label text value to the text received from another component.
	• Trigger the Label to send out its current label text.
	• Hide or show the component when it receives a message with a true (hide) or not-true (show) value.

Content	Use the Label tab to:
	• Enter the name for this component.
	• Enter the label text (which only appears when the Label component is shown on the GUI window or displayed on the page).

Looks	Use the Standard tab to define the appearance of the component:
	• Height and width • Background (color)
	• Enabled • Font
	• Foreground (color) • Show

Note: *For information related to the Label component, see the Text Area, Text Field, and Label3D components.*

Label3D

Palette icon Design icon

Usage	Adds borders, colored text, and 3D effects to a label. Use the Label3D component to dress up label text, or to represent buttons in either a "pressed" or "not pressed" state. For example, a series of Label3D components can serve as navigation buttons, with the button representing the current location appearing to be pressed in. This allows you to represent navigation choices ("where can I go") in the same construct as *orientation* ("where am I").

Input	Accepts inputs to:
	• Set Label3D text and properties.
	• Trigger Label3D to output its label text.

Output	Sends the Label3D label text.

Custom Connectors	Add a custom input connector to hide or show the label when it receives a message with a true (hide) or not-true (show) value.

Content	Use the Label3D tab to:

- Enter the name of the label in the Design window.
- Specify the Label3D Border style and border indent. Border style choices create the following effects:
  - In looks like a button pressed in.
  - Out looks like a button not pressed.
  - Bordered creates a simple rule border around the label text.
  - Not Bordered shows no border around the label (default).
- Specify the Label3D alignment for label text.
- Enter the Label3D text for display.
- Specify the Label3D font name, size, and style (regular, bold, or italic).

Looks	Use the Standard tab to define the appearance of the component:

- Height and width
- Enabled
- Foreground (color)
- Background (color)
- Text (color)
- Show

MontageLite

Palette icon Design icon

Usage	Builds and displays a layered image, each layer of which can contain rectangular areas (called *zones*) that can react to the user's mouse cursor. Each zone has its own input connector to enable the zone and its own output connector to send its label to another component. Each zone's output is triggered by Mouse Enter, Mouse Down, or Mouse Exit actions. Each MontageLite component can have up to five layers.

Use this component to create and display a montage object on your page, and to define the labels or text that the object outputs. |

Input	Each zone accepts inputs to turn the zone's mouse interaction on (true) or off (false).

The MontageLite component accepts inputs to show (true) or hide (false) the component.

Output

Each zone sends its label text when the user's mouse pointer enters (Mouse Enter) or clicks (Mouse Down) on the zone. (On Mouse Exit, the Mouse Enter connector sends an empty string.)

Content

Use the Draw tab to:

- Set the font, size, and bold or italic style of selected text on an image.
- Select a layer (zero through four) on which to create or modify an image.
- Open the Toolbox function to construct or modify an image.
- Specify the color for the interior or outline of selected graphic element in an image.
- Manipulate graphic elements in an image.
- Select and construct component layers before applying them to your design.
- Enter text on the current image.

Use the Toolbox to construct or modify the image content for each layer. Use the Toolbox to:

- Create and modify rectangles, ovals, polygons, and lines, with control over the shape and line and fill colors of each graphic element.
- Insert and modify text, images, and animations. You have control over text content and placement, image sizing and tiling, and painter selection (for special coloration effects).
- Select and manipulate any object on the image, and toggle the display of a background grid to guide or constrain the placement of objects on the image.
- Create a rectangular mouse-sensitive zone on the current image. Specify what triggers the zone to send its label text through its corresponding output connector: Mouse Down (when user clicks in the zone) or Mouse Enter (when the user moves mouse cursor over the zone). You can also show or hide zones from the current canvas on which you're working.

Use the Images tab to enter or browse to the name of an image, and to place the selected image in the Toolbox for editing.

Use the Painters tab to enter, preview, or browse to the name of a painter, and to place the selected painter in the Toolbox for use there. (*Painters* are special colorization effects.)

Use the Pictures tab to enter or browse to a picture created in the standalone version of Montage and copy the picture to the clipboard for pasting onto a layer.

Table

Palette icon Design icon

Usage

Displays data in standard tabular format—table rows and columns. Use this component to display, arrange, analyze, and modify a table's data content. (To modify database content, use the TableOutput component.)

To fill a table with existing data, you must specify a data source for the Table component. This source can be another table or a database. Use the TableOutput component (or another Table component, customized to output data) to pull data from another table. Use the Simple DBAccess component to pull data from a database. By default, you can also enter or edit the Table component's data directly.

Input

Accepts inputs to:

- Add data from a database.
- Trigger the sending of all data in the table in standard table format.

Output

Outputs in standard table format either the user-selected table data or all data in the table.

Custom Connectors

Add pairs of custom input connectors to:

- Identify a specific row number (connector 1), and receive update data (connector 2) for that row.
- Identify a specific column number (connector 1), and receive update data (connector 2) for that column.
- Insert a specific row number (connector 1), and receive new data (connector 2) into that row.
- Insert a specific column number (connector 1), and receive new data (connector 2) into that column.

Add pairs of custom output connectors to:

- Identify a specific row number (connector 1), and send data (connector 2) from that row.
- Identify a specific column number (connector 1), and send data (connector 2) from that column.

Add individual custom input connectors to:

- Enable (yes) or disable (no) the Table component.
- Allow table edit (yes) by the user, or disallow table edit (no).

Content

Use the Table tab to:

- Add a horizontal or vertical scrollbar to the table.
- Allow user editing or sorting of table data.
- Select table display type. Default displays the table with column or row borders. Bubble displays the table column and row borders. Excel displays the table with thick column and row borders. Rainbow Column displays the selected column with a background color of your choice. Rainbow Row displays the selected row with a background color of your choice.
- Specify the number of columns and/or number of rows in the table.
- Clear the table contents to remove all the table data.

Note: *For information related to the Table component, see the TableOutput and Simple DBAccess components.*

TableOutput

Palette icon Design icon

Usage

Displays the found set of a database search in table format. This component works primarily with the Simple DBAccess component to display database query output in a manageable format. To use this component to display query results, connect its input connector to the DBAccess output connector.

Input

Accepts input containing the results of a database query.

Output

Sends output containing the content of selected tables, columns, or rows in standard table format.

Content

Use the TableOutput tab to:

- Enter the name of the component.
- Enable the component to select columns when working with tables.

Looks

Use the Standard tab to define the appearance of the component:

- Height and width
- Background (color)
- Enabled
- Font
- Foreground (color)
- Show

Note: *For information related to the TableOutput component, see the Simple DBAccess and ValidationTextField components.*

Tickertape

Palette icon Design icon

Usage	Scrolls text across a horizontal container in tickertape fashion. Use this component to add dynamic, highly visible text to your Web page.
Input	Accepts input to specify the text and the scrolling speed for display.
Custom Connectors	Add custom input connectors to: • Hide or show the component when it receives a message with a true (hide) or not-true (show) value. • Enable or disable the component when it receives a message with a true (enable) or not-true (disable) value.
Content	Use the Tickertape tab to: • Enter a name and title for the Tickertape component. • Specify the scrolling speed between 1 (slowest) and 100 (fastest).
Looks	Use the Standard tab to define the appearance of the component: • Height and width • Background (color) • Font • Foreground (color)

URL Opener

Palette icon Design icon

Usage	Opens the specified URL in the user's browser. Use this component in an applet to retrieve the target URL. (You can't use the URL Opener component in a Java application, however, due to Java's security limitations.) To configure the URL Opener component to work with a proxy server, select Help from the Java Studio menu bar, then select Registration to display the online product registration form. Click Set Proxy (bottom right), and enter your proxy server address in the dialog provided.

Input	Accepts input to:
	• Display the target URL when the component is triggered.
	• Specify the target URL to be opened.

Content	Use the URL Opener tab to:
	• Specify the targeted URL in IP address format (such as 123.45.67.89) or domain name format (such as **www.sun.com**).
	• Configure the component to automatically display the target URL when it is received.

Toolbox Components

Toolbox components are "construction set" components and functions that you typically use in conjunction with other components to build a more involved Java applet or application. (You can also use them to build Beans or Packaged Designs.) They are among the most useful components supplied with Java Studio. You'll probably find a couple of resources that are so handy that you'll wonder how (or why) you got along without them.

Adapter

Palette icon Design icon

Usage

Stores one or more values for multiple use, and outputs all stored values when new values are received. This component allows you to temporarily store values (such as running totals), strings, or Java objects, and then reuse them as needed. When you place it in your design, the Adapter component defaults to two input connectors, two stored objects with values set to zero, and two output connectors. You can then set its default values to any numeric values or strings, connect other outputs to the Adapter, and connect the Adapter's outputs to the input connectors of other components, as needed.

Each time a new input arrives, the Adapter component outputs both of its stored values (or objects) simultaneously. These inputs (and their subsequent output message) can be any values, strings, or objects.

Use this component when you want to perform running totals, repeated calculations or operations, and other similar tasks. Because it retains its stored values/objects, the Adapter will, in some instances, serve your needs better than other components that automatically clear their input values after generating output—such as the Expression Evaluator, String, Arithmetic, and Relational components.

Input	Accepts one or more input values. By default, the Adapter component has two input connectors.

Output	Sends the stored values when triggered by an input value. By default, the Adapter component has two output connectors.

Content	Use the Adapter tab to:

- Enter a name for the Adapter component.
- Enter the name of the stored object.
- Enter the default value of the stored object.
- Add input and output connectors for the stored object.
- Remove the selected object from storage.

Debug

Palette icon Design icon

Usage Monitors messages between components, and displays or writes the results to file. This component "bridges" between sending and receiving components and gives you the ability to monitor messages between the two. You can direct the debugging output to the Java Console window, an application log file, or a text window. (Due to security constraints, Java applets cannot write debug messages to a file.)

Use this component to help you track down results and progress as you develop applets and applications. For more information on the use of this component in the debugging process, see Chapters 22 and 23.

Input Accepts as input the value being monitored.

Output Sends the monitored value on to the targeted component.

Custom Connectors Add custom input connectors to:

- Set the debug logging mode via input from another component. Specify if debug logging is none, or if debug output is to be sent to console, file, or window.
- Set the log file name in which to save debugging data.

Content	Use the Debug tab to:
	• Disable debug logging by setting it to None.
	• Send debugging data to the Java Console window.
	• Send debugging data to a text window.
	• Send debugging data to a file, and enter the name of the log file to use.
	• Enable debug logging during the running of an applet/ application.
	• Compile multiple debug reports in a Global Debug window.

Distributor

Palette icon Design icon

Usage	Broadcasts an input message to multiple output connectors. This component lets you distribute a single message to multiple components. This single message can be a specific value or a trigger message (allowing you to trigger multiple components from one Button component, for example). Use this component when you want to send the same message simultaneously to multiple components in your design.
Input	Accepts as input the incoming message that is to be distributed.
Output	Provides two default (generic) output connectors for distribution.
Content	To further control the distribution of your message, use the Distributor tab to:
	• Enter the name and a description of a new output connector.
	• Specify the connector's location on the component: top, bottom, left, or right.
	• Add a new output connector.
	• Select and remove an output connector.

Note: *For information related to the Distributor component, see also Merger and Multiplexor components.*

External Connector

Palette icon Design icon

Usage

Connects to external Java resources—JavaBean components, Java Studio components, Java applets, or Java applications—to exchange messages.

Once included in a saved Java Studio design, an External Connector component can export and/or import messages with external resources. When you create a new External Connector to import external messages, Java Studio adds an input connector that can receive messages from other components. When you create a new External Connector to export messages to external resources, Java Studio adds an output connector that can send messages to other components.

If you include an External Connector in an applet or application, it can only import messages, such as parameters or arguments needed when the applet/application initializes. If you include an External Connector in a JavaBean component, it can only import Java events and methods. If you save it as a JavaBean component, it can only receive Java methods and events.

Note: *Unlike other Java Studio components, the External Connector component isn't functional until you have saved it as part of a design, applet, or application.*

Content

Use the External tab to:

- Create a new output connector that can export messages to other components.
- Create a new input connector that can import messages from other components. Save your design as an applet or application, and the External Connector will accept application arguments or applet parameters.
- Create a new External Connector component that can both import and export messages.

Memory

Palette icon Design icon

Usage

Stores values in memory storage areas. When you create a storage area, the Memory component assigns it an associated input and output connector. When the component receives a trigger message from another component, it outputs all stored values to their respective output connectors. There is storage for one value by default. Use other components to send values or objects to storage areas in the Memory component.

Use the Memory component to store a value or object for later reuse or to assemble multiple values for a specific use.

Input
Accepts input connectors to:

- Receive values or objects for storage.
- Trigger the component to send stored values to output connectors.

Output
Sends all stored values to the output connectors associated with their storage areas when it receives a trigger message.

Content
Use the Memory tab to:

- Enter the name for the Memory component.
- Enter the name for the storage area.
- Add or remove a memory storage area (and corresponding input/output connectors).

Note: For information related to the Memory component, see the Constant and Stack components.

Merger

Palette icon Design icon

Usage
Collects messages from multiple inputs and merges them into a single output message. By default, a Merger component has two input and one output connectors. When the component receives messages at either input, it sends them immediately to the output connector. If multiple messages arrive at the same time, the messages are merged in arbitrary order and output as a single message.

Use this component to combine multiple input messages into a single output message for efficiency of design and function.

Input
Accepts input messages that are to be merged through two input connectors.

Output	Sends the merged value to the designated component.
Content	Use the Merge tab to: • Enter the name for this component. • Add or remove input connectors for additional values to be included in the merge.

Note: *For information related to the Merger component, see the Distributor and Multiplexor components.*

Multiplexor

Palette icon Design icon

Usage	Accepts multiple input messages, and redistributes them to multiple output connectors. A new Multiplexor has four connectors that can function either as input or output connectors—their direction is determined on the fly by the connectors that you attach to them. Use this component to establish connections between any kind of components—especially those with bidirectional connectors (such as SimpleDBAccess).
Input/Output	The Multiplexor's four connectors are bidirectional. They can be used as either input or output connectors to the component. Simply attach any external connector to the Multiplexor as needed.
Content	Use the Multiplexor tab to: • Enter a name for the component. • Enter the name and a short description of each connector. • Specify the location of each connector: top, bottom, left, or right. • Add new connectors. • Remove a specific connector.

Note: *For information related to the Multiplexor component, see the Distributor and Merger components.*

Scrollbar

Palette icon Design icon

Usage

Displays a scrollbar widget that, when triggered, sends its currently selected value to another component. Use the Scrollbar component to allow users to select a relative or positional setting, and then send a numeric value representing that setting to another component. You can connect the Scrollbar to any component that expects or handles numeric input.

Output

Sends the number corresponding to the scrollbar's current position.

Custom Connectors

Add custom input connectors to:
- Trigger the scrollbar to send its current value.
- Enable or disable the component when it receives a message with a true (enable) or not-true (disable) value.
- Hide or show the component when it receives a message with a true (hide) or not-true (show) value.
- Set the current (or default) position of the scrollbar.

Content

Use the Scrollbar tab to:
- Enter a name for the component.
- Specify the scrollbar orientation (horizontal or vertical) and the maximum and minimum values for the scrollbar.
- Specify the line increment value that determines the distance the scrollbar moves when a user clicks a scroll arrow.
- Specify the page increment value that determines the distance the scrollbar moves when a user clicks within the scroll track (between the scroll handle and a scroll arrow).

Looks

Use the Standard tab to define the appearance of the component:
- Height and width
- Enabled
- Foreground (color)
- Background (color)
- Font
- Show

Note: *For information related to the Scrollbar component, see the Slider component.*

Sequence Generator

Palette icon Design icon

Usage   Generates and outputs a series of numeric values that it calculates (when triggered) from a starting value and a specified positive or negative interval. Use this component to function as a counter or to otherwise generate a predictable series of numbers. The number sequence continues to increase (or decrease) until the design is restarted or until you set the initial value back to zero.

Input   Accept input connectors to:
- Trigger the Sequence Generator to calculate the next value in the sequence and output the results.
- Set the current value of the sequence.
- Specify the difference value to be added or subtracted in the next calculation.

Output   Sends the current sequence value to the designated component.

Content   Use the Sequence tab to:
- Enter a name for the component.
- Enter the initial (starting) value and the difference value the component adds or subtracts to calculate the next value in the sequence.

Simple DBAccess

Palette icon Design icon

Usage   Connects to a server-accessible database and submits queries to find, insert, and delete records. The Simple DBAccess component can connect to a simple text (flat-file) database or a relational database. To connect to a relational database, DBAccess needs an appropriate JDBC driver or a JDBC/ODBC driver with an ODBC manager resident on the same host.

Use this component to create basic connections to a database so that your Java applet or application can look up, insert, or delete data. (An advanced DBAccess component from Thought, Inc. is available on this book's companion CD-ROM or from the Java Studio Web site at **www.sun.com/studio**. Additional upgrade licensing costs may apply.)

Input	Accepts the following input/triggering connectors:

- Find criteria to perform a search in the specified column for matching records. Sends the results to the ValidationTextField component and (if it's connected) the TableOutput component.
- Row data to insert a new row in the database table.
- Row selection criteria to delete the specified row or rows.
- Retrieve the next row in the current Find result set, and send the results to the ValidationTextField component and (if it's connected) the TableOutput component.
- A triggering message to the security input logs the user into a database.
- A triggering message to the clear input deletes the table contents.

Output	DBAccess provides two output connectors:

- A Status connector to send status or error messages.
- A bidirectional Table Contents connector to send query results.

Custom Connectors	DBAccess creates one bidirectional connector for each column of the database table (visible only when the component is actually connected to the database).

Content	Use the DB Connections tab to:

- Enter the username and password to allow the user to connect to the database.
- Enter the URL of the database location and the driver used to create the database connection.
- Select a table from the database.
- Specify one or more columns to use from the selected table.
- Connect to the selected database.

Note: *For information related to the Simple DBAccess component, see the Table, TableOutput, and ValidationTextField components.*

Slider

Palette icon Design icon

Usage	Displays a slider control that allows the user to select continuously varying or position-based values, such as brightness, speed, and volume. When triggered, the Slider component sends a numeric value corresponding to the position of the slider.
	Use the Slider component to give your users a representation of a physical control mechanism and to send a value from that control to any component that accepts numeric input.
Output	When triggered, sends a numeric value corresponding to the current position of the slider control.
Custom Connectors	Add custom input connectors to this component to:
	• Trigger the slider to send its current value.
	• Enable or disable the component when it receives a message with a true (enable) or not-true (disable) value.
	• Hide or show the component when it receives a message with a true (hide) or not-true (show) value.
	• Specify the default/current slider value or position.
Content	Use the Slider tab to:
	• Enter a name for the component.
	• Enter the maximum, minimum, and initial values for the slider.
	• Specify the slider's vertical or horizontal orientation.
Looks	Use the Standard tab to define the appearance of the component:

• Height and width	• Background (color)
• Enabled	• Font
• Foreground (color)	• Show

Note: *For information related to the Slider component, see the Scrollbar component.*

Sound Player

Palette icon Design icon

Usage	Plays sound files (.AU format) through the user's system. Use this component to launch sound events within your Web pages.
Input	Accepts a trigger message that launches the specified sound.
Content	Use the Sound tab to: • Enter a name for this component. • Enter the name of the sound source file. • Play the current sound for demonstration purposes. • Browse your system or network for a different sound file.

Spin Control

Palette icon Design icon

Usage	Displays a scrollable list of predefined numbers for user selection. Use this component to allow users to select from a fixed set of numeric values (such as days of the month). User editing of the displayed list is optional.
Input	Accepts input connectors to: • Trigger the component to send the currently selected number. • Specify the current number for selection.
Output	Sends the current number.
Custom Connectors	Add custom input connectors to this component to: • Enable or disable the component when it receives a message with a true (enable) or not-true (disable) value. • Hide or show the component when it receives a message with a true (hide) or not-true (show) value.

Content

Use the Spin Control tab to:
- Enter a name for the component.
- Specify the minimum and maximum values allowed in the Spin Control list.
- Enter the increment constant for values in the Spin Control list.
- Specify whether users can (yes) or cannot (no) edit the list numbers.
- Specify the font name, size, and style (bold or italic) for the numbers in the list.

Looks

Use the Standard tab to define the appearance of the component:

- Height
- Text foreground color
- Width
- Text background color

- Enabled
- Button foreground color
- Show
- Button background color

Splitter

Palette icon Design icon

Usage

Splits a bidirectional connector into separate input and output connectors. Use this component with other components that have bidirectional connectors (such as Simple DBAccess).

Input

Accepts one bidirectional connector (from a component such as Simple DBAccess) and one input connector for receiving messages.

Output

Sends messages as they are received.

Content

Use the Splitter tab to enter the name for this component.

Stack

Palette icon Design icon

Usage	Stores values and releases them in either *stack order* (last-in, first-out) or *queue order* (first-in, first-out). This component can function as either a stack storage unit (the default) or a queue storage unit. Use this component as a history-tracking mechanism for data where the sequence of the data is significant, such as page visits, stock prices, or inventory levels.
Stack Input	When this component is configured as a stack, it accepts three input connectors to: • Push a value (which can be numerical, text, or an object) onto the top of the stack. • Pop a value/object through the stack to the Pop output connector. • Clear all values/objects out of the stack.
Stack Output	When this component is configured as a stack, it sends messages through two output connectors: • The Pop output sends the Pop input value/object. • The IsEmpty connector indicates whether the value is empty (true) or not (false). In addition, the Top connector provides the top value in the stack but does not send it to an output connector.
Queue Input	When this component is configured as a queue, it accepts two input connectors to: • Add a value/object to the end of the queue. • Specify a value/object to remove from the front of the queue and send.
Queue Output	When this component is configured as a queue, it sends messages through two output connectors: • IsEmpty indicates whether the value is empty (true) or not (false). • The Remove output sends the removed value/object. In addition, the Front connector provides the first value in the queue but does not send it to an output connector.

Custom Connectors	Add custom connectors to this component to add a Top, Front, Clear, or IsEmpty connector.
Content	Use the Stack tab to configure the Stack component to behave as either a stack or a queue.

String

Palette icon Design icon

Usage	Performs various string formatting and handling functions. This component compares, searches, and manipulates string values. Depending on which function you choose, Java Studio adds one or more input connectors to receive strings and values. Use this component to manipulate string values and formatting.
Input	Java Studio adds one or more input connectors to the String component, depending on the selected function.
Output	Sends to the output connector the results of applying the String component to the designated string content.

Content	Use the String Functions tab to:
	• Enter a name for the String function.
	• Assign a specific string function to this component, selecting from the following options (each string in the operation is represented by a letter):
	  • Append (*a,b*)—Add an initial string to a second string, and send the result to output.
	  • Compare (*a,b*)—Compare two strings (case-sensitive). Sends a value indicating whether they are case-sensitive equal (zero), the first string is greater than the second (+1), or the first string is less than the second (-1).
	  • Ends With (*a,b*)—Perform a comparison matching the end of the second string to the end of the first string. Sends true if they match and false if they don't match.
	  • Equal (*a,b*)—Compare the Unicode values of the characters of two strings to see if they are equal. Sends true if they match and false if they don't match.

- Equal Ignoring Case (*a,b*)—Compares two strings, regardless of letter case. Sends a value indicating whether they are case-insensitive equal (zero), the first string is greater than the second (+1), or the first string is less than the second (-1).
- Index Of (*a,b*)—Search for the index of the first string in the second string. If found, outputs the index of first occurrence. If not found, outputs -1.
- Last Index Of (*a,b*)—Search for the last index of the first string within the second string. If found, outputs the index of last occurrence. If not found, outputs -1.
- Length (*a*)—Count the length of a single input string, and output the results.
- Lower Case (*a*)—Convert to lowercase any arriving input string, and output the results.
- Prepend (*a,b*)—Prepend the first string (literally, "attach it to the beginning") to the second string, and output the results.
- Replace (*a,old,new*)—Replace characters (or a substring) in one string with characters (or a substring) in another string. String *a* is the string being changed, string *old* specifies the characters to be replaced, and string *new* contains the new characters. When all three strings have been received, the String component replaces the characters and outputs the changed string.
- Starts With (*a,b*)—Compares the second string with the beginning of the first string. Outputs true if the first string begins with the second string, and outputs false if not.
- Substring (*a,index,length*)—Extracts the value of a substring of specified length from a string and sends it to the output connector. The *a* value is the source string, the *index* value defines the character position in the source string where the extracted substring starts, and the *length* value determines how many characters to include in the substring. (The index value starts from zero.) For example, *Substring*(12345, 2, 3)=345; *Substring*(0.12, 0, 3)=0.1, and *Substring*(hello, 3, 2)=lo.
- Trim Whitespace (*a*)—Remove blank spaces from either end of the incoming string.
- Upper Case (*a*)—Convert to uppercase any arriving input string, and output the results.

Switch

Palette icon Design icon

Usage	Stores one or more values, then accepts a pair of input values, compares one (the "switch" value) to those stored values, and determines which output to use to forward the second value. This component stores one or more values, each associated with a different output connector. When a switch value is received, it is compared to all stored values. If the switch value matches a stored value, the component sends the second input value to the output connector associated with the switch value. If the switch value does not match, the second input value is sent to the default output connector.
	Use the Switch component to determine the path that a message takes.
Input	Accepts input from two connectors:
	• A Switch value connector that supplies the switch value for comparison to stored values.
	• An Input value connector that supplies the value to be forwarded to the proper output connector.
Output	Sends input values through the default output connector unless switch values match stored values.
Content	Use the Switch tab to:
	• Enter a name for the component.
	• Enter a new value to compare. (The component adds unique input/output connectors for the new value.)
	• Specify the location for the connector: top, bottom, left, or right.
	• Add a connector and value to the list of existing values.
	• Remove a selected connector and value from the list of existing values.

Note: *For information related to the Switch component, see the Distributor, If, and Logical components.*

Timer

Palette icon Design icon

Usage

Sends out a trigger message automatically at specified intervals. Starting at zero, the timer's counter increments by one each time the specified interval has passed. At each increment, the component sends a triggering message to all output connectors.

Use this component to send repeated messages separated by a set time interval. Multiple timers cannot be synchronized within a single design—two timers placed in the same design will not send out synchronous trigger pulses.

Output

Sends out a trigger message at scheduled intervals.

Custom Connectors

Add custom input connectors to:

• Reset the timer count to zero.
• Set the time-delay interval to a new value (requires a numerical value).

Content

Use the Timer tab to set the time-delay interval in milliseconds. The minimum value is 200 milliseconds.

Appendix B

Other Resources

We couldn't resist an appendix of resources, but we were determined not to include the kitchen sink. We've mulled over lists in other books, checked the contents of the Bookmarks file, pulled out our Favorites lists, and gathered all the Post-It notes stuck on our monitors.

The sites listed here are the ones left after we threw out the sites without useful content or an intriguing perspective. Sometimes, we've listed a site that is a personal site, but the person happens to be writing Beans for Java Studio in his or her spare time. We hope you find these sites as useful as we do. Please keep in mind that all information and opinions in this appendix were current at press time. Also, this appendix is provided on this book's companion CD-ROM as an HTML document. You can use the HTML version of this appendix to jump directly to any of the sites we've listed.

The categories in this appendix include:

- JavaBean developers
- Individual Bean developers
- Bean collections
- Other Java-related resources
- Sites that address improving performance of applets
- Sites involved with Java security

JavaBean Developers

Software Technologies
www.sw-technologies.com/javabeans

Provides a good collection of links to articles, documentation, and tools.

Gensym Corporation
www.gensym.com/java

Sells a utility that converts an ActiveX control to a JavaBean component.

Jscape Corporation
www.jscape.com

Provides several Beans in Java Studio, on the palette and in the contributed directory. The Jscape Corporation Web site is set up to easily find and download evaluation versions of their Beans as well as purchase the Beans online. However, their black-background Web site is rather difficult to read and loads rather slowly. Jscape Form sells for $120; Jscape Widgets sells for $800.

KL Group
www.klgroup.com

Offers several Beans in Java Studio, in the contributed directory. Their Beans include:

- Jclass DataSource, which helps you access databases.
- Jclass LiveTable, for creating tables.
- Jclass Chart, for creating charts.
- Jclass BWT, which extends the Java class Abstract Windowing Toolkit (AWT).
- Jclass Field, which allows you to validate user input in a field.

Thought, Inc.
www.thoughtinc.com

Dedicates a page on their Web site to Java Studio, but it's pretty limited.

Halcyon Software
www.vbix.com

Provides Java developer tools. Halcyon Software developed a few of the contributed Beans in Java Studio, and the company appears to be fairly active in the Visual Java arena.

Wildcrest Associates
www.wildcrest.com

Provides Java components for developers and consulting services. Wildcrest Associates created the MultiLineLabel Bean we used in Chapter 14. It costs $29 for an individual license.

Scotty's Minibeans
www.geocities.com/SouthBeach/Inlet/5085

A personal Web site for developer Scott Straw that happens to offer some components for Java Studio. Straw was part of the original development team for Java Studio. Now, in his spare time, he writes Java Studio components for fun.

Weborg.com
www.weborg.com

Offers a WorldTime Bean, which costs $356. The Bean allows you to display the time in 531 cities. The demo version enables you to show the time for 12 cities.

alphaWorks
www.alphaworks.ibm.com/foundry

Provides some particularly useful Beans, including WiringHelpers. WiringHelpers has four Beans: Iterator, If, ObjectsComparator, and NumbersComparator. Iterator and If are useful additions to Java Studio. alphaWorks is an IBM organization dedicated to becoming the largest online repository of Beans.

Prospero Software
www.prosperosoftware.co.uk

Provides some very useful Beans. Their PSPNum Bean allows you to perform mathematical and array operations on a floating-point number that uses Java's BigDecimal class. So, the results are extremely accurate. The Bean also offers masking to display the number, so you can specify how many digits before and after the decimal, whether to use commas or dollar signs, and a variety of other display features. The PSPNum Bean is adaptable for displaying currency in multiple countries.

Prospero Software allowed us to put the demo version of their PSPNum Bean on the CD-ROM, so you can try it.

ProtoView
www.protoview.com

Offers a collection of JavaBeans and ActiveX controls. In their WinJ Component Library, for example, they offer multiple buttons, MaskEdit, EditText, NumericEdit, TimeEdit, Currency, StaticText, DateEdit, DateEditLong, SpinButtons, and ComboBox.

Individual Bean Developers

Biorhythm
www.jot.com/bio

Provides a Bean that plots your biorhythms. It's not compliant with Visual Java, so it can't be imported into Java Studio. But you can play with it.

Joe's Puzzle Bean
ourworld.compuserve.com/homepages/jozart/puzzle/puzzle.html

Contains a fun Bean found at JARS.com—Joe's Puzzle Bean. This clever Bean simulates those little plastic puzzles from when you were a kid. The puzzle has 15 tiles in a frame that has space for 16 tiles. The tiles go in a specific order, and the game is to scramble and unscramble the tiles.

Joe allowed us to put the Bean on the CD-ROM.

Bean Collections

Java Applet Rating Services (JARS)
www.jars.com

Provides an independent collection of Java-related resources. One of the best collections of Java Beans around, this site rates each resource. The site is organized so you can look for Beans in categories—look for the link called JavaBeans Listings.

Gamelan.com
www.developer.com/directories/pages/dir.java.html

Supplies a list of some 120 Beans without categories or subdirectories. Gamelan.com was one of the most well-respected and well-known online collection of all things Java. They later became part of Developer.com. It is still a good collection of JavaBeans, and they award blue fan icons to Beans they have determined to be "cool." But the Beans are not organized in any way.

Yahoo-Not!
Does not offer a category for JavaBeans collections or developers. We suspect that will change, so you should check **www.yahoo.com** and search for JavaBeans.

Other Java-Related Resources

Phoenix Technologies (Now Called Nova Labs)
www.phoenixtech.com

Offers information about their seminars. This company partners with Sun Microsystems to offer seminars they call the *Developers Kitchen*. They don't offer any Beans on the site.

ZD University
www.zdu.com

Offers a groundbreaking collection of online courses, including many on Java-related topics.

Jcentral
www.ibm.com/java

Acts as IBM's search site for Java-related items. At press time, it didn't actually point to any Beans, but it appears to have potential.

Java 1.1.1 Plug-In For Browsers
java.sun.com/products/plugin

Provides a plug-in, free of charge from Sun Microsystems, that enables browsers to use newer versions of the JDK before the browsers themselves have implemented support.

Improving Performance

CAB Files For Internet Explorer 3
www.microsoft.com/workshop/management/cab/overview.asp

Provides a utility for using Java with Microsoft's Internet Explorer. You can use CAB files to store CLASS files for Internet Explorer, just as you use a Zip file to store CLASS files for Netscape Navigator 3. This reduces the overhead needed to download the individual CLASS files by using one socket connection to download all the CLASS files at once.

JAR Guide
java.sun.com/products/jdk/1.1/docs/guide/jar/jarGuide.html

Provides documentation and advice on using JAR files. You can use JAR files for Navigator 4 or Internet Explorer 4. JAR files compress the CLASS files for an applet.

Bandwidth Conservation Society
www.infohiway.com/faster

Provides articles and tips on reducing the burden on the Internet by minimizing the size of Web sites. This group is a loosely knit organization of Web developers dedicated to the idea that bandwidth-friendly Web sites are good Web sites. This group primarily focuses on how to reduce the size of images, but they also address other ideas for coding sites that load faster.

OptimizeIt
www.optimizeit.com

Offers a profiler, called OptimizeIt, that tells you where your applet or Java application spends most of its time and suggests ways for you to improve its performance. At press time, OptimizeIt costs $389 for a Windows or Solaris license.

DashO
www.preemptive.com/DashO

Provides a product to improve Java performance. DashO, from Preemptive, improves the performance of your applet or Java application, and it also reduces the size of the applet file. At press time, DashO for Windows lists at $1,145 and is on sale for $895. For platinum support, the list price is $1,695 and is on sale for $1,295.

WinZip
www.winzip.com

Provides a utility from Niko Mak Computing, Inc., to unzip Zip files and then compress the CLASS files into a JAR file.

CaffeineMark
www.webfayre.com/pendragon/cm2/index.html

Provides a utility to measure Java performance. CaffeineMark is a benchmark developed by Pendragon Software, and it measures performance of a Java system. The test includes evaluating performance of JIT compilers, Java byte code interpreters, and applet viewers.

CaffeineMark Results
java.sun.com/products/jdk/1.1/performance/caffeinemark.html

Reports the improvement in performance between JDK 1.0.1 and JDK 1.1 in running the CaffeineMark benchmark.

Security

Princeton University's Secure Internet Programming
www.cs.princeton.edu/sip

Provides articles and analyses of various security-related issues for the Internet. They are studying the security of Internet software, especially Java, ActiveX, and JavaScript. They are respected for their research and independent status.

Sun's Frequently Asked Questions About Java Security
java.sun.com/sfaq

Offers the best collection of FAQs about Java security online, as long as you understand that it's maintained by people who are presenting the structure of Java and not necessarily pointing out the potential holes. For holes, review the information at the Princeton site.

Mark LaDue's Hostile Applets Home Page
www.rstcorp.com/hostile-applets

Provides applets that are hostile, so you can test the security of Java. Mark LaDue is a noted security expert. He had alumni privileges at Georgia Tech's School of Mathematics, and he maintained a page of example hostile applets and other opinions on Java security. He lost his privileges when he wrote a scathing review of a company's Java security products, so Reliable Software Technologies now hosts LaDue's page.

World Wide Web Consortium (W3C)
www.w3.org/Security/Faq

Provides the World Wide Web Consortium's FAQ on Web security. The World Wide Web Consortium is the ruling body of the Web.

Computer Security Institute
www.gocsi.com

Provides membership information for the Computer Security Instititue. The Computer Security Institute is an organization focused on offering training to information security professionals.

Computer Emergency Report Team (CERT) Coordination Center
www.cert.org

Tracks reports of computer security problems. As soon as an information security professional encounters a problem or hears a rumor about a problem, they go to this site.

Creating Digital Signatures For Applets
java.sun.com/security/signExample

Provides information on creating digital signatures. Future versions of the JDK (after 1.1) are implementing digital signatures for applets. Use this resource at Sun Microsystems for more information on implementing digital signatures.

Index

A

What's On The CD-ROM

The *Java Studio Blue Book's* companion CD-ROM contains elements specifically selected to enhance the usefulness of this book, including:

- *Java Studio 1*—An evaluation version of the application from Sun Microsystems. Java Studio is a dynamic authoring tool that provides a faster and easier way to create Java applets and applications—without ever writing a single line of code.

- *Java WorkShop 2*—An evaluation version of the application from Sun Microsystems. Java WorkShop offers a complete, easy-to-use tool set for building JavaBeans, Java applets, and applications.

- Three third-party JavaBeans that you can import into Java Studio as new components:

  - *MultiLineLabelBean*—From Wildcrest Associates.

  - *Joe's Puzzle Bean*—Developed by Joe Bowbeer.

  - *PSPNum Bean*—From Prospero Software.

- *Sample Java Studio design files*—The files contain finished applets, applications, JavaBeans, and packaged designs.

- *Class, JAR, and SDF files*—These files are needed to develop and complete the designs described in this book.

- *An HTML version of "Appendix B: Other Resources"*—You can view and link directly to the resources listed, using your Web browser.

System Requirements

- An Intel (or equivalent) Pentium 100MHz processor is the minimum platform required; an Intel (or equivalent) Pentium 133MHz processor is recommended.

- Your operating system must be running Windows 95, 98, NT 4 or higher.

- 32MB of RAM is the minimum requirement.

- The Java Studio application requires approximately 50MB of disk storage space.

- A color monitor (256 colors) is recommended.

- A Java-compatible Web browser is needed to view the output of your Java Studio designs outside of the Java Studio applet viewer. You'll also need a Web browser to view some of the resources on this book's CD-ROM.